?

*among psychics and
sets him apart —*

*"My interest in being a psychic
medium is not to use the ability to
go out and do what other mediums
are doing, or trying to duplicate
them in hopes of being John
Edward or James Van Praagh or
any of the others. I am using it
to unlock the deeper possibilities
inherent within people and to
discover more about what it means
to be a Soul. Yes, I can connect
and pass messages and there's
incredible value in that (which I
do a lot of the time), but I am also
wishing to apply it to what I feel
could answer the greater questions
of life and consciousness. I am
using the ability to learn more
about what we are, what we are
capable of, and hopefully reach a
greater audience with it — in the
hope of making the world a better
place when I leave it than when
I entered it. I think, ultimately,
that has the most value to me in
the nature of this work."*

YOUR
MAGICAL
SOUL

How Science and
Psychic Phenomena
Paint a New Picture of
the Self and Reality

ALSO BY JEFFREY A. MARKS

WEB

Spiritual Exploration and Eduction (S.E.E.)
www.spiritualexploration.com

BLOG

The Inner Voice:
a dialogue on the nature of consciousness,
spirituality, psychic living,
and paranormal science
http://jeffreymarks.blogspot.com

MUSIC CD

Into the Light (The Marks Brothers)
www.marksbrothersmusic.com

YOUR MAGICAL SOUL

*How Science and
Psychic Phenomena
Paint a New Picture of
the Self and Reality*

Jeffrey A. Marks

Psychic Medium, Paranormal Researcher
and Consciousness Explorer

ARAGO PRESS
AN IMPRINT OF ARAGO OMNIMEDIA, LLC

Published in the United States by Arago Press (Lynnwood, Washington)
an imprint of Arago Omnimedia, LLC

Visit us on the web at www.aragopress.com

Managing editor: Heidi Marks
Editor: Heather Babiar
Design, cover, and production: Heidi Marks
Illustrations: Jeffrey and Heidi Marks

Grateful acknowledgement is made to Hay House, Inc. (Carlsbad, California) for permission to use excerpts from *The Biology of Belief*, ©2005 by Bruce Lipton, and *Everything You Need to Feel Go(o)d*, ©2006 by Candace Pert. Other permissions listed in the notes at the end of each chapter.

Publisher's Cataloging-in-Publication Data

Marks, Jeffrey A. (Jeffrey Allan), 1970-

Your magical soul : how science and psychic phenomena paint a new picture of the self and reality / Jeffrey A. Marks. -- Lynnwood, Wash. : Arago Press, c2011.

p. ; cm.
ISBN: 978-1-936492-00-8 (tradepaper: acid-free paper)
Includes bibliographical references.

1. Soul. 2. Metaphysics. 3. Spirituality. 4. Consciousness. 5. Parapsychology--Research. 6. Psychophysics. 7. Mediums. I. Title.

BD421 .M37 2011   2010917803
129-dc22   1101

First Edition

TO MY PARENTS
DONNA AND GARRY MARKS
FOR ALWAYS ALLOWING ME
TO EXPLORE
THE WORLD HERE
AND BEYOND

CONTENTS

Acknowledgements

This book would not have come about without the tremendous support, encouragement, guidance, and wisdom from numerous people throughout the years. Many special thanks go to Jodi N., Astara B., Linda and Jodi P., and Terri S., just to name a few – without you, I certainly wouldn't be where I'm at; you've brought me peace, trust, and a sense of ability. I would also like to thank the many wonderful people in the Washington State Ghost Society, who opened a much wider door for me regarding the nature of consciousness and spirituality than I could've hoped for on my own. I would also like to give special thanks to my best friend from high school, Marcus C., and my brother, Russell, as they have actively supported and engaged in my development – in some ways, more than they will ever know. In addition, special nods to my psychic brothers and sisters in arms, without whom I would not be here with my sanity intact: Marci C., Randy (you're missed), Kim S., Carol G., and Dave K. (you know you're psychic, just accept it), and my fellow sensitives at WSGS. Also, many warm thanks to my editor, Heather Babiar, for without her this book would not flow or be nearly as coherent as it is – the sharing of her insights and editorial savvy made the construction of the material a joy. Most of all, I wish to thank and praise my wife, Heidi. In many ways, this book is more hers than it is mine. Without her tireless dedication and commitment, it would not be in anyone's hands – from page layout, design, cover art, and much much more, I am grateful beyond words. I love you!

INTRODUCTION

What you have in your hands is not a science book, though I will often quote scientific findings to frame a point. I am not a scientist, yet I do believe in the scientific method and its value in examining phenomena. I also don't consider myself a superstitious person or one who easily accepts reported paranormal events, though I have engaged in a personal study of such experiences for nearly the whole of my life and have learned a great many things from it. In fact, one could consider me a provisional skeptic—I need experiential proof before I simply believe something and take it on faith, especially when it comes to the matter of my own eternal Soul.

The subject of the Soul has been pondered since the dawn of recorded civilization. Usually it has fallen under the wings of religion, faith, and superstition; rarely has it ever been considered for scientific scrutiny. Under the auspices of religion we have been asked to embrace a series of ancient texts that can hardly be verified as truly historical events. First thrust upon a populace who was unable to read or write, and was thus mentally ill-equipped to validate or debunk the tales and their notion of spirituality, the texts were carried forth into history by the prose of tradition (and in some cases the fear of death by inquisition or other power plays) and foisted upon uneducated individuals, who were led about by a fear of the unknown (death) by the handlers of the doctrine. As a result, we have all been left to either kneel or toss up our hands in a final act of taking the notion of our Soul and its attributes on "faith."

Even if the aforementioned texts were in some way indicative of actual historical incidents, then we cannot say with any conviction that they reveal the nature of an individual's Soul. They reveal only a culture's perception of the Self and the supposed guidelines of how to "protect" or "save" it, according to the universally accepted hierarchical view, giving the individual a sense of hovering over a chasm. In other words, it is all a matter of opinion, relative to the nature of a series of elusive events and written by persons whose interpretation of those stories stemmed from the same minds who believed that the sun rotated around the earth, that epilepsy was the effect of demonic possession, and that everything sprang into existence already fully and biologically complete.

These ancient people, as a matter of course, believed that man had an immortal spirit, but they failed to describe just what that spirit *was*. Only in terms of its nature did they agree: It fell short of God and was therefore sinful or somehow less than perfect. Ranging from the ancient Egyptians to the early Judeo-Christian faith, humankind was always at the mercy of Universal Creators, hanging on the edge of an abyss where the Lord (or lords) may act on impulse to purge humanity's evil ways through fire, lightning bolts, bloodshed, or flood. On a completely different level, it was inferred from the doctrine that the Soul possessed an individual's personality and traits, much like the ancient Egyptian idea of the *ka*, and was susceptible to earthly pleasures and woes—physical pleasure or physical pain. Living in this way, with the course of their lives under the sway of the gods, the ancients were left without self-empowerment or appointment. Instead, they succumbed to the dogged wishes of the almighty through the prospect of a certain "chosen" elite who had (or had been afforded) the ability to decide—through voting and agenda—just what was considered Divine

Revelation and what was not. To ponder one's self in discovering the Soul was to inquire about the role and purpose of the deity in controlling the individual, something far too complicated for the lowly sinner to comprehend—again, one must take it on faith. Granted, how could the mind conceive the magnitude of something (or someone) that could create the stars in the sky, the leaves on the trees, and the beasts that roam the earth? In the face of such incomprehensible power, best to resort to what the ancient texts alluded to: Don't question—just obey.

Science, on the other hand, hasn't provided any better alternatives. In fact, one could argue that science hasn't merely ignored the possibility of a Soul—it has often sought to negate it. In some cases, science-minded individuals have become just as dogmatic as their religious counterparts, touting that we are simply epiphenomena, the result of brain synapses firing and a conglomeration of cells and organs working together that gives rise to the abilities of introspection, reflection, and ultimate sense of "consciousness"—and that when we die, we are gone forever. To speak of a Soul would be akin to talking about that which does not exist.

In the nineteenth and early twentieth centuries, rampant materialism knocked down anything considered nonphysical or "spiritual." If something couldn't be measured or quantified or repeated with definitiveness, then it was considered idle superstition, false, or wrong. No wonder material science has never tackled the concept of a Soul. How could it? To the materialist scientist, personality and the nature of existence are the result of a biological machine simply churning its gears. It would be sheer quackery to ponder questions such as, "Who turned the machine on in the first place?" and "Who, what, or where is the observer within the machine?" To scientists, even if we were to grant a dispensation for the idea of a Soul and ask them to consider other mystical and/or elusive phenomena seemingly related to individual experience—such as telepathy, clairvoyance, or the like—we are ridiculed as playing with fantasy, coincidence, and mental aberration. How can anything nonphysical, such as telepathy or "second sight," be legitimized from a materialist scientific point of view, when everything in the known universe is simply a cog and wheel turning? Quite frankly, it can't. For many, from a purely scientific point of view, this is where the line in the sand has been drawn.

Fortunately, not all scientists have been so dogmatic. In the 1800s, physicists, psychologists, and revered university professors skilled in conducting scientific experiments and protocols, set about studying unexplained "mystical" phenomena. Amassing a huge amount of documentation, whilst risking both professional credibility and social standing, the founding members of the Society for Psychical Research, or SPR, in both Europe and America, uncovered experiences common to all, ranging from crisis apparitions, telepathy, and clairvoyance to the controversial "correspondence from the other side of the veil." Naturally, though they did their best to entice honest inquiry from their scientific peers and tackle what they felt to be the most valuable of scientific pursuits—the nature of consciousness and spirit—the shroud of materialism had settled in, and to most, it pushed aside such "nonsense" in favor of the new-fangled view of reality. During that time, Darwin reigned supreme. Newtonian physics and its cogwheel science were spitting out new inventions every year for the advancement of materialist society. For the religious, psychic phenomena had many interpretations: proof of spiritism, or—more threatening by far—proof of Satanism (and, needless to say, much confusion about which was which). Unfortunately, at the time, spiritist fraud was widespread, with conjurers and illusionists making it even more dangerous to delve into such murky waters in search of Truth.

Slowly but surely, however, things started to change. With the introduction of quantum mechanics into the scientific realm, the old, materialist paradigm suddenly no longer seemed so solid. The further one looked into the center of the atom, the more it revealed empty space rather than material properties. Quantum mechanics, it seemed, mocked scientists. This mysterious new science twisted their understanding of reality, introducing such concepts as nonlocal space, as well as wave/particle duality. It plucked physics out of the cog-and-wheel mentality and suggested that reality had something to do with the inclusion of the observer. Meanwhile, psychic science continued, albeit without fanfare or much academic acceptance. J. B. Rhine began doing telekinesis experiments by tossing dice. The branches of the SPR continued to study mediums and perform experiments in telepathy. The concept of distant mental influence was explored, as well as long-distance healing.

As time marched on, men of honor and prestige came out of the woodwork to discuss such mysteries. Early in the 1970s, one such luminary was astronaut Ed Mitchell. He spoke about his paranormal experiences while traveling in space, and thus began the Institute of Noetic Sciences. Russell Targ and Hal Puthoff studied remote viewing, which is the description of distant locations by using the mind's eye from the confines of a small electrically shielded room, hinting at something extraordinary about the abilities of human perception. Due to their incredible success, the U.S. government secured them for the purposes of psychic spying on the Soviets (while it was also well known that the Soviets were working their own psychic programs). In the 1980s, a resurgence in spiritualism occurred, referred to as the "New Age." Trance-channeling mediums and further explorations into psychic phenomenon became more mainstream, eventually morphing the taboo terms "spirit" and "soul" into a more acceptable designation: consciousness. Had spiritual explorations not been shoved under the rug in the early twentieth century, the public (who were kept in the dark about such research) might have realized that there was nothing "new" about these phenomena, and we would probably have been better prepared to explore and analyze them as a society. Nevertheless, the cry for a better understanding of our natures and capabilities in relation to the divine became just as insistent in the new era as it had been in the Victorian age. This time, however, with recent advances in communication technology, it wasn't going to be suppressed as it had in the past.

With the transitioning of the words "soul" and "spirit" into "consciousness," the counterparts of early SPR investigators came onto the scene, eager to tackle new inquiries into psychic phenomena and hoping to make the subject more acceptable to mainstream science. These were, as their earlier brethren had been, bona fide researchers: specialists in physics, medicine, psychology, and neuronal sciences, just to name a few. They delved into such phenomena as near-death experiences, telepathy, and biofeedback. With technology vastly improved since the early 1900s, new ways of measuring phenomena were available, revealing definitively that information can travel between individuals without a physical intermediary—paralleling results in quantum physics and its theories of nonlocality.

In short, the combination of quantum mechanics and consciousness research has opened new doors into the possibilities inherent within our beings. These possibilities reveal something about us that defies the boundaries of our flesh and harkens right back to the notion of the eternal Soul, something that up until now has only been the providence of the clergy and philosopher and never synthesized with mainstream science. What's more, these findings, I discovered, corresponded with what I have learned on my own personal quest within the realm of metaphysics and psychic phenomena as a paranormal researcher, consciousness explorer, and psychic medium.

The first part of this book outlines those experiences, offering a brief glimpse into my life in dealing with psychic and paranormal phenomena as I have experienced them—from investigations into haunted houses to receiving messages from discarnate beings. Only as I got older and agreed that such experiences *were* a part of my life—and not simply my imagination—did I start paying attention to the lessons about the nature of the Soul coming to me from these resources. It is my hope that by examining this first section, the reader will find that while I am not a scientist by profession, I have a wide basis of experience and the credentials upon which to elucidate the nature of the Soul and multidimensional living. I offer a unique perspective into the nature of the Soul, as I have come to understand it. Moreover, since I am not confined by scientific dogma or religious ideology (meaning that I do not belong to any particular class or institution with which I identify), I am also free to offer up an independent interpretation of scientific findings in support of my thesis, so long as the assertions parallel the possibilities suggested by the scientists themselves. The second half of the book deals with the message I have gleaned regarding the nature of the Soul through the combination of metaphysics, psychic phenomena, and the synthesis of science in the fields of consciousness research and quantum mechanics. In the end, a whole new picture of who (and what) we are and are capable of reveals what I believe is a most startling composite: *You are a Magical Soul.*

—*Jeffrey Marks*
Seattle, Washington

Part One

THE
MESSENGER

Chapter One

COOKING UP A LIFE:
FROM RARE TO MEDIUM

"You are supposed to be a teacher." I cannot tell you how many times I was told that while growing up and how much I resented it. My desire was not to teach, it was to write movies. My creative energies were lit by the fire of the silver screen, not to stand in front of people, droning on in monotone.

"You are here to change the world." Yeah, right. I figured every kid was told that, as children are always heralded as the "way of the future." And kids want to believe they have such power, too. But I didn't buy it. I mean, sure—changing the world sounded fantastic, but it certainly wasn't logical or realistic—it was too much like fantasy: A child is born into a broken-down world, is offered signposts toward achieving enlightenment, and then uses them to transform everything into "perfect" order. It was his destiny—no, wait, let's make this like a movie—it was his prophecy! At least, that's how it all sounded to me. I guess you come to ridicule such "prophecy" when it's spoken by a psychic or intuitive person, simply because no psychic is ever 100%

accurate, which makes it easier to label them "kooks." But as "fate" would have it, I was not only informed of this prediction by psychics when I was as young as fifteen, I was also told by healers, consciousness explorers, hypnotherapists, and people I encountered in life to whom I had given a friendly dose of advice.

"I'm going to write movies," I kept insisting to myself. But I began to feel on the inside, as much as I rallied against it, that becoming a screenwriter was, sadly, not for me. Not when every cornerstone pointed elsewhere.

"You are going to be a teacher...of the soul and spirit." That incredible phrase wasn't offered to me by any psychic or healer, but by a group of seven luminescent beings that surrounded my bed one January night when I was fifteen years old, after I opened my eyes during a moment of reaching a deep, meditative state.

I know, I know. *Seven luminescent beings?* I can only imagine the way this makes me sound. And, yes, at times I did wonder if I was going crazy, but I knew, from a scientific standpoint, that if I could reproduce such a fantastic result again by reenacting the same conditions, then I couldn't be *completely* out of my mind. For the next week, every time I went to bed, I turned the event over in my mind. I concluded that one of two things had to be the case: Either (a) the encounter had been nothing more than a figment of my imagination and so, indeed, I might be losing my marbles, or (b) if these "beings" were some kind of ghosts who wanted to scare the daylights out of me, they had been gone for a whole week and hadn't done anything about it, and (c) well...what the hell *were* they, if they *were* real? After some initial trepidation and preparation, I put myself back into that same meditative state. Upon opening my eyes, something deep inside me leapt in astonishment—the beings were back again! It wasn't my imagination after all. "I'm not insane," I repeated to myself over and over, "but I am scared out of my wits." Very gently, one of them reached out and *touched my hand.*

The sheer electricity of his touch made my hair stand on end. His voice, albeit loud, was gentle enough to quell my anxiety.

"Do not be afraid."

At that moment, I knew that my life was going to be different—and somehow, that it always had been

For as long as I could remember, I could "see" things. My five senses were not the only senses I used to navigate through life. My feelings often told me what others were thinking, whether they voiced their thoughts or not. Only later, after events unfolded, did I learn the truth about my suppositions. I could also sense potential events in the future by the feel of the air—"Later this afternoon, something good (or sometimes bad) is going to happen." Nine times out of ten, I was right. It was just a feeling—very rarely did I get specific information, but I was always right about the time frame when the event would occur and how it would feel "inside" my body. For instance, if the event was going to be joyful, I would feel light and tingly inside. Conversely, if it was going to be bad, there was a sense of heaviness and being pulled down by gravity. Both feelings would ensue when the event actually unfolded. Both were often accompanied by mental imagery of either white light or darkness, as well as images of a timeline, whether it be blocks of seven squares representing the seven days of the week, with one block being "pulled out" to show which day, or a simple "ruler," showing the time of day the incident would happen by a splash of luminescence covering a sequence of hours.

No, this was not something we ever talked about in my family.

These days, people often ask me if I thought everyone was this way while I was growing up. Honestly, as a child, I didn't know. But by my mid-teens, I was smart enough to realize that it wasn't likely. I was born with a gift. Yet my parents weren't religious or spiritual, and so this type of thing wasn't part of my upbringing. Spirituality just wasn't a focal point in the family—we never really talked about it. We did acknowledge the possibility of "strange" things occurring in life, such as telepathy, precognition, ghosts, and reincarnation, but we never dwelled on them (though we did once live in a very haunted house when I was three). My family didn't give me this gift—if anything, I have since given it to my family.

Throughout my entire life, there had been this sense within me of coming into the world from some "other place," as if to say that this world was somehow not my original home. My mother loves to tell the story of how I always told her, "I came from space." I assumed she thought, *"Isn't it nice, the stories my children can make up?"* As I have delved deep into the regions of my inner being and my mind, I now realize how literal I might have been! My "gut feelings" told me, while growing up, that my core self (as well as everyone else's) was much greater than what our beliefs and our ancient religious histories had been teaching us to perceive. And so, I made it my life's work to understand why—and to discover what "all this" is all about.

From early childhood, I seemed to know, first-hand, about life's mystical realms. Even from a very young age, I could "recall" images of desert lands, pyramids, and the sensation of being blown apart by artillery fire every Fourth of July. These memories weren't simply fly-by-night imaginings, for they contained intense feelings, as well. Sometimes I got confused because I felt like I was actually in these locations, instead of crawling around on the floor at home—that's how real they were. Was this reincarnation? The feeling of direct experience certainly made it seem so; however, there was also a sense of there being "no gap" in time between my current reality of being a small child and the "remembrances" that I was experiencing. What's more, with regard to the luminescent beings, my whole family had encountered spirits in the past. As I mentioned previously, we lived in a haunted house when I was three—a place and a series of events that we all hoped to forget (the experiences we had in that house weren't all pleasant).

Leading up to that stunning January night when the mystical seven appeared, I knew something was happening. It was my sophomore year in high school, and already I had memories of what seemed to be past lives, odd coincidences during my youth, and encounters with ghosts. My "extra" senses were already partially developed, because I had learned to be on the lookout for these types of phenomena. Several months prior to the appearance of the radiant beings, these senses suddenly sharpened, as though on high alert. I started to notice things out of the corners of my eyes—quick blurs and flashes of light. The subtle vibrations of energy inside my body ramped up to a loud roar, acting like a Geiger counter. One day at school, something inside me told me to look up, where I saw the transparent shape of a female; faint but noticeable nonetheless. She was gliding over the kids in the hall between classes. She was following me, often watching from the upper corners of the corridor. My reaction was natural: fear. Being sensitive to this type of nonphysical energy—which is everywhere—I felt like I was plugged into an electrical outlet every day of my waking life. I slept with the sheets over my head every night. However, that fear vanished the moment the glowing being gently touched my wrist, and I heard (and felt) the words, "Do not be afraid."

The sudden appearance of these visitors was an initiation into a very strange and mysterious school. They told me they were my "soul-guides" (or "spirit-guides," as known in metaphysical circles). With them came the sense of something wonderful about to happen, yet there was also something comfortably familiar about them—that they weren't strangers. Not in the least. Every night for several months, they greeted me at bedtime and talked to me about energy, about the thrust of thoughts (the power and energy behind thought that shapes our perception and molds reality), and about reincarnation. All of us, they said, had been together in other perceived lifetimes, and they told me that I had asked them to join me in this incarnation, to help guide me through my life. This message is what gave me a sense of recognition. Some of them harkened back to my earlier memories about reincarnation from my childhood.

For the first few years, the luminescent beings instructed me about the ins and outs of personal validation and "spiritual cohesiveness" in the midst of "reality"—quite a topic for a fifteen-year-old high-school sophomore! As time progressed, their teachings branched out to affect my friends and family. After a while, I bit the bullet and revealed to my family and a few close friends the details about my glowing friends (and consequently hoped they wouldn't escort me out in a straight jacket). As it turned out, my guides welcomed the chance to interact with others, and my family and friends were willing. I learned to trance-channel a few of the beings, as other spiritual mediums were doing at the time (such as J. Z. Knight with Ramtha, and Kevin Ryerson of Shirley MacLaine fame). Eventually, I stopped, as it was too taboo for my own comfort. However, I still communicated with the beings, and they enabled many physical encounters to continue to happen between them, myself, and my friends.

As an example, one of my favorite incidents occurred when I wanted to read a three-dimensional comic book that required those special red-and-blue spectacles for viewing. I knew I had a pair somewhere, but was unable to find them. I asked for my guides' assistance, expecting a visual to flash into my head that would lead me to the correct location. Alas, that didn't happen. Several hours later, I came back into my room to find the glasses propped on my pillow (thanks, guys!). Another time, one of my guides approached me in meditation and dropped a wooden scarab in the palm of my hand. Later that day, while driving home from an errand, I had an incredible urge to stop at a bookshop that just happened to be selling the same wooden scarab that was handed to me. It was remarkable! On a different occasion, I was with some of my family and friends, and we asked one of my guides to appear before our eyes. After about 5 minutes of waiting (my guide said that he was building up the energy), we saw a shape suddenly appear against a wall. It was brief, but everyone saw it. It took the form of a light falling across a body, like a medical scan in a sci-fi movie that outlines the shape of a human figure. In a less dramatic way, although it happened often, nearby tables or objects would vibrate to reveal when my guides were physically present.

At seventeen, I was directed by a friend to check out the Seth material by Jane Roberts. Seth was an entity channeled through Roberts during the 1960s up until the time of her death in the early 1980s. The Seth materials consisted of verbatim transcripts of Jane's channeling sessions, as chronicled by her husband, Robert. The material was so insightful that, to this day, it has a special place of recognition at Yale University. When I first read *Seth Speaks,* I was blown away. It mirrored so much what my own guides had taught me, but was so much more detailed and intricate in its execution. *The Nature of Personal Reality,* which was the follow-up to *Seth Speaks,* became my Bible—to the point that I wore out the binding and had to buy a second copy. Armed with the material I had from Seth, plus my own education through my guides and childhood experiences, I knew I was on the road to accomplishing my mission in understanding the nature of reality and the Soul.

"Scooter. She said scooter."

The words, OH MY GOD! THAT WAS HER FAVORITE THING! flashed on my computer screen. My chat-room friend, who went by the name Goldenfawn, was stunned, excited, and curious. By this time, nearly 7 years had passed since I had last spoken with my guides. I was 30 and married, with a house and a cat—trying to live the "normal" life, chatting online just like everyone else at the time. I had a two-hour commute to my job every day in the bustling clog of humanity that was downtown Seattle. My brother and I were in a band plagued with noncommittal lead singers, keeping us confined at our home recording studio without much hope of playing in front of a live audience. In a word, I was miserable. It seemed like everything I was doing—including screenplay writing—always fell flat.

In June of 2000, during the height of my banging-my-head-against-the-wall days, my mother called me on the phone and said, "Turn on the Sci-Fi channel." It was the start of John Edward's "Crossing Over" program. I had seen James Van Praagh on television in the past and found him intriguing, but I was absolutely enthralled with John Edward. Here was a guy who wasn't afraid to show his connection with spirit and was actually able to help people with it. What's more, he had no trouble admitting that sometimes his interpretations were mistaken, and that sometimes he would receive no insights at all. His connection with spirit reminded me of my own lost relationship with my spirit guides. I could sense a stirring within myself for change, and for some reason, it felt right to explore it. I wondered if I could do the same thing as John Edward, so I tested myself out as a medium. I had no idea if I could do it, but I figured that if I used to have the ability to talk with my guides, then I should be able to receive information from the dead.

Internet chat was just coming into popularity, and I hung out in a few spiritual chat rooms. This is where I met Goldenfawn, along with a host of others. I knew I needed someone to experiment with for a reading, and Goldie had mentioned the passing of her grandmother. She graciously allowed me to give it a shot. It was short, sweet, and not 100% accurate, but the word "scooter" was all Goldie needed to validate a connection. After all, it was her grandmother's favorite piece of equipment to help get herself around during her final years. A few other items came out that also fit the bill—and thus began a new journey into the world of spirit and learning more about the nature of life in the cosmos.

Things moved quickly. I began doing private readings for friends at work. From that, oddly enough, strangers who worked in the same building started seeking me out. Word seemed to be spreading about what I was doing. I must not have been too bad, as they kept coming back for more.

Then the bottom fell out. My company was downsizing, and I was laid off, along with hundreds of others. My pool of friends and acquaintances thinned out, as they all lived too far away to gather for a simple reading, and it wasn't something I was willing to do over the phone. I knew I had to grab my fear by the horns and try to do readings for complete strangers that I had never met before (without my former crutch of having received prior introductions from coworkers). The thought terrified me. Would it work? Could I really read somebody I'd never laid eyes on before? Was it possible that all the readings I did in the past were simply flukes?

When I arrived at my first sitter's apartment, all I could do was go for it.

Wow! What a reading! It lasted ninety minutes, with information coming from her deceased grandmother, her aunt, and even her sister, who had died a few years earlier. What was even more amazing was that I picked up the fact that the sitter was learning a Native American language *before* I met her. Prior to my arrival at her home, I had meditated to prepare myself. During the meditation, a Native American spirit approached me, who said he had come for the woman I was going to see. When I mentioned this to my client, she produced the book from which she was learning the language.

I was floored. It was a great experience, which led to many others. Every reading went the same: Beforehand, I would doubt and fret about whether or not I could pull it off psychically, right up until the moment the first message came through. Once things got started, it usually ran smoothly. I say "usually," because these experiences are based mainly on the energy of the individual receiving the reading, as well as their expectation level.

The worst reading I ever did was for a mother and son. When I do readings, I don't allow people to talk to me for the first five or ten minutes—I ask them to let me offer any initial impressions I might be receiving without interruption. After that first initial burst, everyone knows whether or not the reading will be successful, at which point I allow the client to ask personal questions or offer further insights. In the case of the mother-son duo, the first 15 minutes was like pulling teeth. Their energy was reserved, almost to the point of being completely shut off. My delivery was choppy and not at all smooth. I was only able to come up with tidbits of information in a sporadic manner. The son would validate that the information I was receiving was accurate, yet he and his mother still had a disinterested look. Finally, I asked, "What did you hope to gain in coming to see me?"

"Where Grandmother hid the inheritance money in the house."

They were treasure hunting! Any of the other information that was coming through didn't matter—they were only interested in finding the deceased woman's money. I was so let down and disappointed. The whole time I had been working with them, the uphill struggle of trying to receive any information of value had me seriously doubting my psychic abilities.

Alas, that reading came and went, and other readings reassured me of my ability to tap into a frequency through which a deceased loved one could pass information or which allowed me to see what was possible in a sitter's life at some point in the future. All this was feeding my curiosity about the nature of the Soul and reality, little by little. Here I was, experiencing the incredible dynamics of the energy I had learned about from my guides.

By this time, the relationship between me and my spiritual teachers was much different than it had been when I was a teenager. Before, they had been instructors, providing guidance on an emotional/psychological/spiritual level. Now they were physically guiding me to get out and use my abilities to help others. The most poignant way of demonstrating this was when they wanted me to go out and find a bookstore in which to do my readings. They provided me with the location by showing me snapshots of directions in my mind and by guiding me there through a feeling of "magnetism." And so, I went to check it out. The store they showed me was out of business—closed. They assured me that the directions were not incorrect. A week later, they urged me to try again. I hopped in the car and drove back to the storefront, fully expecting to find the place shut up tight. It never pays to doubt the spirit guides! A new shop was just opening, making preparations for its first psychic fair. I introduced myself to the owner, offered her a private reading to demonstrate my skills, and with that— off I went, embarking on the next leg of my spiritual journey.

Word got out in the metaphysical community about how well I was doing as a psychic, and it wasn't long before I was requested to participate in psychic salons and fairs. I was always one of the last psychics to leave because I was so booked up with readings via word-of-mouth and repeat customers. They were fun and nerve wracking at the same time. I consider myself a down-to-earth psychic, which means I'm naturally skeptical and require some sort of proof that the information I'm receiving is not simply a figment of my imagination. There is always a distinction between the two, and for the first several years, it wasn't until I was actually doing the reading that I believed anything was going to come of it. It was always a struggle, an inner fight within myself to believe, yet I knew that it was possible and that I had to go through with it, even if I felt uncertain in the beginning.

As my psychic-reading hobby took off, I began to realize there was a heavy weight building within me—my wife at the time was not a part of this. It became evident to me that total strangers receiving readings from me knew me better than she did. What's worse, it dawned on me that I couldn't be myself at home. My wife and I had no real interest in each other's lives, even though we were living together. We had to shut our true selves down in order to do anything together. We were both walking on eggshells around each other, and I knew it. In the summer of 2003, we divorced. Only my faith in spirit and the reassurances of my guides kept me going during our tumultuous separation and legal interactions. "You're doing the right thing. This was the intended course of the relationship from the beginning." This was the mantra of my spiritual team. As an aside, a few years later, it was revealed to me that my ex-wife and I were fulfilling a karmic pattern set forth by the two of us in the 1700s. The answer came to me in two parts—starting with a dream I had during the week before our separation. The dream took place in the eighteenth century. Since I never have historical dreams and hadn't recalled reincarnation-related existences since childhood, I knew it must have meant something important regarding my marriage. In the dream, my wife and I were engaged to be married in this past time. For some reason, she felt I was not being loyal to her, so she committed suicide. Her death left me to wander through my life, carrying the pain of loss and guilt. When I was doing some past-life regression work with a hypnotherapist a few years after our divorce, an extension of the dream occurred that tied everything together. At any rate, our relationship had deeper roots than what was apparent to us on a surface level, and its energy was playing itself out in this life, when its origins had begun 300 years earlier.

Alone, divorced, with only my job and my cat to hold onto, I knew there were only two directions I could go: down in the dumps, or upward and onward. The psychic salons had stopped and I was getting burned out on fairs, so I took a breather from psychic readings to focus on my personal life. Here was a great opportunity to take the spiritual lessons I had learned about consciously creating my future reality by focusing my energies on the type of person and relationship I did want to have. I had used plenty of tools and techniques in the past to consciously create a new job, a new car—even my ex-wife was the result of a previous, conscious creation. I put together a program designed to keep my energy up, my focus clear, and my expectations high. The only problem: How do I tell a future girlfriend about being psychic and talking to spirits? It was an inescapable dilemma. Would she believe me? Would she think I was a lunatic? Whatever the outcome, it was destined to be yet another personal experiment in learning the fundamentals of reality and the abilities of consciousness. Once again, the ostensible purpose of my life which I had attempted to subdue almost a decade earlier by trying to live a "normal" life—managed to bob to the surface.

My fears were completely unfounded. When I met my future wife, Heidi, the first question she asked was, "Are you psychic?" The cat was out of the bag from day one—I was rescued from having to fumble around with broaching the subject on my own. We had attended a lecture by the author of a book called *Living Kindness* (Donald Altman, Inner Ocean Publishing, 2003). I knew, and so did Heidi, that the kind of person I wanted to meet and spend quality time with was not going to be found in a raucous bar or lounge. Instead, I spent time in places that catered to multispiritual and open belief systems similar to my own—bookstores, fairs, and similar locales. I knew that energy attracted "like energy"—I did specific things to move the universe in the direction I wanted to go. As a result, I found myself at this nexus point, meeting Heidi for the first time. Interestingly, we had both contemplated not attending that lecture—it was a rainy night, and we had both felt a lack of energy. As luck would have it, however, each of us had made a commitment to get out and meet people in the hopes of finding that special someone. How wonderful was it that each of us listened to that inner voice, pushing us out of doors into the rain! She knew by my responses to the author's arguments that I was "different." She explained that she had a friend who was psychic and had a similar way of interacting with others. Acting on a hunch, she spared me the agony of having to find a way to spill the beans.

On that note, it's one thing to *say* you're psychic—it's another thing entirely to have to *prove* it. I knew that for Heidi to truly understand who I was and what I was capable of, she would need to see me in action. However, I wasn't willing to give her a reading—that wouldn't have allowed her to watch me objectively and make up her mind about me as an observer. She would need to see me read for other people. The opportunity came two months after we met.

Though I had wanted to take a break from psychic work after my divorce, my guides had other plans. On one hand, they did give me the space I needed to go out and meet people and deal with the mental and emotional aspects of my new life. On the other hand, they did not want me to "slack." Not long after meeting Heidi in October, the spirit guides were knocking at my proverbial door again. This time, they wanted me to do psychic readings in front of a group. "It is the next step in your development," they said.

This…was a frightening prospect. On the inside, I knew they were right. But in my own egocentric brain, I was scared out of my wits. What if I froze up? Or couldn't make a connection with anyone? I'd risk looking like total fool, especially in front of my new girlfriend! "Go do it, go do it, go do it," they repeated.

Okay. I figured I could rent a small room somewhere, invite my friends (who had already received readings from me in the past), and see what happens. As it turned out, there was a wellness center nearby with a metaphysical/spiritual bent. As I was chatting with the owner—a kind and warm soul named Linda—I told her about my plans. She had a room available for me to rent, and I booked it for a date in December.

"How many people do you plan on inviting?" she asked.

"About eleven or twelve," I said.

"Would you mind if I invited a couple others—people you don't know, to see if you could pick anything up from them?"

"Sure," I said. What difference would a few extra people make?

On the night of the event, as the crowd ballooned to nearly 30 people (more than twice the number I expected), I realized I didn't recognize most of them. Inside, I cried out in terror. Here I was, getting ready to do my impression of John Edward for the very first time, with my girlfriend watching. This was either going to be a great success or a flaming Hindenburg of a failure. After Linda introduced me to the crowd, I took a deep breath and waited. I could feel thirty pairs of eyes on me. I had to do my best to ignore them and begin to "feel" the room.

Out of nowhere, there was a tug. In the back row, off to my left. It was a young boy, who died before his time—very, very young. That's all I knew. I pointed to a lady who I felt the energy was connected to, explained what had appeared in my mind, and off I went. Two hours later, people were anxious to come back and see me again. It had worked, just like my guides said it would! I had stood in front of a group and just let the energy flow. I was amazed. I could feel the joy emanating from my guides. This was going to be the start of something new and different. I had no idea what was going to happen, or where all of this was going to take me. All I knew was that I had to have faith that I was pursuing a course true to my life's purpose.

Linda asked if I would be willing to talk about being a medium at an event the following month, at her healers' group. In the past, these groups had three or four speakers, so I surmised I would get up, talk about connecting to spirit, then sit down and let somebody else talk. When I found myself standing alone in front of a group of thirty, however, I realized my mistake. These people had all come to find out if a deceased relative had anything to say! Again, fear coursed through me like water through a sieve. It didn't matter that it had all worked out the month before—could I pull it off again? As always, I bit the bullet and went for it. In the end, it went off without a hitch—the results mirrored those of the original experiment! It all worked out beautifully. Linda felt it was such a success, she asked me to come back to do a monthly event. For the next two years, I met with groups as small as eight or nine, to larger audiences of twenty-five to thirty.

It got harder. Like I said, I consider myself a skeptical, down-to-earth psychic, so I found that I had to overcome my fears each and every time I got up in front of people. There were many times I told myself, "If this evening turns out to be a struggle to receive information, I'm going to stop doing these things." Naturally, such thinking creates such reality, and that's what came to be. When the monthly gathering began, things picked up and went smoothly after the first one or two "hits" (validated pieces of information that I had received psychically). As time progressed, after about the first year, I was struggling. The reason for this was simple—expectations.

When you stand in front of a crowd for more than a year, you realize that people have heard you do this. And when they come with friends who have already been to a group reading, there's a certain level of expectation from everyone in the audience. Second, my own expectation level was out of tune. Instead of simply opening myself up to allow spirit to provide the messages, I grasped for connections because I felt that was the only way to get "more"—as though what I normally received wasn't already enough. In essence, the combination of perceived high expectation from the audience and high expectations from myself resulted in less than stellar evenings—in my opinion, at least. Messages were still getting through, but I struggled with them—they just weren't as smooth or as "powerful" as they had been originally.

The stress level finally taxed me to a point that I was ready to quit. Linda and her husband, Jodi, would never allow such a negative attitude. Thank heaven for those two angels! They encouraged me to simply change the format and approach it from a different angle. Their advice guided me to create a new style that I use for all group readings to this day. I have no desire to be a superstar psychic or medium—my passion is the exploration and experience of soul-spirit, of which being psychic is only one layer. Twice I have been approached about doing television, and twice I've refused. Let John Edward and James Van

Praagh do that—I want to help others realize the potential of their own Souls, while I learn about my own. The new group format allowed me to do just that. Not everyone who goes to see a psychic in a group setting is interested in hearing from a deceased relative—they are hoping for answers regarding some of their own problems. Plus, standing in front of a crowd, waiting to get "pulled" by a "tug" of energy doesn't guarantee that everybody will receive a reading.

I wanted to open people's eyes to their own magic, as my guides had done for me. The new group-reading format facilitated all that. It was simple: Write a question or concern on a piece of paper and throw it in a hat. I randomly picked questions from the hat, asking the person to come up so I could focus strictly on them, and off we'd go. This way, I wasn't always pressured to seek a connection to the dead, and I was able to talk about the multidimensionality of a person's spirit. Eventually these gatherings became a mixture of psychic reading and spiritual counseling, involving much less stress and pressure than before. And everyone who placed a question in the hat was guaranteed a shot at some kind of answer.

Times change, though, and new tides create new needs. After two years of consistent monthly gatherings, Linda and Jodi decided it was time to end the groups and focus their energies in other directions for the wellness center. I was really the only psychic intuitive working at the location, while the rest of the center focused on massage and acupuncture. At any rate, it gave me a welcome break.

I knew I wouldn't be out of work for long.

I was approached by one of the regulars to the monthly gatherings and asked if I'd be willing to do group readings out of her home. Ever since, home gatherings have been a great source of continued practice and development, which I am so very thankful for. With most gatherings averaging between ten and fifteen participants, they can be intimate and entertaining, with people lounging on couches and in easy chairs. Still fashioned in the "questions from a hat" format, the gatherings continue to allow a flow of good information and wisdom, from sources on "the Other Side" to the source of one's own higher self. These events always turn out being half psychic reading, half spiritual counseling. They are a tiny encapsulation of what I am here to do on earth: To learn and to be a teacher of the Soul and spirit.

Chapter Two

GHOST STORIES

Some would say an ordinary garden slug has more of a social life than I do. Although I perform monthly group readings, these interactions are conducted strictly to help others and to continue developing my psychic muscles and to do a bit of teaching. Outside of that, rarely do I visit people or attend events. Occasionally, I wonder if I might have a tinge of agoraphobia. If I find myself in a large crowd, I feel borderline paranoia because of all the energy whirling around, like a thick soup. This lack of interaction became a concern for Heidi shortly after we married in 2005. She suggested that because of my background and my ability to connect with people's deceased relatives, I should check out a group she found online, called the Washington State Ghost Society. As always, I resisted. Sure it would be interesting, but the web site made it appear that they were looking more for the scientific type than an ordinary person. My initial reaction was that they would probably prefer someone with a science or engineering degree.

"You? *Ordinary?*" you may ask.

Yes.

My interest in ghost research was purely scientific—no psychic stuff. I didn't have any scientific credentials, but I was interested in investigating such phenomena in hopes of either debunking or validating them by using standardized equipment, such as recorders, electromagnetic field detectors, digital thermometers, and night-vision video cameras. In the end, I reasoned that by applying solid research methods, I could develop a better understanding of the nature of consciousness and being. Logically, it was also the next step in my evolution in terms of communicating with the realm of spirit (though I wasn't looking to do it psychically). But like I said, I figured they would want someone with a more scientific background. However, Heidi did have a point. My history as a medium gave me a unique edge in dealing with spooks. It took courage, but I finally swallowed my fear and contacted the group. I detailed my history but mentioned that I wasn't interested in using my psychic skills. I was surprised when they extended an invitation to attend one of their meetings.

They were far more welcoming than I anticipated. It was a ragtag bunch of curious individuals, some with scientific backgrounds, some not, representing all age groups. When we went around the table for introductions, there was a woman who was also visiting for the first time, who claimed to have psychic abilities. "This is good," I thought. "I could focus on the technical gear, rather than having to be the medium." Plus, I wasn't sure if they were going to test my psychic skills, which would have made me incredibly nervous (though I could easily supply references from my group readings).

To make a long story short, even though I was more interested in operating the gear and approaching the subject from a more scientific angle, they still asked me to work primarily as a "sensitive." At some level I was disappointed. However, I was willing to participate in whatever capacity they needed—I suppose they must have been short-handed in that department. I knew, at least theoretically, that the ability to connect with a ghost should be no different than communicating with a deceased relative. But at the time, I wasn't so sure. When a person approaches me and asks for a reading, that person is the primary conduit of energy. It's their energy that "opens the door" to communication with a relative that has crossed over. In ghost hunting, there is no primary conduit. It is hoped that the ghost alone will provide the energy required to connect. If anything, I thought, trying to talk to a ghost without an intermediary would make for an interesting experiment.

Truth be told, I had already done it once before at the request of a woman who attended one of my group readings. She lived out of town, in a rural area surrounded by thick woods near a pristine lake. However, her quaint two-story home lacked the charm you might expect from the outer facade. Her friends were afraid to spend too much time in the house. They saw lights, shadows, and even heard footsteps coming down the stairs from the second story. The atmosphere was heavy and dense. Without a doubt, things were not normal in the home. I arrived with a pair of dowsing rods (simple wire clothes hangers, straightened out and held easily in the hands) to assist me. I had read that spirits could twirl the rods for simple "yes" and "no" communications and thought it would a good visual for the client to see, if such a thing were to happen. I had never tried it before, but I figured that if my guides could put 3D glasses on my pillow, it shouldn't be too hard for a ghost to twirl a wire hanger.

As I navigated the house, there was an undeniable magnetic pull for me to go upstairs. It felt like something grabbing my torso and announcing, "Up here, up here." Not knowing what to expect, I quickly checked in with my spiritual guides, who gave me a psychic nod to go for it. The client—I'll call her Jackie—asked if she could follow along with a tape recorder. I agreed, and upstairs we went.

Anticipation boiled up in me as we climbed the stairs. Every inch of the ascent carried me closer, I felt, to my first encounter with a new type of supernatural event. Would it be like the haunted house from my youth? I wondered…my senses were on red alert, waiting for anything to come at me out of the walls. As we neared the landing, Jackie told me about some of the incidents her son had experienced in the bedroom above—witnessing a dark shadow and objects moving around and hearing noises. When we reached the threshold, I paused to "feel out" the surroundings. We were standing in a converted attic, with a room tucked off to the left. If there was something there, it was doing a good job of hiding. All I knew was that I was pulled up there for a reason.

Jackie showed me into the cramped bedroom and pointed to where her son had seen a black mass. The fear in her eyes took hold of me, and I knew that if something was there, I needed to find it. I took a relaxing breath (as relaxing as possible under the circumstances) and opened myself up wider. Boom! There it was—a pool of masculine energy, waiting just outside the door. It coursed through my cells, almost weighing me down. I padded out of the room to engage him, and he disappeared suddenly. "Oh—a cat-and-mouse game," I thought. Taking another relaxing breath, I opened up again. Like some kind of human GPS unit, I could sense that he had moved down to the other end of the attic. It seemed that wherever he transported, I could find him at will. I noted how easy it was to recognize him after he disappeared. After feeling his energy the first time, I knew through the science of quantum entanglement—where two particles, once joined, can still "communicate" with each other across any distance in no time—that we were now linked. It didn't matter if he disappeared. All I had to do was visualize the interior of the house, and I would be able to recognize where his energy stood.

Then, I felt another pull. Feminine energy was hiding in one of the shaded corners of the dusty open attic's spread. I approached with the dowsing rod. The closer I got, the more the energy became prickly and agitated. I could tell she was frightened. She darted here and there, trying to get away from me. After the first minute of flight, as I worked to convince her that she would not be harmed, we began to have a conversation through a combination of psychic impression and spinning of the rod. She told me that she was afraid to move on, for fear of being judged by God. She had lived during the late 1800s, the pioneering time, and was still bound by her beliefs of being cast into Hell for her transgressions. During a warm, heart-to-heart dialogue, I coaxed her into the realization that she had simply bought into a lie—that the source of life does not judge. I asked her to look into the core of my being, so that she could see I was telling the truth. Then, within my mind, I asked one of my guides to take her hand—and I could sense that the tunnel was opening. At first she resisted, unsure of whether or not my guide was going to hurt her.

"Do you see the hand of the bare-chested man reaching out for you?" I asked. The rod spun in the affirmative. After a full minute of palpable anxiety, in my mind's eye, I could see this frightened young woman reach out for my spirit guide. Then—whoosh! She was gone. The sense of agitation in the air transformed into one of stillness and peace.

But this encounter wasn't over yet—there was still the male to deal with.

Jackie and I returned downstairs to confront him. He was in her bedroom, where she had often seen him as an apparition. I tried to think of a way to keep him there and not play cat-and-mouse with me again. His desire to flee was not because he was frightened of me—he just didn't want to deal with someone who obviously wasn't scared of him and somehow knew instinctively how to track him. I told him that I wasn't going to harm him—that I wanted to hear what he had to say.

Why was he in the house?

Was there a message he wanted me to relay to Jackie and her family?

I kept myself open to receive any communication he might offer. That's when I realized there was a second entity in the room. However, the energy of the newcomer was light and freeing. I knew this was not another ghost haunting the house. If anything, this stranger was here to help.

I asked our spook if he could also see the new entity. He responded, "yes," via the dowsing rod. At that point, a flood of tingling washed through my body. The positive energy of the newcomer was coming closer. I convinced the ghost to take this entity's hand, and assured him that the entity would lead him to happiness. Within seconds, Jackie and I saw a spark of light—and the heaviness inside the house was sucked out, as if God had turned on a powerful vacuum cleaner. Our spook had departed.

The following month, Jackie came to my group reading with her tape recorder in hand. She insisted I listen to one short clip from the encounter. It was the moment when I had picked up on the entrance of that second, lighter entity. On the recording, I heard myself ask, "Do you see someone else in the room?" A voice on the tape exclaimed in disbelief, "Grandpa?" The second entity was the ghost's own relative, who had come to help him cross over! It was amazing.

When I joined up with the Washington State Ghost Society, I wondered if I could do the same thing again. The Society made it a challenge, because they did not provide any background or historical information about a location to any of the "sensitives" (aka Yours Truly) prior to an investigation. It's a practice they still uphold to this day. When you're on an investigation, it's a psychic's job to lead team members to the phenomenon, and having advanced knowledge of where a haunting occurs and any accompanying historical information could not only taint the sensitive's impressions, but it could assist a fraudulent psychic in maintaining a false identity and detract from the exploration and understanding of the haunting. I wasn't sure how this whole psychic-ghost-hunting thing was going to work out.

Date: February 2006. Location: A private home north of Bellingham, Washington. The family had been experiencing apparitions, noises, and even voices emanating out of radio speakers that were supposedly switched off. It was going to be a small team: the Society's vice-president, Sandy; her husband, Russ,* who was a tech (he operated the cameras and other gear); and me, functioning as the sensitive. We headed upstairs. From the psychic eye (or "my mind's eye," take your pick), I spotted a young girl in the master bath, trying to hide behind the shower curtain. I tried to coax her out. During the exchange, Russ was videotaping. The girl put her hands out from behind the shower curtain to reach me, and all of us saw the shower curtain *move*. Validation was established—not only was I connecting with a little girl, but I successfully knew where she was and she was trying to reach out to me. Her essence was so compelling, Russ and Sandy even thought they saw her hands at the same time I did.

The girl said she was afraid of the older man—referring to another ghost in the house. As with the investigation at Jackie's home, I used dowsing rods to allow my teammates to have visual confirmation of the conversation. Sandy, Russ, and I did our best to console the child. By telling her how safe she would be going into the tunnel of light and having new toys to play with, we were able to successfully cross her over.† Similar to the encounter at Jackie's, at the moment she left, there was an instant change in atmosphere. In physics, this would be considered the "gauge symmetry" of the room—that is, the properties of the environment have definable characteristics that somehow changed upon the departure of the entity, which all of us could feel.

---

*   Russ and Sandy are no longer members of the Washington State Ghost Society, but can be found online as their own investigative group F.O.G. (Friends of Ghosts).

†   The Washington State Ghost Society does not make it a part of their mission to help spirits cross over. They arrive at a location strictly to debunk or capture evidence of the claimed paranormal phenomenon. On occasion, members have made attempts to move ghosts to the Other Side, but the Society makes no claims or support to such endeavors. At that point, it is strictly a personal act by the investigators and is not sanctioned by the Society during the course of the investigation. No guarantee can be made that when a ghost is perceived as "crossing over" that the entity has actually done so. Only the absence of the haunting phenomenon can be said to validate such an occurrence.

Soon afterward, we caught up with the male ghost the little girl had warned us about. He was not a nice fellow. His energy was heavy and murky, domineering to the point of being combative, and he did not like us being there. Focusing in on his energy, I was able to glean that his name was William. This was later confirmed by reviewing historical documents the homeowners obtained. He claimed the land as his own and didn't like other people trying to run it themselves. He wanted to be in charge, and made sure that the little girl we had helped was kept in line. In the end, we caught him off-guard—he wasn't aware we had helped the child cross over. As we were getting ready to pack up the gear to go home, my audio recorder picked up his voice asking, "Where's …" CLICK. I had turned off my recorder before he could finish the sentence, unaware that he was asking the question, since I couldn't hear him audibly with my own ears. In the end, we didn't cross William over (it's really not standard Society policy)—and he, quite frankly, wouldn't have been interested in that sort of thing anyway.

Not all of the homeowner's complaints had paranormal origins, however. The problem with the voices coming out of the radio speakers resulted from the speakers being wireless. It would occasionally pick up random signals from cell phones or other radio stations. I knew this from years of being in a band, as my brother was a guitarist and he used a wireless remote to connect his guitar to the amp. Every so often, faint radio stations would bleed through the speakers. The client's problems with lights turning on and off centered around a single lamp, and it was determined that the lamp had faulty wiring.

The more investigations I attended, the more questions I had regarding the nature of consciousness. My guides had taught me that consciousness is the base—the beginning of all experience—after that, the way an individual interacts with his or her view of reality results from the framework of perception adopted by the individual. For example, does one see reality as a series of events that happens to him or that is created by him? Once you have that framework figured out, there are myriad responses possible—joy, frustration, fear, anxiety, excitement. It's an incredible web of psychic possibilities. I wondered, why do some people go directly into the light to another dimension at the time of death, while others do not? If consciousness is the base of experience, how does one person's consciousness accept one option, while another's does not? Why do some see a tunnel, and others don't? Or does everyone see a tunnel, and some simply choose not to enter it? These were the questions that emerged from the sense of distinction between communicating with deceased relatives and an earthbound ghost. Though both were considered to be real people who had died, there was a distinct difference in terms of energy and psychic impression between those who were earthbound and those who had crossed over.

My zeal for answers made my thirst for ghost research bloom. I tried to handle each case as cleanly and scientifically as possible, by using a combination of gear and my psychic senses to make contact with disembodied entities. Other members of the Society took notice, and I was voted in as the group's president in October of 2006. With the inclusion of my brother and other science-minded individuals, we brought in more technical gear, night-vision video cameras, and audio-enhancing computer programs, and set to work to create various tests we could run to validate phenomena. We also re-evaluated how investigations were set up and handled, from start to finish. This continues to be an evolving process, though I am no longer the president of the Society, just a regular card-carrying member.

"Moments disappear." A second later, the electromagnetic-frequency (EMF) detector let out a final beep and fell silent. At the time, neither my brother, Russell (not to be confused with Sandy's husband of the same name), nor myself had heard the voice inside the small room with us. But it was clearly there on the recorder. It was as if the entity wanted to show he had complete control over the device. We also heard a second voice announce, "That's it," after the meter began beeping a moment before.

There's a theory in ghost research that says the EMF detector goes off when encountering the energy of a spirit. Does this mean that my brother just happened to shove the device through an entity's abdomen at random, without any of us even realizing there was a spirit in the room? That by sheer coincidence, he "ran into" the spirit, and the meter responded? Sometimes, the encounters turn into a game of hide-and-go-seek, like at Jackie's. One moment the detector goes off in one area, then it stops and goes off in another. It's as if the ghost is trying to lead you somewhere. Again, is it all happenstance? When these voices showed up on my recorder, it made me think, "perhaps not." To say, "That's it," and the meter starts beeping, and "Moments disappear," and the meter stops, suggests that the ghosts can manipulate the gear according to their choosing rather than us running into them by coincidence. There have been many times when I sensed an entity in the room, even recorded a voice, but failed to receive a hit on the EMF detector. Likewise, members have had conversations with entities by using dowsing rods, but any EMF detectors at the same location remained silent.

Since ghosts are an energy form without a physical body, the question became, How do they bridge the gap? How do they manipulate the energy manifesting in the physical realm to move dowsing rods, light up lights on a detector, and create tapping noises on the walls? Something unique and mystical must be going on, and it must be a power all of us share, otherwise detectors would not be going off and dowsing rods would not spin. I have conversed with ghosts about how they physically twirl the dowsing rod—I have seen window frames buckle as a ghost hits it in answer to a question. That these phenomena occur points to the reality that we can affect the material world without using material means. The implication is that with enough concentration of energy, the physical fabric of the universe *can* be impacted. Remember when my guide manifested before a group of us in the last chapter? It took several minutes to occur because, as he said, he was building up the energy to do it. It is quite possible that all of the effects of a haunting are a building of energy created by the conscious intentions of the dead, reaching a state that energizes and moves quantum bits of prematter into the world of actual matter—a threshold experience that bursts into material reality.

Electronic voice phenomena, or EVPs, also raise questions. EVPs occur when a recording device picks up the voice of a spirit that you didn't hear with your own ears at the time of the investigation. Since our ears cannot hear the ghost, yet our recorders can pick up the frequency, what is the mechanism of that recording? Are we hearing an actual voice or the electronic manipulation of the recording sensor, which results in a voice being heard? I have heard EVPs that have an electronic quality to them, like a computer voice from a laptop, but I have also heard speech that sounds just as real as that of your next-door neighbor—there is a natural difference in tone and oscillation of a male versus a female voice, and these are discernible in EVPs. When investigating an old school turned into a community center, we picked up several children's voices, which where higher pitched, without an "adult" baritone quality. One child even asked, "Why aren't you finding me?" Several of the Society members have noticed that a second before an EVP is heard on a recording, there is an audible popping sound. Is this a result of energy from the nonphysical realm reaching a specific frequency and breaking some kind of energetic barrier, where their voice then makes it onto the recording?

There are many questions that will probably require decades of research in both paranormal and energy sciences to enable the deduction of reasonable conclusions.

As I said earlier, talking to entities who have crossed over and conducting ghost investigations have their differences. There is a sense of peace with crossed-over people, whereas earthbound spirits retain a more rugged and sometimes charged energy that doesn't speak to a unity with the cosmos. Both types, cross-overs and earthbounds, still have their own personal issues, likes and dislikes. But cross-overs feel like they have a handle on the understanding that they must own their issues rather than lay blame. Perhaps this comes as a result of instruction or learning from the Other Side itself.

In either case, we, as physically manifested living beings, have the ability to go in either direction. We may cross over, or we may stay earthbound, and I believe that somewhere in the equation this results from personal choice, whether conscious or unconscious. What ignites my curiosity is this: What is life as an earthbound spirit like? If our perceived reality is a result of our mental/psychic filters, how does a ghost live in this universe, in contrast to a spirit who has crossed over?

I surmised that a predesigned set of EVP questions might grant me some answers. My years of interacting with spirit guides and deceased relatives of clients had given me a fairly good idea of the crossed-over dimension and the nature of the Soul in that arena, but not what life was like for an earthbound entity. I created a list of targeted questions to ask at every investigation, in hopes that a potential ghost might answer. Over the course of four years, I have received replies to some queries, but not all. Why not ask my spirit guides, you ask? Because I prefer to hear it from the horse's mouth.

Now, some might argue that the answers I have received on my EVP recordings may not be legitimate. How do you know if the ghost is lying? Technically, if I'm not psychically tuned in, I don't. On the other hand, if the ghost is a real person and is capable of the basic understanding that we are trying to figure out the nature of consciousness and the Soul's existence, then what motivation would he have to lead us astray? For example, one of the questions I always ask is, "Do you ever notice a tunnel of light following you?" The query revolves around the tunnel that most people report flying through during near-death experiences to reach the Other Side. It has also been noted that people under the influence of certain altered states of consciousness, such as deep trance meditation or intense drugs, can also see this tunnel. In two infrared photos of potential apparitions taken by a member of the Society, there is a distinct glowing orb overhead that could possibly be the tunnel entrance. It was because of those pictures that I was inspired to ask the question. In one case, a ghost exclaimed on the recording, "You know about the tunnel of light?" I believe so long as I approach these questions with a sense of openness and genuine curiosity, I have no reason to think the answers I receive are going to be lies. The questions don't pertain to me personally, nor do they necessarily pertain to the entity on a personal level—just the life of a ghost in general. Overall, only a few of the twenty-two questions I ask have ever received an answer.

In some cases, there are conflicts. Consider the tunnel of light question. I have received both a yes and a no answer from different ghosts on different investigations. Does this mean one is lying to me? Not necessarily. It is quite possible that the ghost who does not see the tunnel doesn't believe in a heaven or other dimension of where one can go—therefore, it is not within his perceptual range on the basis of his belief system.

The level of the mind, the psyche (from which comes the term *psychic*), plays a much larger role in the experience of life than we normally consider. Modern thought posits the brain as the source of all perception; it is mechanistic and epigenetic. That is, it is a series of neurons and neural networks simply firing off impulses that gives us the experience of life. In metaphysics, however, the brain is seen as an outgrowth of a much richer foundation underneath: The psychic (mental) framework becomes the foundation. Those neural exchanges occur on the basis of the psychic scaffolding that a personality builds his or her life around. Those interconnections of ideas, beliefs, and attitudes—all invisible in terms of actuality, since they only exist in the Soul—in turn inform our actions and reactions, resulting in the way we view the world and how the physical brain fires.

We can see this quite clearly through hypnosis.

Medical reports have shown the use of hypnosis as a means of keeping burn victims from feeling the pain of the trauma. In contrast, by hypnotic suggestion, people have been shown to create blisters when told their hand was being burned—in the absence of a flame. With respect to a ghost, a departed spirit could hypnotize himself into seeing or not seeing certain aspects or possibilities of reality, such as the tunnel and other dimensions, by using similar self-hypnotic suggestions. This becomes part of the challenge when dealing with certain spirits. They believe so strongly in their hypnotic state, it can be difficult to urge them out of it. For instance, on one investigation, my team encountered the spirit of a teenage girl who had died while having a seizure. She didn't realize she was dead and was continually having self-induced/perceived seizures, which resulted in the homeowner's dishes vibrating and clanging together in the kitchen, just on the other side of the wall from where the spirit stood. She resisted the notion of her death when we attempted to convince her.

It's not always black and white between earthbounds and crossed-overs, however. There are some similarities that the two do share —the perception of Time being the most poignant. Sixty-seconds-equals-one-minute is not relevant, once outside the constructs of physical space (and really isn't relevant in physical space either, but we'll get to that later). To those who have departed, there doesn't appear to be a sense of how much Time has passed. One of my favorite EVP questions (and one that frequently gets answered) is, "Are you affected by the passing of Time? Do you still age?" To date, no one has responded, "Yes," and a few have replied, "No," meaning that Time is not something they are bound to. The most compelling response I have received is, "It's all wrapped up." As we get into the chapter on Time, we'll see that this particular response may be the closest to the actual truth.

Ghost research is something that will go on forever. Each ghost or haunting is unique—it has myriad permutations and factors that set it apart from other hauntings and spirits. There may be common threads, such as footsteps, voices, and apparitions, but the reason for each of these could be as many as there are stars in the sky. Some ghosts may choose to stay behind, while others may have no idea they have died at all. Again, it is a function of consciousness. And consciousness can manifest into countless varieties—aware, unaware, happy, sad, anxious, beautiful, hideous—for countless reasons.

The synthesis of knowledge regarding the Soul through communications with spirit-guides, talking with deceased relatives of clients, and interactions with earthbound spirits offers an amazing picture of the magic of an individual's consciousness and what is possible. It is astonishing how we can be our own saviors or our own jailors. I have experienced all of these first-hand—but even these occurrences have not provided "enough" to satisfy my quest to unravel the Soul and the nature of reality. I still crave to understand the multidimensionality of the Soul and how spirituality can (and ultimately does) unfold in our everyday lives. Just how much of a role do we play in our own existence and the reality of life around us? Aside from what the paranormal has taught me, I am equally curious about the discoveries within the "world of the mundane." The combination of the two can only give me a much more rounded and complete picture of the reality of the Soul. To that end, I decided to tread squarely into the domain most psychics and "woo-woo" people avoid: science.

> "If anything we do in this life matters, then everything we
> do matters. There isn't living and Living."
> —Greta D. Sibley, photographer

Chapter Three

SCIENCE AND THE ANALYTICAL

My own insatiable curiosity drove me to learn more. My quest to understand the nature of the Soul and its relationship to reality went beyond the borders of the paranormal. I had to find out what researchers in the "everyday" world were discovering.

On September 11, 2001, the world watched in horror as the twin towers were reduced to a heap of smoldering rubble in New York. It was one of those defining moments in history that drew the attention of the entire world.

It also seized the interest of several scientists who were studying the effects of consciousness.

The Global Consciousness Project began in 1998 as the brainchild of Princeton psychologist Roger Nelson. Its purpose was to investigate field consciousness in relation to mind-matter events. The project was an outgrowth of experiments conducted previously with random number generators (RNGs), where it was determined that observers with conscious intent were able to affect the outcome of the numbers produced by the generators.

RNGs are machines that figuratively simulate a random coin toss, but instead of tossing coins, the machines alternate between 0's and 1's. If everything were indeed random, then 50% of the time, the results would be analogous to "heads" on a coin, and the other 50% of the time, "tails" would prevail. Over a course of nearly two decades, tests were performed by groups such as Princeton Engineering Anomalies Research (PEAR) to see if an individual's intent could, in fact, influence the test results and sway the outcome away from the 50% range.

In the PEAR tests, participants were asked to mentally influence the generators to yield numbers more often than the expected chance-average, such as creating more 1's than 0's. Conversely, the subjects were also asked to shift the other direction, to influence the outcome to yield fewer numbers than the chance-average—for example, creating fewer 1's than 0's. Finally, for a baseline result, the participants were asked to not place any attention on the generators—this way, if the machines were truly generating at random, the 50/50 results would occur. In 1997, after conducting twelve years of research involving more than 100 participants, Robert Jahn and his colleagues at PEAR published their results. They discovered that the intended results of the experiments matched the intentions of the subjects. When they were hoping for higher-than-chance-average results, the machines produced such findings. When they were hoping for lower-than-chance-average outcomes, the results followed suit. In the end, they reported that the psychokinetic effect was equal to 1 bit out of 10,000 being shifted away from chance. Though this may seem like a small difference at the surface level, when considering the entire database of experiments, it resulted in odds against chance of 35 trillion to 1.[1]

These experiments, and others like them, had Roger Nelson wondering if the machines would be susceptible to mass awareness. He surmised that if a group of people uniformly focused their minds, the effects of such focus could be picked up as a purveying field that would disrupt the randomness of the generators, forcing them to move one way or the other. He designed the Global Consciousness Project (GCP) to focus not on solitary groups, as the PEAR studies and others like them had done, but on the awareness of the entire world. The theory was this: By placing RNGs around the globe and studying the generated outcomes on the basis of the timing of newsworthy events, the GCP could determine whether or not the field (collective) consciousness of humanity could have a measurable impact on the generators, advancing our awareness of consciousness. The "impact" would result from the collective consciousness reaching a state known as *coherence*— the energy of consciousness being affected by newsworthy events and reaching such a point that it creates an effect capable of manipulating quantum reality indicative of the RNGs, thereby forcing the machines to produce outcomes outside a state of randomness.

By 2005, a total of 185 global events had been tested and verified by means of independent analysis, including the death of Pope John Paul II and the Asian Tsunami of December 2004. The overall results of the 185 events showed a clear deviation from chance. The outcome of the RNGs had been affected, with odds against chance of 36,400 to 1. Scientist and author Dean Radin stated about these results:

> "This suggests that when millions to billions of people become coherently focused that the amount of *physical* coherence or order in the world also increases. These moments of unusual coherence would not just be limited to RNGs, but would affect everything. That is, presumably every animal, plant, and rock would behave slightly differently during moments of high global coherence."[2]

These test results indicated that the effects of consciousness can be felt beyond the confines of the physical body and are capable of interacting and combining with other forces around the world. Here we have something similar to what ghosts produce, in the sense that the power of Mind can affect physical matter. Believe it or not, science was speaking to what my experiences in the paranormal had already demonstrated.

The events of September 11, 2001, gave the GCP an unprecedented chance to examine their field-consciousness hypothesis. The results were not only staggering—they were mystifying. RNGs around the world created a bell curve that peaked nearly four hours *before the first plane smashed into the first World Trade tower.* In other words, it appeared that the generators were experiencing some sort of premonition of what was to come! In actuality, the machines themselves could not have had this premonition, but consciousness *en masse* knew in advance on some deeper level, which in turn created the effects in the RNGs. Moreover, the lowest point of the curve occurred at about 2 P.M. that day, roughly eight hours later, when—by that time—the entire world

Terrorist Attacks on the WTC, September 11, 2001

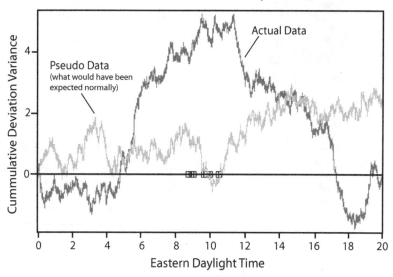

GCP's exploratory analysis of the RNG data on the day of the September 11, 2001, attacks. The spike of the curve shows the generators coming out of randomness as early as 4 A.M.—hours before the attacks actually occurred. (Graph based on image from the Global Consciousness Project web site, http://noosphere.princeton.edu. Used with permission.)

knew what had happened, and the flames of fear swept across the U.S. It was the largest drop in a bell curve experienced by the GCP network for the entire 2001 calendar year. Is it merely coincidence that, on that day, the entire RNG network around the world created a bell-shaped curve that effectively "rang" the same tone? These machines were located hundreds to thousands of miles apart, scattered all over the globe, yet they all behaved in the same way on that fateful day.[3]

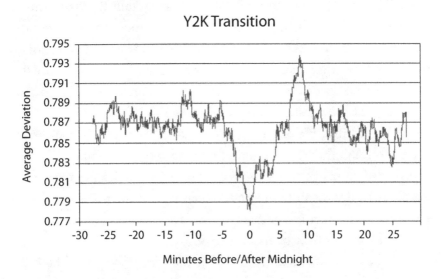

Note how the RNG data shifted out of randomness as the clock ticked closer to midnight. (Graph based on image from the Global Consciousness Project web site, http://noosphere.princeton.edu. Used with permission.)

It gets more interesting still. Prior to September 11, another major world event provided excellent testing grounds for witnessing the effects of mass consciousness. When the clock was ticking down from the year 1999 to the year 2000, millions of people were concerned that the computer chips in their cars, the mass transit systems, and the power grid would all fail and that the planet would collapse into utter chaos (we'll likely see a similar scenario again the closer we get to December 21, 2012, with the end of the Mayan calendar). Like September 2001, RNG machines around the world began to shift out of randomness the closer the clock ticked toward midnight. Amazingly, this happened in each of the planet's nineteen tested time zones! Indeed, the analysis of the data provided by the GCP confirmed that as the stroke of midnight neared, humanity in each time zone metaphorically (and perhaps literally) held their collective breath and somehow affected quantum reality within these machines.[4]

Studies like these fascinate me. They always reflect what my guides had taught: "You create your own reality. Your thoughts inform the physical fabric." Being instructed by spirit guides that the foundation of life comes as the result of consciousness is indeed captivating, but to discover that scientists are uncovering evidence to support this supernatural claim is astounding. Being a skeptical psychic, for my own sense of balance I couldn't take the words of my guides or other people's dead relatives on faith—I needed more than just their assurances. To fulfill that end, my mind became very critical and analytical and turned to fringe science and quantum mechanics for answers. It wasn't that I doubted the supernatural entities or their message, I simply needed confirmation of their treatises in the world-at-large, outside the confinement of my own experiences.

When I went searching for what the "everyday world" had discovered, I quickly learned that I couldn't go with a straight materialistic science, which maintains that reality is only what you can see with your own two eyes, along with anything our current scientific instruments can measure. I knew intuitively that such reductionist thinking was missing crucial facts and was also undeniably arrogant in its approach. To say that our current level of science is the best it will ever be and that it has all the instruments capable of recording every bit of reality is utter nonsense. What's worse, materialist science doesn't account for the greatest variable in its computations: consciousness. It considers consciousness to be the result of matter, not the other way around. Yet, quantum mechanics has clearly demonstrated the importance of consciousness by revealing the nature of the observer and one's effects on quantum systems. If anything, quantum mechanics states that consciousness is inseparable from and interwoven within matter—indeed, it is an essential component in the manifestation *of* matter. The results of the GCP confirm this. Additionally, when stacked with the anomalies of the paranormal—recording the voice of a departed spirit with a voice recorder, witnessing things that seem to appear out of thin air, and receiving authenticated messages from a client's departed relative—the experiential knowledge, combined with these other mounting bodies of evidence, substantiate the deduction that the materialist philosophy is intrinsically flawed. I knew that the materialist paradigm lacked key components to unlocking the mysteries I had been living, and therefore, this limited paradigm could not speak to the true nature of the Soul and its expression in the universe.

Fortunately, there *are* other fields of scientific inquiry. And the results from some of these researchers, in time, may redefine the world as we know it. When one gets into the bizarre reality of the quantum, the special theory of relativity, the idea of a holographic universe, the incredible aspects of light, the test results that have shown Time to be an illusion (which will be discussed in the chapter on Time), and the sheer intelligence of one's own body to reproduce itself millions of times over in a single lifetime, you can't help but realize that what is being uncovered in laboratories by pioneering scientists can significantly add to our knowledge of the Soul and reality. As they risk their reputations to identify truth, we should honor these scientists' efforts and not simply toss them aside because their findings don't necessarily fit into the standard materialist paradigm. Is it not the greatest endeavor of all the sciences to uncover these mysteries? Granted, the scientific method can at times be incredibly slow, but nonetheless, at least the inquiries are being made.

For me, although I didn't doubt the existence of my spirit guides or the psychic signal, which offered up information that I was able to assimilate into my body and brain (though I was often skeptical that it would be easy to do), I developed a hunger to find scientific studies that either disproved or proved such phenomena.

I do believe the process of giving psychic readings should be open to such analysis.

What is the method or function of receiving information?

Obviously, something mystical is happening—what are its mechanisms?

These are valid questions, and ones worth answering. Gary Schwartz, professor of psychology, medicine, neurology, psychiatry, and surgery, did his best to ask these questions at Arizona State University, where he tested such famous mediums as John Edward, George Anderson, and Suzanne Northrup. Dr. Schwartz walked away a believer in life after death and the possibility of mediumship, owing to the statistical "hits" of the mediums in completely controlled environments—such as the sitters being hidden from the mediums and the mediums not having any prior knowledge of who they were going to be reading, and still walking away with accurate details that were statistically much more unlikely than the chance average (such as names, past events, and medical conditions). Dr. Schwartz reported changes within the mediums' electrocardiogram (ECG) and electroencephalogram (EEG) readings during times when readings were being conducted versus control times during which no readings were performed, which suggests the possibility of something unique happening.[5] Still, we don't know the mechanism for receiving psychic information. We can only theorize its processes through some kind of nonlocal quantum field network. However, it's still good to ask the questions.

And when asking them, it must be done objectively.

When it comes to communicating with ghosts during an actual ghost investigation with the Washington State Ghost Society, the psychic impression is not considered evidence unless it can be validated either by historical record or by hard evidence collected with the gear. Even then, the psychic impression may not be completely valid, but circumstantial. For instance, if I say that I am picking up the ghost of a woman in her thirties with dark brown hair and we capture an EVP of a woman's voice, that's some good circumstantial evidence. However, there's really no way of knowing if the voice belonged to the spirit of a woman I described (unless the spirit herself could confirm it by saying on the recording, "I have brown hair and I am thirty-two," or if we had an historical photograph of her to lend more weight). Since the level of accuracy of the Society's mediums is known by its members, much of it is taken on faith that our impressions are highly accurate; but to be truly scientific and provide the best evidence for a client, without something more substantial than a feeling or psychic description, the psychic impression has to be taken with a grain of salt. And I'm okay with that. From a scientific point of view, it's reasonable.

I sought out scientific studies that were at least objective to the possibility of my own experiences, which consciousness research and quantum mechanics are. What's more, if these studies could also paint a picture of how consciousness interacts with and creates reality, so much the better. By "sheer coincidence," I discovered that "psi" phenomena—interactions dealing with the mind independently of matter—had been investigated in the 1970s, starting at the Stanford Research Institute (SRI). Prior to that, however, organizations such as the Rhine Research Center and the British Society of Psychical Research (and the American counterpart, ASPR) had also studied parapsychology and the paranormal in the early twentieth century. It wasn't until the 1970s when the U.S. government came knocking, though—and when that happens, you know it's pretty serious. Such was the case with SRI's remote-viewing program, headed up by Russell Targ and Hal Puthoff.

Targ was so intrigued by the results of his newly coined "remote-viewing" experiments that he decided to give a demonstration to some of his pals in the CIA. This quickly landed him and his team in a whole new line of work: psychic spying. At times, Targ's group was asked to perform top-secret remote viewings for the government, hoping to gain glimpses of enemy installations around the globe by lying down in a small room and "seeing" these obscure locations through the mind's eye. Word had gotten out by 1981 that the Soviets were also using such methods and that we needed to meet the challenge, as evidenced by a U.S. House of Representatives Science and Technology committee report:

> Recent experiments in remote viewing and other studies in parapsychology suggest that there is an 'interconnectedness' of the human mind and other minds and with matter…Experiments on mind-to-mind interconnectedness have yielded some encouraging results…The implications of these results is that the human mind may be able to obtain information independent of geography and time…Given the potentially powerful and far-reaching implications of knowledge in this field, and given that the Soviet Union is widely acknowledged to be supporting such research at a far higher and more official level, Congress may wish to undertake a serious assessment of research in this country.[6]

That's a heavy recommendation! If you would, stop and think about this for a moment. The U.S. government, after analyzing top-secret reports and demonstrations, came right out and used the words "independent of geography and time" with regard to these psychic abilities. That should give everyone a moment of pause.

To demonstrate just what they were referring to, here is a documented case to sink your teeth into. During remote-viewing sessions, a target would be selected from a pool of potential locations. In many of the experiments, these were chosen at random. A team would travel to the target, while the viewer, in this case Pat Price, remained behind with Russell Targ. Neither Price nor Targ had any idea of the location the target team had selected. The two moved into an electrically shielded room and waited until they believed enough time had passed for the target team to arrive at the location. At that point, Price leaned back on a couch and closed his eyes, while Targ began a typical interview with him to find out what he was seeing.

In this particular case, Price spoke of a large, circular pool of water about 100 feet in diameter. He also saw a smaller, rectangular pool about 60 by 80 feet off to the side. He then proceeded to describe a house made of concrete blocks as being a part of the complex. As was typical with Price, he created a drawing of what he was witnessing. The result: He described the Rinconada Park swimming pool complex in Palo Alto, California—the exact location of the target team, 5 miles away. The large pool measured 110 feet, not 100, and there was a smaller rectangular pool 75 feet by 100 feet, not 60 by 80. However, this was still within 10% of the correct value, and the pools were situated on the complex in the location where Pat had drawn them. In psychic circles, that's a huge hit.

This case gets even more intriguing. Pat went on to describe two storage tanks and thought that the site might be a water purification plant. He even added rotating machinery to his drawing. When the target team returned, they confirmed the pools and the concrete-block house, but not the towers or machinery. These, they surmised, were simply errors on Price's part.

Twenty-two years later, Targ learned differently.

On March 16, 1995, he received a copy of the *Annual Report of the City of Palo Alto*, celebrating its centennial year. On page twenty-two (a convenient twenty-two years after the remote-viewing experiment with Price), the report read, "In 1913 a new municipal waterworks was built on the site of the present Rinconada Park." The accompanying photograph showed the two water tanks exactly where Price had drawn them![7]

This case is just one of hundreds that were conducted during the SRI trials and is indicative of many of their findings. Though SRI is no longer in existence, some of the experiments and subsequent results are still considered top secret—another reason to consider just how accurate and spine-tingling the reality of supernatural consciousness was considered by our own government.

It was a fascination for me to study the psychic phenomena that occurred with Targ and his team. They tapped the skills of everyone from top-rated psychics to ordinary people off the street in their experiments. After decades of research, Targ has commented that the skills associated with "being paranormal" should simply be considered typical, as it appeared everyone had them to some degree or another. As with anything, and in my own personal opinion and experience, the more you use a skill, the better you become at doing it.

Again, here I found an example of where scientific findings paralleled what I had learned through my experiences with the paranormal. The science pointed clearly to the interconnectedness of being and to the abilities of the Soul extending beyond the confines of the flesh.

Targ's studies didn't end with remote viewing, either. They also tapped into the realm of remote healing.

Russell Targ's daughter, Elisabeth, conducted a landmark study of patients with AIDS that was published in the *Western Journal of Medicine*. In her study, she chose experienced healers from all around the U.S. to focus on a population of patients with advanced cases of AIDS in the San Francisco Bay area for a period of ten weeks. The healers came from all backgrounds—Christian, Native American, Jewish, Buddhist, as well as those from shamanic traditions and "bioenergetic" schools. In a series of double-blind tests, the healers were instructed to direct prayers toward certain patients, and not toward others. Neither the patients nor their doctors knew who was being prayed for and who wasn't. The results indicated that those who received healing prayers felt more mentally positive about themselves, experienced fewer opportunistic illnesses and trips to the hospital, and spent fewer days in the hospital than those who did not receive the prayers.[8]

Time and again, tests have shown that people have the ability to connect in what is termed "nonlocal reality" to both transmit and receive telepathic messages, intentions, and healings—and this is being confirmed by science! Nonlocal reality refers to the fact that Time and Space simply are not relevant in these kinds of interactions. Information in the form of mental intention is transmitted and received in virtually no time at all, across any distance, from anywhere around the world—and we seem to have the ability to consciously affect reality (again, something that I learned from paranormal sources). Being able to call it "nonlocal" simply gave me a scientific name for it and a wonderful sense of validation as I made my way through the "everyday" world.

Another example of one's ability to affect our environment (and hence another clue to the nature of the Soul and consciousness) is when William A. Tiller, professor emeritus at Stanford University, gathered together four experienced meditators to perform an experiment on water. Their goal: Change the pH balance of the water by up to one unit, plus or minus. They utilized a small "black box" device that Tiller invented as a way to "capture" the intention. They would meditate for about fifteen minutes over the boxes, intending to fill up the devices with the power of their thoughts, then wrap up the intention-induced devices and send them off to four different laboratories. Once received by the labs, the boxes were unwrapped, switched on, and placed next to test beakers of water.

The results were a resounding success. When the meditators intended to increase the pH level by one unit, they did. Conversely, when they intended to lower the pH level by one unit, they did that, as well. They also performed a control test, using black boxes that had not been impressed with intention, and placing them next to the water subjects. The black boxes that had not been subjected to meditation had no effect on the pH level of the water, proving that the intentions of the meditators were indeed the reason for the changing pH levels.

Then Tiller noticed something strange. The more experiments

his team did, the quicker the results came. In fact, he noticed that the effects of the meditations lingered inside the laboratories for up to a year! In other words, the energy of the intentions somehow changed the environment of the labs, to the point that the black boxes *were no longer needed,* because the atmosphere already demonstrated the charge of the intention within it.[9] In a second experiment, by using meditative intention via the intention-induced black boxes, Tiller and his group were able to increase the metabolic cellular ATP/ADP ratio in developing fruit fly larvae, causing a reduction in the larval development time. The results of this experiment demonstrated that the intentions of Tiller's team yielded an effect on the development of life itself.[10]

In one final example, a neuroscientist by the name of Dr. Larry Farwell performed an experiment in which conscious intention was used to affect the quantum mechanical event of alpha particles being released from an alpha particle source. An experimental apparatus was designed so that an individual could have the opportunity to "influence" the pattern of the particle emissions. Since the expected distribution of particle detections in a given amount of time is precisely known, the system provided a statistically accurate method for testing the possibility of the influence of consciousness on matter at the most fundamental level.

The experiment ran as follows: The experimenter sat in front of a computer screen that provided information about the detection of alpha particles. A small alpha particle source nearby emitted alpha particles, which were detected by a detector. A computerized system timed the intervals between alpha particles to the nearest microsecond (one millionth of a second). The experimental data collected consisted of the number of microseconds that elapsed between each particle detected and the previous particle. In the absence of any outside influence, 50% of the time, an even number of microseconds would elapse between the release of detected particles; and 50% of the time, and an odd number of microseconds would elapse between the release of detected particles. In other words, half the time, the number of microseconds between one particle and the next would be a number like 2, 4, 6, or 8 microseconds, and half the time it would be a number like 1, 3, 5, or 7 microseconds.

In the experiment, the intention was to influence the particle emissions to deviate from the 50/50 split between odd and even intervals. During one experiment, it was the goal of the intention to move the emissions to a more even than odd interval, and in another, the experimenter intended to move it to a more odd interval than even. In a third experiment, the experimenter was asked to simply turn away from the screen, so as not to project any intention; this was to act as the control test to show that the alpha particles were not biased toward either odd or even intervals. In the end, the results showed conclusively that human beings can, in fact, influence quantum-mechanical processes to a highly statistically significant degree—through the intervention of conscious intention alone.[11]

These are some significant examples of tests that have been conducted over the course of the last thirty to forty years, demonstrating that science is taking amazing leaps toward sneaking a peek into the nature of consciousness. As I said earlier, however, science can often be a slow process. Paradigms are incredibly difficult to change. Typically, if a new result or scientific hypothesis conflicts with the current paradigm (in our case, the materialist paradigm), that result is ridiculed or ignored. If it continues to appear, then it becomes the product of "hidden variables," meaning that somewhere, it can still fit into the current paradigm—we just haven't uncovered the missing piece of the puzzle that's "obviously" right before us, until finally it is acknowledged that the current paradigm is a flawed product, and the new paradigm not only provides the answer to the anomaly but also supports everything that came before it.

As it stands right now, scientists who study the effects of consciousness are still very much at the infantile level of understanding, due to the nature of scientific progress. Several will admit (and are currently postulating) that the view of the current findings is leaning toward the notion that consciousness *is* the creator of the universe and of experience (see the research of Drs. Fred Alan Wolf and Amit Goswami). Yet, there are others who would argue that the jury is still out on such a claim. At any rate, it is wise to keep an eye on what these scientists are discovering, for it does give us a broader understanding of our individual and mass capabilities. So far, these handfuls of examples are nice complements to what I have learned through my own experience as a medium and ghost researcher and all-around explorer of my own personal consciousness. Hopefully, they have wet your whistle to seek out more evidence for yourself. I have included a bibliography at the end of this book for further suggested reading.

The findings in quantum physics (which will be expanded on later) and the results of consciousness experiments have kept me at the forefront of trying to discern the truth when it comes to (a) the nature of our Souls and reality and (b) keeping it within the bounds of some type of reason. Though I do not believe current science has all the answers, and I am not willing to limit myself strictly to the scientific process, I do feel that I can better understand what is happening in the realm of metaphysics because of what modern researchers are discovering. As I said, they are still in the infantile stages of understanding just what our consciousness is and what we can do with it. Nonetheless, psychic phenomena and my own abilities are slowly being converted from taboo to an acceptable manifestation of reality via the experiments in consciousness research and possibilities inherent within quantum mechanics. I also feel that as these discoveries come to light, they offer more clues as to the question of "how" all this stuff works.

If I simply relied on the scientific method, I could not believe in my experiences as a medium or ghost researcher, for such things—according to "traditional" science—do not, as yet, exist. However, my experiences and those of my peers provide a direct contradiction to such a notion, so I have to accept that science is still playing "catch up." In some ways, this means there will still be detractors to what I do and what I theorize and postulate. This is nothing new, as Copernicus and Galileo found themselves in the same boat. So I suppose I'm in good company.

The examination of consciousness with black-and-white laboratory tests has its merits, but we shouldn't stop there. There are other types of researchers that can also shed light on our experiences as Souls—namely, those that study near-death experiences and past-life recall.

Significant research in near-death experiences (NDEs) has been going on for decades. In his groundbreaking book, *Closer to the Light*, Dr. Melvin Morse documented dozens of cases of NDEs in children. Not yet affected by adult beliefs and viewpoints and therefore dismissing certain inner events as "dreams" or "hallucinations," these children gave first-hand accounts of floating above the body, seeing and hearing the events surrounding the body, traveling down a tunnel, and going into a different dimension where they were greeted by a deceased relative or a perceived religious figure.

> All I remember was my hair getting stuck in the drain and then blacking out. The next thing I knew, I floated out of my body. I could see myself under the water but I wasn't afraid. All of a sudden I started going up a tunnel, and before I could think about it, I found myself in heaven. I knew it was heaven because everything was bright and everyone was cheerful. A nice man asked me if I wanted to stay there. I thought about staying; I really did. But I said 'I want to be with my family.' Then I got to come back.[12]

Dr. Morse's continued research uncovered the realization that the effects of the NDE experience were long lasting and life altering. He discovered that individuals who had experienced NDEs lived generally healthier lives and had fewer psychosomatic complaints. They also reported stronger family ties, more zest for living, a greatly diminished fear of death, and, in many cases, psychic abilities, such as clairvoyance.[13] It is hard to believe that the hundreds of NDE cases that Dr. Morse studied could be anything but a testimony to the nature of the Soul and its continued longevity in the fabric of reality.

In another type of research that demonstrates the survival of the Soul after death, Dr. Ian Stevenson is credited as being the father of reincarnation studies. Working as a psychiatrist at the University of Virginia, Dr. Stevenson traveled the world to document cases where people claimed to have lived past lives. He and his colleagues amassed more than 2,500 cases in which the claimants were able to describe, in great detail, the lives of previous personalities. In his riveting book, *Life Before Life,* Dr. Jim B. Tucker, an associate of Stevenson, documents several of the cases reported by young children. Their statements were often found to be accurate for a particular deceased individual—in many cases naming the previous individual's town, occupation, and description of home life. Some children have "recognized" members of their families from previous lives, citing them by name and relation, such as brother, sister, cousin, or—in a few cases—the previous personality's own child. A number of children also had birthmarks or defects that matched wounds on the body of the deceased person.[14]

Several wonderful books have been written by Raymond Moody and Brian L. Weiss, which detail past-life experiences through the conduit of hypnosis. This can sometimes be controversial, but nonetheless, both psychiatrists report the incredible healing effects that patients have after uncovering past-life memories. What's more, in many cases, the subjects are able to describe the past in such intricate detail, it is quite convincing that they were the people living in the times they describe. (See the bibliography for more information.)

There are some psychics who shy away from science and from seeking out the kind of research I've introduced here. Whether this is because they do not feel they can understand the results, or they are afraid the results will conflict with their perception of reality and refute their abilities, I can only speculate. (Or, perhaps they believe they already know everything and don't need to go looking elsewhere for validation.) In my opinion, we need to remain open to information from all sources. The combination of science, spirituality, and ghost research can only give us a more complete picture of our universe and our place within it. At times, data from different sources may conflict. But remember that, at one time, the perception that the earth rotated on its axis and traveled around the sun was also discounted as absurd and entered into direct conflict with what was "known." In the end, we were able to let go of our centrist notion of everything revolving around us, and guess what—not only did we survive, but we moved into an even greater reality. I believe we are still on that path.

Physical sciences are still geared toward the physical. However, the deeper scientists probe, they are finding that what we call "matter" or "physical reality" is actually made up of primarily empty space, to the tune of 99.9%. They are also finding that something outside of our perceived "physical reality" plays a role in the 0.1% that does make up the tapestry of material life. It is that 99.9% that science has yet to penetrate. This perceived "vacuum" constitutes most of the universe, yet it operates at frequencies beyond what the filters of our brain are capable of translating and perceiving as light and sound. All the bodily equipment we possess is designed to attune ourselves to a teeny, tiny fraction of what is considered to be "out there." It is within that immense, imperceptible void that consciousness bursts—where we all return to when we die—where we all continue to exist and create our lives, whether it be here or on the Other Side. It is a basic law of physics that the energy constant of the universe never changes, no matter how many things come into existence or how many things go out of it. It is known as the first law of thermodynamics. This law alone speaks to the eternal nature of a person's Soul, for a Soul simply cannot disappear out of existence if the energy level of the universe always remains the same.

It will no doubt be hard for science to shake the hand of someone who claims to psychically talk to the dead and receive information from the potential future, and one who also interacts with ghosts. They may never catch up to or be able to penetrate that emptiness where these abilities reside. Our reality is shaded with limitations to keep our focus in this dimension; to try and create experiments and devices to supersede the illusion will take not only time, but courage. Scientists will first have to admit that physical reality is not the only reality that exists—that their theories and devices are limited by the very nature of the dimension in which we live. This, to me, is the glorious message of quantum physics.

But it must go further. When it does, the questions will be, How do you prove it? How do you prove another reality if you are confined by the attributes of the one you are currently living in? If the limitations of our current reality prevent us from having direct experience with the scientific equipment we need to validate other such phenomena, how can we ever move beyond a certain investigative level? At this point, someone will need to stand up and say, "The true measure is not the readout from a computer or measurement device, but rather the observation of the individual experiencing it, the consciousness and Soul itself that had a hand in creating it in the first place."

It all comes back to the observer. The consciousness. The Soul. This is the real message of reality. This is what I have been learning, and this is what I have been inspired to teach.

NOTES

1. Reprinted with permission of Pocket Books, a division of Simon & Schuster, Inc., from *Entangled Minds* by Dean Radin. Copyright ©2006 by Dean Radin Ph.D. All rights reserved. See p. 154.

2. Ibid., p. 198.

3. Ibid., p. 204.

4. From the Global Consciousness Project web site, http://noosphere.princeton.edu. Used by permission.

5. Gary E. Schwartz, Ph.D., with William Simon, *The Afterlife Experiments* (Pocket Books, a division of Simon & Schuster, Inc., 2002). Used by permission.

6. From the book *Miracles of Mind.* Copyright ©1998, 1999 by Russell Targ and Jane Katra, Ph.D. Reprinted with permission of New World Library, Novato, California. www.newworldlibrary.com. See p. 36.

7. Ibid., pp. 42-44.

8. From the book *Limitless Mind.* Copyright ©2004 by Russell Targ and Jane Katra, Ph.D. Reprinted with permission of New World Library, Novato, California. www.newworldlibrary.com. See pp. 146, 174.

9. William A. Tiller, Walter E. Dibble, Jr, and Michael J. Kohane, *Conscious Acts of Creation* (Walnut Creek, California: Pavior Publishing, 2001), pp. 394-397. Used with permission.

10. Ibid.

11. Larry Farwell, *How Consciousness Commands Matter* (Fairfield, Iowa: Sunstar Publishing, 1999), pp. 142-144. Used with permission from the author.

12. From *Closer to the Light* by Melvin Morse, M.D., Paul Perry, copyright ©1988 by Melvin Morse and Paul Perry. Used by permission of Villiard Books, a division of Random House, Inc.

13. From *Transformed by the Light* by Melvin Morse, M.D., Paul Perry, copyright ©1992 by Melvin Morse and Paul Perry. Used by permission of Villiard Books, a division of Random House, Inc.

14. Jim B. Tucker, *Life Before Life* (New York: St. Martin's Press, 2005).

Chapter Four

SYNTHESIS

Sometimes, the lunch rush at the restaurant where my brother and I worked in our late teens was horrendous. Being the only bus boy on duty meant that I had to fly around the establishment at breakneck speeds to clear tables and make way for the next round of customers. Similarly, my brother, who worked in the dish room, had to deal with the onslaught of dirty dishes I brought in, plus whatever pans the cooks discarded. Some days, we just weren't up to the physical challenge.

But we also knew it provided ample testing ground for what we had been learning from my guides: You create your own reality.

Our solution to the crazy lunch rush was to mentally think and feel differently about it—to intentionally infuse the environment—so that it would be *slower than usual* (at least that way, we had some hope of keeping up!). These were always spur-of-the-moment experiments, but we did our best to take what we had learned and to use it to our advantage. (After all, boys will be boys!)

Similar to the RNG test results from the last chapter, we certainly didn't keep customers from coming in, but there was a noticeable difference in the size of groups that came and the pace at which the lunch rush passed. Again, our goal was to slow things down, and whenever we put that focus out into the environment without succumbing to any thoughts or feelings of doubt, the lunch hour did move smoothly into the afternoon lull. I didn't have to careen around the restaurant, and my brother didn't have to deal with a clogged up dishwasher and sweat through a heap of crusty kitchen pans. In essence, we had synthesized spiritual teaching with practical reality and achieved a measurable result, albeit one that was never documented on paper (though it was potentially recorded on the daily restaurant receipts).

Years later, I had another chance to try a similar experiment. At the time, I had just started my first office job, answering phones and doing data entry. It was extremely hectic and oftentimes stressful. Very early on, I sensed it was going to be a challenge working there and often wondered why I had created such a reality for myself. Nevertheless, I was committed to seeing it through as long as I could—but some days, it became too much.

One morning I decided—no, I prayed—that I could take matters into my own hands. It was my week to be answering the phones, and with all the bad energy floating through the atmosphere from various sources, I had had enough. I had no idea what to do in order to change things—all I knew is that any outcome had to at least get me off the phone and a moment of pause to squeeze in a breath. I pushed that sense of interruption with such mental intensity…it short-circuited the phone system. Literally. The multiple lines came down, and we were forced to use a single phone in the warehouse. It was perfect. One of my coworkers took over the phone, while I stole a breather. An hour later, everything was back up—but by then, I had recharged my batteries and was able to better handle the stress of the day.

Some people might say that the phones going down was mere coincidence, but factoring in the odds that it would happen after I had specifically asked for a disruptive change—statistically speaking, it's unlikely that the two were unrelated. When you become sensitive to your inner energies in relation to your outer environment, you learn very quickly there is no such thing as coincidence.

How could this happen? How was I able to create such an event? On a fundamental level, I knew it was a combination of thoughts, feelings, attitudes, and expectations. In this case, I expected some kind of a breather—even if it was only momentary—in which to experience some semblance of freedom from my stifling surroundings. I wasn't willing to accept anything less. In retrospect, it was an aggressive move. But if you were a lobster getting boiled in the pot, wouldn't you wish for the flames to go out?

To my surprise (and ecstasy), I later discovered that here, in the context of forced intention, was a series of scientific studies being conducted by large groups of practitioners interested in transcendental meditation (TM).

The first studies were performed in twenty-four U.S. cities in which 1% of the population was studying the TM technique. The TM practitioners were asked to put forth an intention of less crime in previously specified cities when they meditated. By using FBI crime statistics, it was noted that crime rates decreased significantly in the twenty-four cities in which the TM practitioners focused, while crime increased in demographically matched control cities. The crime rate was also significantly lower over the next six years for the cities in which TM had been performed. These trials were so intriguing, they were replicated three times.[1]

The first published research on the society-wide influence of group practice of the TM-Sidhi technique (a slightly different form of TM practice, the goal of which is to train the mind to think from the mind's source) was reported in 1987 by Dillbeck et al. They reported statistically significant crime reductions in Manila, Philippines, during two specific periods when large groups practiced the TM and TM-Sidhi techniques. There was an 11% reduction in crime from November

1980 to March 1981, and a 12% reduction in crime from August 1984 to August 1985.[2]

In 1983, during the war in Lebanon, a group of TM-Sidhi experts went to Israel after submitting predictions in advance in the presence of U.S. and Israeli scientists regarding reductions in war deaths and other societal measures. In a 1988 study published in the *Journal of Conflict Resolution,* Orme-Johson reported highly significant decreases in war deaths, war intensity, and numerous other measures related to stress, such as crime rate, traffic accidents, fires, and increases in measures of overall well-being and in the stock market. These results have been replicated seven times.[3] Factor this jaw-dropping phenomenon in with what we've seen regarding the GCP and its work with RNGs, and again—something remarkable about the nature of the human Soul emerges.

On three separate occasions, large assemblies of TM-Sidhi and TM experts turned their attention to the well-being of the entire world. During these assemblies, international conflicts decreased by more than 30%, and terrorism worldwide decreased by 70%. World-wide stock markets also increased significantly.[4]

A few years ago, best-selling author Lynn McTaggart launched a new inquiry into the power of intention with her book, *The Intention Experiment.* The book chronicles the amazing pursuits of scientists into measuring the power of conscious intent and its effects in the world. Using her findings as a primer, Lynn decided to use her own seminars and the power of the Web to conduct intention experiments in conjunction with scientists around the world. Her experiments have yielded spectacular results.

The first pilot experiment was performed in 2007. Sixteen meditators based in London were asked to direct their thoughts on four remote targets in Germany: on two types of algae, a plant, and a human volunteer. They were asked to attempt to lower certain measurable biodynamic processes through meditation. The results showed significant changes in all four targets while the intentions were being sent, as compared with times when the meditators were "resting."[5]

A second experiment was performed on a pair of geranium leaves. Dr. Gary Schwartz of Arizona State University, who we discussed earlier, assisted with the experiment by measuring the results. The two leaves were identical in size and in the number of light emissions, as recorded by a super-cooled digital charge-coupled device, or CCD, camera system. One leaf was to receive an intention, and the other leaf was not (to act as a control). The leaves were then punctured sixteen times to provide more than thirty data points that could be measured for statistical significance.

On March 11, 2007, during one of Lynn's conferences, the leaves were projected on a screen for Lynn and her audience via webcam. The audience was asked to choose one of the two leaves as the target by flipping a coin. At the time, she didn't tell Dr. Schwartz or his assistant, Mark Boccuzzi, which leaf had been chosen to receive the intention, thereby providing a blind experiment for the researchers. For ten minutes, the group focused on increasing the light emissions of the chosen leaf by using their thoughts, to make the leaf "glow and glow." After the experiment was over and the calculation for each leaf was tabulated, it was determined by the CCD camera that the target leaf did, in fact, show measurable increases in light. Further, Dr. Schwartz revealed that the changes in the light emissions of the leaf were so strong that they could readily be seen on the digital images captured by the CCD cameras. Numerically, the increased biophoton effect was highly significant. In fact, he said, all the punctured holes in the chosen leaf were filled with light. All the holes in the control leaf, on the other hand, remained dark.[6]

These experiments always leave one asking: How does it work?

Look back upon your own life and count how many times you desired something and then it "magically" came to you, or how many times it seemed that everything "fell magically into place" to make it happen. It seemed like coincidence, right? I have personally manifested some pretty complex stuff—a new car, a new job, a wonderful new marriage, and a new house, just to name a few. For each intention I set forth, I included specifics that I considered a requirement for each item. The manifestations of the intentions, which have always arrived with my requirements intact, provide statistical evidence that these manifestations were not simply coincidence. Take a moment to review your own past successes. How many are there? Could they *all* be attributed to chance?

"Sometimes it doesn't work." Yes, I can hear you saying that. "Why not?" you might ask. And how does this relate to the Soul?

Let's start with a talk about energy. Your Soul is energy. And energy travels in waves. Waves behave in certain fashions. If two cresting waves meet, they create a more powerful, larger wave. This would

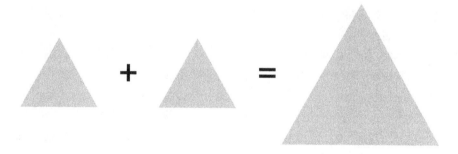

Two cresting waves come together to create a larger, more powerful wave.

be analogous to the TM group performing mass meditation to reduce crime in conflicted geographical areas. However, if the two waves are opposing when they meet—that is, one is a crest while the other is a trough—they cancel each other out, and the power of each wave is nullified. This is why some thoughts come to pass while others do not: The frequencies cancel each other out.

A cresting wave meets with a trough, cancelling out the energy packets for a null effect.

Again, this speaks to the idea of *coherence,* a term used in physics.

The energies of doubt and skepticism introduce trough-like formations in the wave potentials of an intention, which can then lessen an outcome. I have seen this happen in my own personal life, as well as the lives of others. The reason certain things fail to materialize is not because the universe is out to get you or because it's beyond your control, it's because you have yet to work the energy properly. In other words, the energetic wave of creative power is still filled with too many instances of troughs—negative energy dips—that keep the positive peaks from growing and instigating the literal quantum leaps necessary to affect the foundations of basic matter. Beliefs about your current reality can hinder the process, as they contribute to the buildup of emotional energy (which definitely impacts the creative process).

Much of this becomes strikingly clear in communicating with an individual's deceased relatives. In cases where the personality lived a hard life, there is always an apology and recognition that things could have been different. The deceased always seem to recognize that the power was in their control while alive, they just failed to acknowledge it and went about their downward spiral. In one case, a client's deceased grandmother insisted, "You have the choice—you have the power to choose. Stick to your guns." This was her way of saying, "Don't let the appearance of outside forces dictate how you think and feel on the inside." It's a moniker that should be adopted by everyone. As I was taught, and as has been my experience, the opposite is wholly true: "Your inner thoughts and feelings dictate the circumstances of your 'outer' reality."

I had one client whose deceased father vehemently apologized for all the abuse he showered on his son during his life. He admitted that the anger was his own and that he simply could not see beyond his own shortcomings. Even at the time of the reading, he mentioned that he was still "getting counseling" on the Other Side. When his son had called to book the appointment, I had no inkling of the nature of the client's relationship to his father. After hanging up the telephone, however, I could hear his father screaming in my ear, the way he had done to his son while he was alive. This was his way of notifying me what the nature of the reading was going to be about. Once on the Other Side, the client's father was able to see his inability to move beyond his own mind during his life—and that there were other choices he could have made that would have spared his son a great deal of pain, as well as his own remorse.

The message that is paramount is that we do have choices, and that we do have a direct hand in the creation of our lives. The spirits admit that had they thought differently while alive, new events would have come to pass, resulting in a much better life than they ended up living. From the Other Side, they could see the course of their lives as resulting of an inner point of view. This inner perspective, which originated within themselves, manifested outward into the world, as opposed to life "happening to them" in a way that was beyond their control. We can see this with our own friends and family, who are alive with us in the here and now. Haven't you ever wanted to smack a friend or family member, in an attempt to get him or her to think differently, or to change how he or she might approach something?

Earthbound spirits, as mentioned earlier, oftentimes don't have the view of personal responsibility like their brethren on the Other Side.

They still believe they are at the mercy of events happening *to* them—hence, some of the haunting activities. When delving into these cases, I usually wind up playing psychologist to the deceased to get them to leave the homeowners alone or to help them to simply move on. A lot of people, even when they're dead, can still remain locked into old patterns of thinking and behaving, oblivious to all other options available. This keeps their frustrations going, their fears, and their lack of control.

The only reason I believe crossed-overs are different is because of the "life review."

Life reviews are a common theme in near-death studies. When a person enters "the tunnel" and emerges into a new dimension, what often happens is they are greeted by a deceased relative or a religious figure who then "replays" the newcomer's life. The unique aspect about a life review is that not only are you visually seeing your life played out before your eyes, you are also able to *feel* the emotions and energy of everyone involved in your history as it unfolds before you. In this way, you become intimately aware of how your energy—your choices—impacted everyone and everything around you. In that sense, you could say it was an "eye for an eye" and a "tooth for a tooth." This realization becomes an unmistakable tribute to the idea that we are all connected and One. In hurting others, we only hurt ourselves—and this becomes a literal truth from the standpoint of a life review. Afterward, the knowledge gained segues a being into a different psychic framework, helping one to better interact with others and evolve one's future life experiences.

An earthbound entity, having not gone through the tunnel, more than likely has not had the benefit of a life review, and therefore still lacks the knowledge of how his choices impact others and how they ultimately impact himself. Those that have gone through the tunnel and into the light are forever changed—this has been documented, time and time again, by those who have come back from an NDE. Conversely, someone who has passed and has ignored the calling of the light would still be somewhat attached to his previous psychic framework of how he lived his life on earth and how he interacted with others. If a ghost knows he has died and is simply hanging around, then we would have to say that the death experience had a very negligible impact (if any at all) on the overall psyche of the deceased. In some way, he is still attached to his environment, to certain people, or to previous emotions or events (or any combination of these). In a sense, although he has died and departed his physical body, he has yet to "die" to these other intangibles in his life. In so remaining, he neglects his own evolution and any options he may have for growth, experience, and enjoyment.

In many ways, billions of people alive on earth right now are in a similar predicament. In my years of doing readings and paranormal investigations and just simply interacting with others, I have seen how people keep themselves cut off from the magnificence of their Souls. They walk in lockstep with a belief system, an emotion, or a mental attitude that inhibits the innumerable possibilities available to them. Stuck in a rut with these blinders on, I have seen people give up and make no effort to change their lives and discover their own immutable power. Yet they are their own creators! They perceive no magic in their lives, yet the very act of life itself is magic in motion. They feel they are trapped inside their bodies, always relegating freedom as something outside that must be given to them, yet scientific experiments have shown that the mind affects matter—revealing the very gateway to freedom! Every spiritual discipline on earth believes in the power of faith moving mountains, yet all faith in the creative source—one's self—is completely ignored. Marcus Aurelius said it best when he opined, "Your mind will be like its habitual thoughts; for the soul becomes dyed with the color of its thoughts."

I have spent my entire life inquiring into the nature of the Soul and its capacities, both esoteric and everyday. The seat of consciousness, your Soul—your life—is a magical one. Every coincidence is created by you, whether you are aware of this consciously or not. When you begin to pay attention to your Soul and the possibilities inherent in your divinity, you begin to see how the subtleties of life are instruments in an orchestra of incredible creation, and that *you* are the conductor of every minute detail of the song. It is your song you are hearing and experiencing. Your experience is also an instrument in an even larger orchestra: the symphony of all life happening on earth, at this very moment.

Do you contribute to the song as a vibrant, lilting melody, making it a joyous piece of music with which to be enamored? Or do you drag out each note in a low, sometimes off-key defiance?

Do you invite the other instruments to enhance your theme, or do you find yourself sitting out in silence, feeling that your song simply doesn't belong?

Either way, you are a part of the music. And you have every ability to guide the entire chorus, once you realize that you, the orchestra, and the conductor, are one in the same.

NOTES

1. Larry Farwell, *How Consciousness Commands Matter* (Fairfield, Iowa: Sunstar Publishing, 1999), pp. 153-154. Used with permission from the author.

2. Ibid.

3. Ibid.

4. Ibid.

5. Based on the book *The Intention Experiment* by Lynne McTaggart, published by Free Press, an imprint of Simon & Schuster. Referenced from Lynne McTaggart's web site, http://www.theintentionexperiment.com. Used with permission.

6. Ibid.

Part Two

THE
MESSAGE

Chapter Five

GETTING IN TOUCH
WITH YOUR SOUL, PART I

CONTEMPLATION
OF THE SPIRIT-SELF

Have you ever stopped to consider the REAL you? When you think about yourself, do you automatically envision that person you see standing in front of the mirror? Chances are, you do. But you are much more than that. Indeed, you are a far more fantastic creation than the trillions of atoms circling about your Soul, creating that visage you behold in the reflection of your mind.

Think about it.

No one knows where the real "you" resides inside your flesh. Where is that Being that creates your personality? That makes decisions? That reacts to events and circumstances—and, in fact, even creates them? As a professional medium and ghost researcher, my experience has told me that you are ultimately no such body at all—that you exist very much beyond it.

When somebody without a physical body can transmit images or words into the frontal cortex of my brain, which I can then recognize and pass on to a loved one sitting before me, the experience suggests something more than a mere epiphenomenon of organs and tissues churning out a personality. Or when a deceased spirit, without the same physical apparatus as myself, is able to somehow manipulate the electronics in my voice recorder to allow his or her voice to be heard during playback—this, too, suggests something wonderful and magical about the nature of our Beings.

So, you may ask, what does this reveal about you and your own life?

Can you imagine yourself without a body?

If we are all spirit, "encased" in flesh, consider what your true Soul looks like.

One morning as I was sitting in meditation, I took up the challenge. I resolved to travel through my inner landscape and discover that ultimate observer within myself. My objective was to pin it down in some sort of three-dimensional perception, if possible, so that I could somehow better relate to it in my physical experience. Since I believe that I am a Soul, and that my Soul came before my body and will go on after it expires, I wished to know what the face of my true spiritual Being looked like.

It was a surreal adventure. The answer that was offered to me revealed something I knew to be true for every living thing throughout Time and Space. It was like turning away from the movie screen of my life and becoming aware of the projectionist in the booth.

I ask you to do the same.

Look inside yourself, for You. Ask yourself: Where am I inside this body? If I am Spirit, and if I have a Soul, what does that mean? If you are to take this journey with me in attempting to understand your magical Soul, it is not going to entail simply reading and absorbing information from this book. Life is about experience. And if you have picked up this book, some part of you wishes to experience a greater dimension within yourself that can only come as a result of deep inspection and reflection, not basic reading and comprehension.

The exercise of trying to find the real You may startle and inspire you. I guarantee it will give you a sense of magic about your Being, which has been hidden behind the wall of flesh you've perceived yourself to be walking around in.

Here is the answer I received when I asked the question (and since you and I are made in the same way, you be the judge as to whether my experience also holds true for you). The "I"-ness of me and of you is an invisible spirit, ultimately without form and preceding form: You are *less than a mist*. You cannot truly, really, be seen—only felt. Your flesh, your face, your façade, is an aftereffect of your life energy and Being, but it still is not You. You make Yourself known through subtle vibrations of energy. At its root, that is all life is anyway—vibrational energy—energy that is sifted and translated through the senses of your body, reconstructed within your Mind, and thrust outward again into the universe. You—your Soul—is volition. You are movement without a First Cause, other than your own invisible Mind. When I say Mind, I do not mean your physical brain, but rather the invisible psychic framework you think from. Creation, therefore, springs from You. Nothing came before you—you have *always been*.

Consider the movements of your body, as it moves according to the subtle vibration of your thoughts. You think, "move arm," and energy responds to the command and your arm waves.

Realize that your thoughts emanate even further outside your flesh to mingle with the universe in creating circumstances, events, and coincidences. Remember the scientific studies from earlier, about the geranium leaves and the alpha particles? Remember your own mental list of previous coincidences that "magically" came together for you, after you desired something and then it appeared or happened? This notion of being able to create your own reality may seem fantastic and even dubious at first. However, I hope to show you that as you open yourself to the possibility that you are indeed the projectionist of the circumstances of your life, you will come to know, for yourself, that this is the truth of You. Moreover, since the source of You is formless and thus invisible within the context of matter, you *must* create form and develop form. Yet, form is always fleeting, for you can never find You within that matter.

"Doctor, can your instruments find Me?"

No. The "I," the essence of your being and my being, your very personality, cannot be found anywhere inside your bodily tissues and organs. The physical body will still exist, albeit without movement, after you have vacated it, eventually decomposing into a different material state—but it will still consist of an atomic structure nonetheless.

Indeed, molecular biologists even concede that our thoughts affect molecular events.

In his paradigm-shattering book, *The Biology of Belief,* Bruce Lipton, Ph.D., acknowledges that the trillions of cells in the body are affected by the environment they swim around in, and guess what: That inner environment of the cellular world is controlled by the emotions and beliefs You create! He discovered this by conducting numerous experiments with cell cultures.

In one study involving the use of endothelial cells—the cells that line the blood vessels—Lipton discovered that the cells reacted differently to "positive" and "negative" environmental stimuli. When he offered nutrients, the cells gravitated toward the nutrients. When he created a toxic environment, the cells retreated.[1] We offer the same types of environments to our cells on the basis of our thoughts and emotions! When you think and feel "positive" thoughts, this provides a nutrient-filled environment for your cells to propagate a healthy inner experience. By contrast, feelings that are considered "negative," such as anger and hate, have the opposite effect. They create a toxic residue at the cellular level that can not only make you sick, but can propagate the development of debilitating health conditions, with potentially life-altering effects.

A similar type of event is referred to as the *psychosomatic communication network,* as coined by pharmacologist Candace Pert, Ph.D., who (in conjunction with her husband, Michael), discovered that the body works as if it has a mind all its own, that it communicates within itself, between all the cells and organs, and that the Mind of You, in combination with the body, can control how the "molecules of emotion" work and interact. Pert found that the Mind can inform the body to create certain peptides to fit particular cellular receptors. Once the peptide "hooks" into the cellular receptor, like a key in a door, the cell then reacts on the basis of the information provided by the peptide. As an example, Pert discovered that the brain can produce a peptide to fit into a cellular receptor that would produce the same effect as taking morphine![2] What this means is that your brain has the capability to create all the chemicals necessary to balance and maintain health, or completely knock it asunder. Can you guess what creates the impulse to manufacture the peptides? That's right—You. Your consciousness. Your Soul.

And, may we ask, who perceives the senses? Who registers the sights, smells, sounds, tastes, and touches we encounter in everyday life?

To my dear Doctor: If you try to find the Observer in our tissue and cells, you will still come up empty-handed.

To my dear Reader: You are not trapped inside a body or in any kind of physical mold—for a physical mold presupposes substance, of which you are not. Since you are ultimately a Soul, form cannot capture you—you cannot be caged. If you have never thought about yourself this way, consider this your wake-up call—you are free! You are not—and have never been—bound within your physical body. Far from it. In which case, if you are not truly bound here in the flesh but have only come to experience an aspect of soul-life through the filtering mechanism of a body, then where are you? What are you? What does it mean to be a Soul?

You are a Force—a Force from which you *evoke* form. *You call form into existence.* This was demonstrated to me through my work as a medium and a ghost researcher. Likewise, it has been demonstrated by scientists seeking to identify the effects of consciousness on matter.

As a medium, I have heard countless stories from people of how a deceased relative has come to them in the form of a physical sign. One of my clients told me that her father often appears to her as dragonfly. During one of his visits, a dragonfly actually landed on her leg and remained there for an entire minute! Oftentimes, when he communicates with me during a reading, he excites my olfactory nerves to smell smoke, because he was a smoker. One of my wife's deceased cousins makes himself known by manipulating dimes—he'll leave dimes in places where there had been none only moments earlier. This tells us that even without a body, a person still has a *force*, and it can be used to evoke form into existence and/or provide the impetus to *make something happen.*

The evidence points to the realization that You are less than a mist, but You sing through the *objects and events* you create. Spiritual language, the language of the Soul, is not a string of words uttered through the lips—no, the voice of spirit is the environment and the events of one's life. Your voice can be heard through the life you live—not the words you speak, but the Reality your invisible volition effectuates.

If you feel that you are living in a form of oppressive prison, release your spirit from its invisible enclosure, through the realization that it is merely a figment of your own creation. It is no more than a mental construct generated within your own mind. It is made…of nothing at all.

Since you are less than a mist, you are the embodiment of Nothing. Your Word—the very thoughts that give your spirit a communicative voice—is your Reality. Your Reality, then, is a manifestation of your psyche, your Mind, which in itself is Invisible. Your self-created prison is a simple house of cards—no, it's less than that. It is an illusion—a digital green-screen of *effect*. Recognition and consciousness give the illusion life—and the only way the illusion can live is with your consent.

And so, it is truly only in the Mind of You, the observer, ultimately looking in upon yourself, that you perceive this self-limiting prison to exist at all. This is the reality proven by quantum physics, where the introduction of an observer affects the way quantum particles and waves react and behave. It is further substantiated by cellular biologists, who continually demonstrate that our beliefs affect the very health of our cells, tissues, and organs, in the most powerful ways.

Here is a basic example of how you create reality in your mind. Take a look at the following picture.

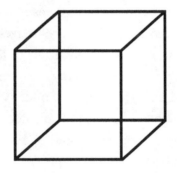

Here, it appears we have a simple box. When you look at it, do you see it pop into three dimensions? If so, do you see part of it jut out from above, angling toward the right? Or, do you see it sticking out and down, toward the left? Either way, the reality is that it is a two-dimensional drawing on a piece of paper, which your mind perceives to be a three-dimensional box. If two people look at this drawing simultaneously, one person may see the box from an upper view, while the other may view it from below. This proves that it is indeed the mind-set of the observer, *inside*, that creates the perception of what is going on *outside*, and that no two people see the exact same thing in the same way.

When light strikes the retinas of your eyes, it passes through filters shaped like cones and rods. These filters take the incoming wavelengths of light and break them down into hues, saturations, and intensities, which then zip down the optic nerve into the visual cortex of the brain. Here, the Mind organizes the data into an image *inside your head*, to allow you to "see" what is actually out in front of you. The fact of the matter is, not everything that exists before your eyes is being shown to you, since we can only see a very narrow band of the light spectrum. We can feel ultraviolet light on our skin, but we cannot see it with our eyes, because it vibrates at a frequency that we are unable to translate optically. The opposite is true for certain insects, who can tell what flower to land on by the ultraviolet light that they *can see.*

The play of light being assembled inside our heads offers us a perception of spatial distance outside of ourselves. In contrast, if you were to blindfold a bat, he would still be able to fly easily through the branches of any tree and snatch up any insect of his choosing. His perception isn't based on light, but on sound, as bats travel by echo-location. Bats emit high-pitched sounds outside the range detectable with our ears, and those frequencies bounce off of their surroundings and create within the bat's brain a kind of picture that informs him of the creature's path. If bats could talk, and you asked one what a tree looked like, his perception would undoubtedly differ from yours! Put a blindfold on most people, and they would run into that tree. Place earplugs in a bat's ears, and he would do the same. It's all a matter of perception.

Life is a play upon itself, which unfolds in the Mind of the ob-server, who in turn creates the framework of that Mind.

You are ultimately Nothing in terms of physicality as a Soul—and you are constructing Reality within a framework of an invisible Mind.

No two people will ever see the same object or event in the same way. At the same time, it has been demonstrated that you have the ability to affect all things through the efforts of your Mind. All this combined reveals an inherent truth, that there are no walls that can contain the "I" of You or Me.

Let Freedom by your new cry.

Let Abundance be your new Word.

If you are Nothing in terms of form, then you are the inherent potential of ALL THINGS, because Nothing has *no limits.* It is indestructible. It is infinity wrapped in eternity. And since Nothing has no limits, then the potential for all things exists within that formless "void." *Nothing has no limits.* It is All—therefore, the unseen essence of You is also All.

You have no bounds. You are a boundless force, working with other invisible forces, whether those forces be other people, the planet, or the stars spinning above your head. Everything cooperates in a vast cosmic orchestra, of which you are a major player (yes, you!). Your Mind constructs the ultimate observation of the music, but You are, in fact, the conductor. You are both the instrument and the composer. You are simultaneously an instrument in your own song, as well as in someone else's. One instrument missing from the ensemble changes the dynamic of the entire symphony—so know that you are here on purpose, creating a beautiful melody, espoused by the energy of your unseen, boundless, creative Being. It is an orchestra in which the members are not distinguishable by personality, age, or race; it is a song of pure energy, vibrating at all possible frequencies, like an ocean undulating across the infinite bounds of the earthen sphere.

When you "embody" a desire, you are creating a new Spiritual Body, wrapping it around your invisible Being. Your new flesh becomes the people, places, and things you experience. Again, You are without form, but You create form by your own volition of your Spirit-Self. Contemplate upon this. Contemplate upon the nature of your own Soul.

At night, when I dream, I completely lose connection with my waking appearance. Instead, I create a whole new one. It's just as valid, for I can feel the wind brush up against my new flesh as I'm flying over the ground; I can also feel my feet sluggish upon the floor as I try to outrun a sinister monster. It seems that when I sleep, a whole new world opens up, and the one I just spent sixteen or more hours in becomes a different reality.

Envision yourself in your own dreams for just a moment. Don't you react to your dream experiences as vividly and intensely as you would during "normal" waking life? Do you not also feel the imagined heat of the sun on your dream body's skin? Or the wind rustling your hair or chilling you to the bone? I have yet to find someone who doesn't. In fact, some people experience more intensity in their dreams than they do in their waking lives.

When we dream, we completely disassociate from the existence we had been living before we laid down to rest. It vanishes entirely. Our consciousness during the dream state is not worried about what happened to our physical bodies from that "other" physical reality, for it does not exist while we're dreaming; we don't even acknowledge it lying there on the bed. If you were to take an honest approach toward your Being while in the dream state, you would find yourself totally dismissing this other body you inhabit during your "waking life," because what is real at that moment is the body you are experiencing in the dream. In your dreams, too, you experience a three-dimensional reality, with spatial separation and perhaps even Time. It is only because we are taught in the Western world to downplay our dreams that we completely dismiss the dream-body and its experiences altogether.

Some cultures don't do this. They consider their dream lives to be experiences just as valid as their normal waking ones. In their dreams, they fulfill goals and obligations and continue to grow and expand in ways not only identical to those in their waking lives, but in ways that could not be achieved in this waking reality. The dreaming life, for them, fits naturally within their own consciousness and is not separate from it. Indeed, they would feel a loss without it.

As an example, the Achuar and the Huaorani Indians of the Amazon gather together every morning to discuss their dreams. To them, the experiences of the dream state foretell what is to come in the waking hours. In those dreams, they connect with their ancestors and the rest of the universe. The dream is what is real. It is their waking life that is the falsehood.[3] For others, dreams provide opportunities and present possibilities that could carry over into one's awakened state. For those who have made an effort to journal their dreams, it is not uncommon that, upon reflection of these nightly passages, startling precognitive information has been discovered, which helps to warn or reveal certain events to come. Continuous dream symbols, once considered ambiguous, after journaling and conscious inspection, reveal themselves to be harbingers of intellectual wisdom couched in a visual camouflage that can then be decoded for waking life. Both realities sing to an individual the proof of one's *multidimensional* existence and signals to the consciousness of our invisible Souls.

If we can traverse different bodies—those in an awakened state, and those in a dream state—and realize that our perceptions arise from inside our Minds and not from outside, then we automatically know, from a consciousness point of view, that we are not solely the bodies we walk around in—we can travel between worlds and realities. Therefore, we ultimately transcend *a* body. The You, the real You, is not something encased within a single form—You can be in many. You may simply choose to downplay one over the other, but this does not negate the existence of the other. Secondly, whenever you participate in an event, whether it occurs in an awakened state or while dreaming, no matter how trivial the circumstance, you either act or react, actively or passively, on the basis of your mental interpretation of the events you are experiencing. In other words, your own unseen (yet valid) psychological interpretation informs your next course of action. The bodies that we live in (physical and dreaming) respond to our *mental* wishes, independent of whether we're operating within our waking or dreaming body. The body does not produce the thought, the thought produces the body—how it will react, what muscles to move, etcetera. Some scientists even suggest that the brain is not the originator of the thought itself, but an amplifier.

As Itzhak Bentov states:

> For those who can quiet their minds as a result of long years of prac-
> ticing meditation, a thought is a very coarse, big thing. It's like a truck
> rumbling through the head and disturbs the very fine equilibrium achieved
> by balancing the mind in a nonthought state. I suggest, therefore, that our
> brain is not the *source* of thought but a *thought amplified*...It takes a tiny
> impulse, magnifies it for us, and only then does it become a thought. It
> appears that thought does not originate within the brain; rather, the brain
> picks up the tiny impulses implanted there by our astral, mental, or causal
> bodies...It is the function of the brain to amplify this signal for us into a
> useful form.[4]

Indeed, where is it that impulse and thought originate from, that sparks the brain to fire in the first place? These would be the astral, mental, or causal bodies Bentov speaks of—suggesting that the real You actually resides in multiple dimensions at once.

No molecule inside the suit of anything alive on earth reveals the actual animator of the clothing. This physical stuff that moves around from day to day is one step outside the realm of who You are. The body does not create circumstances, it can only perform movement and function. *It is the invisible Soul that creates events, for it is the Soul that creates the psychological frameworks and embeds them with the color of experience.* It is the Soul that records and reviews these moments of Time and says unto itself, "It is good."

For some, this realization may constitute your first experience with the true nature of your wonderful Soul. You are boundless and eternal. You are *perfect*. Contemplate on this. And you, too, will know that it is so.

NOTES

1. Bruce Lipton, *The Biology of Belief* (Carlsbad, California: Hay House, Inc., 2005). Used with permission.

2. Candace Pert, *Everything You Need to Know to Feel Go(o)D* (Carlsbad, California: Hay House, Inc., 2006). Used with permission.

3. The description of the Amazonian Indians was based on a study conducted by The Institute of Noetic Sciences, which appeared in the following article: Marilyn Schlitz, "On Consciousness, Causation and Evolution," *Alt Ther.*, 4(4):82-90 (1998).

4. Itzhak Bentov, *Stalking the Wild Pendulum* (Rochester, Vermont: Destiny Books, 1988), pp. 115-116. Used with permission.

Chapter Six

GETTING IN TOUCH
WITH YOUR SOUL, PART II

SO—WHERE DOES
THE SOUL RESIDE?

It's time to take a look at ourselves in an effort to come to some sort of conclusion in the dilemma of locating the Soul, which exists somewhere in Time and Space. Let's face it, if a Soul—you and me—is "less than a mist," than just where the heck are we? To try and answer this question, I will examine myself at this very moment (I also invite you to do the same).

As I sit in this chair and write, I can sense not only the top of my head, but also the bottom of my feet. If I cared to, I could feel sensations throughout my body, from top to bottom, all at the same time. There's tingling all over, as organs work together and blood courses through my veins. I can feel my heart beating and my feet receiving the pulse all within the same moment.

"So what?" you might ask.

Stop and think about it. I can feel all this going on *simultaneously*.

Try it for yourself. Feel your feet. At first it might just be a gentle warmth that gives way to a tingle, perhaps followed by the recognition of weight from your bones. Then, without turning your attention away from your feet, focus on your hands. You might feel a rush of energy streaming through your wrists and down to your fingertips. Maybe your palms also have a slight tingle to them. Then, once you feel both your hands and feet together, turn your attention to your head, or any other part of your body, and take in the sensations there.

I used to wonder if the Soul rested in the head, because that was where my sight came in and where I got most of my sensory information. Hearing, sight, taste, smell…but is the head really the entry point? No. I receive sensory information throughout my whole body. For instance, when giving psychic readings, if a member of the family is diabetic, my right foot tingles like it's asleep. In ghost investigations, if I walk onto the site and my legs feel weighty, as if I were walking through thick mud, I know there's an entity hanging around. If you've ever had a "gut feeling," then you know your body gets sensory information from other places than simply your head. For me personally, I find myself entranced by the visual sensations of my eyes more than my other senses, it seems.

All this talk, however, presupposes that the Soul is a tangible entity that contains mass and resides "inside the body," as a driver resides within the physical space of a car. However, if such a driver could simultaneously feel all parts of the car—from steering wheel, to the rear window, to the tires—one would have to deduce that such a driver does not actually sit anywhere inside the car, but in fact exists throughout the entire vehicle! What's more, does such a traveler stop at the edge of the car, or can he (or she) extend beyond it?

Remote viewing and various other psychic phenomena certainly indicate that this is so.

In 1974, Pat Price successfully described a Soviet weapons factory in eastern Russia. In a joint American-Russian experiment in

1984, Russell Targ, along with his daughter Elisabeth and Russian healer Djuna Davitashvili, successfully remote-viewed a location in San Francisco from Moscow. Not only was it a 10,000-mile-long viewing, Djuna also perceived it two hours in advance of the target team's arrival![1] Remote-viewing descriptions during these tests ranged from a sense of floating above a location and "seeing" the objects below (visually), to sometimes feeling where objects were and what they might be.

The most astounding remote viewing story Russell talks of is when Ingo Swann decided he wanted to remote-view the planet Jupiter. At the time, he said he saw a ring around the planet and admitted that it sounded inaccurate. At a later date, pictures came back from NASA to reveal that, indeed, Jupiter did have a noticeable ring!

Now, I can sit here and pour my consciousness into this chair or into the wall several feet away from me. That is, I can think "chair" or "wall" and actually "feel" myself within those areas, as if a part of me is somehow existing within these other structures. I can immediately sense a different "frequency" of feeling than that in, say, my feet. Indeed, I can even sense the width of the wall, its height, and its length. I can also perceive (if the wall had eyes) its "view" of the floor. If this sounds at all strange to you, I encourage you to stand next to a wall. Put your hand on it and sense through your fingertips not just its textual surface, but look inside your mind, that area you would typically call your imagination, and other areas of your body. You may feel a small but recognizable difference from your usual sense of self. You may even have quick flashes inside the visual cortex of your brain, revealing things about the wall itself—where studs are located, and the insulation and wires, etcetera. Once you have done that, go sit in a chair elsewhere in the house and focus your attention back on that wall. You may again feel, inside yourself, the sensation of the wall. Now, in order to not relegate the sensation to simple memory, place your mind in a different wall, or better yet, an entirely different object. On the surface, this may sound foreign and uncertain to you, but it is, in actuality, an exercise in remote viewing and alternative consciousness perception. Take a walk in a forest or grove, and try the same experiment with the plants and trees. If you have never done this before, you may find yourself filled with awe and wonder, as you allow yourself to feel the majesty of nature from the inside for the very first time.

As another example, I can sense the television I have in this room, off to my left. Something in my energy can feel the hardness of the glass screen, and beyond that, a sense of something within the unit itself. This is not my imagination, for I am not "seeing" anything in my mind—I am actually "feeling," within the tissue of my inner being, the television unit itself. The sensations of outside objects may not be as "intense" or "vibrant" as sensations within my own body, but they are undeniably present, and this may be the same way with you. The energy is subtle, but recognizable nonetheless. Keep this subtle feel of the energy in mind, because we'll be coming back to it later in the book. For now, practice this. Try to "feel" and "be with" the other objects you perceive as being outside your body.

So—and this is a very important follow-up question—if an individual can learn to feel the essence of these outside objects inside herself, and even "travel" thousands of miles to remote-view objects or places on the other side of the earth, one must again ask: Where does the Soul reside?

If the driver of a car fills the whole car itself, and can also somehow feel the life of the trees and the gravel on the road, this indicates that the driver must be a part of his surroundings, as well. When I say I "feel the wall" or "feel the television," I'm not talking about running my hand over the objects. If I turn my attention inward, I find that I seem to be aware of the objects *within me,* as discussed previously.

This, in turn, must mean that my Soul exists *within everything.* That access can be granted to travel "within" or "around" something isn't enough. That a form of cohabitation and union occurs as I interact with my surroundings reveals that the focus of consciousness can be and go anywhere, and that the "fabric" of consciousness itself is not a physical body or thing; rather, it is All Things that come into view and sensation by the act of conscious intent.

Most of us don't believe or know that we can have sensations like this, however, because we're so caught up with the stimuli we receive through the body and its five physical senses. Yet, one way we know we are not limited to these five senses of sound, touch, feel, smell, and taste, is by paying attention to the tingling feeling of life moving through our own bodies, just as I sat in my chair and felt the tingling in my feet and hands. That is not something felt by using any of my five senses, for when I do that, I am not *touching* anything, I am not *hearing* anything, I am not *seeing, smelling,* or *tasting*—and yet, somehow, I can "feel stuff" going on inside my body. Even if it could be argued that I am using my nerve endings to feel these processes, it must be conceded that nerve endings are *not* one of the five. Emotions are also not defined as a sense, yet we know how the emotions of pleasure and fear provide us with sensory "information."

Indeed, modern medicine acknowledges that we receive sensory information beyond the realm of the standard five senses identified thousands of years ago by Aristotle. The somatosensory system inside our bodies is made up of receptors and corresponding processing systems that can translate heat, body position, and pain. The receptors cover the skin, skeletal muscles, bones, joints, and other areas.

Since most of us learn only a single language from the time that we are young, we can actually find ourselves unable (or unwilling) to learn the nuances and syntax of another language because we have focused so strictly on our native language—yet, we know that multiple languages exist. To this analogy, I posit that with the teaching of the five basic senses, this strict focus on these five methods of sensation has disconnected us from the validity and value of all the other wonderful senses at our disposal, which may be a contributing factor in why we appear to be so "disconnected" from everything else in the world around us. This reliance and narrow belief of "physical validity through only five portholes" makes such things as remote viewing and psychic information seem unnatural and "paranormal." Yet, if at a young age we were taught that we are equipped with many more forms of sensory input than just our five basic senses, as a multilingual child is taught more than one language, then these other sensory inputs might seem just as natural in expanding the life of the Soul-traveler as multiple languages are to the world traveler. It would also serve to nurture the premise that the Soul resides not in any body, but in *every body*. The input of sensation from the walls, trees, and rocks would be just as vibrant as that of my toes and hands, were I taught at a young age to include them in the makeup of my own "body" and "sensory system." Perhaps I could even feel ocean waves…not only here on the Pacific, where I live, but also in the Atlantic and beyond.

"How is that?" you ask.

The Soul, which exists everywhere, makes such sensation possible. Even if the Soul had some kind of "structure," like a quantum particle (and I use this example only to assign a thought-*thing* to it, even though quantum particles aren't really *things* in the conventional sense), the nature of quantum mechanics makes such sensation achievable.

It has been indisputably proven that quantum particles can interact and exist in a nonlocal state, communicating over vast distances, without confinement of Time or Space. That is, two particles, once joined and then separated, can communicate over vast distances without any lag time. This is one of the factors that so exasperated Einstein, for it flew in the face of the notion that nothing can travel faster than the speed of light. For instance, let's say you have two particles that exhibit a "Y" axis. Then you separate the two particles by thousands of miles, and switch the axis of one particle to a "Z" axis. Due to the nature of nonlocal reality, the second particle will switch its axis to "Z" *at the exact same time*. What does this mean? That you could be standing on the west coast, projecting your mind to the east, and gather an experience of the Atlantic Ocean via this phenomenon of nonlocality.

Now, quantum physicists state that such an action requires the two particles to have been once joined together. You might argue that if you can feel the Atlantic Ocean from a distance, then to make use of the nonlocality concept in quantum physics, you would have to have been at the Atlantic Ocean at some point in order to sense it. Fair enough. And to that point, if my suggestion is correct that the Soul exists everywhere at once, covering all space (and I dare to suggest Time, as well), then this means that the Atlantic Ocean is indeed already joined with me, and was connected with me even before I physically came into the world.

"Well perhaps you are simply projecting your Soul into these environments," you say. "How do you know that you are them and they are you, all at once?"

Again, I return to my own body. How can I say that my foot is my own? Only because it seems to be connected to the rest of me.

"But isn't that only what the eyes tell us?"

Where my own flesh *appears* to stop is where the real illusion begins. Where is the true "edge" of my body? My body is a configuration of energy, atoms, and molecules, all jumbled together at a different frequency than what is perceived to be "outside" of me. What is "outside" of me *is made of the same molecules and atoms as my flesh*—it is simply combined into different patterns. This holds true for everyone. The air between your flesh and a nearby object is teeming with billions of atoms and molecules, just as the inside of your body is. Your eyes, only being attuned to certain frequencies, cannot see them in their various organizations and can only recognize them as macrocosmic objects on a larger scale. If you could see down to the molecular level, you would notice that everything is a jumbled-up, undulating soup of particles, with adjacent clumps of energy assembled together in different configurations. The fact of the matter is, the edge of your body is just a quantum blur that the eyes sharpen to a fine-pointed edge in the visual cortex of the mind. Even stranger than that, scientists concede that the body "blinks" on and off at the cellular level, as the atoms of our bodies are oscillating at a high frequency. This cellular "blinking" happens so fast that our eyes cannot see it. Where do the parts of You go when you blink "off"?

If you were to cut into me, you would see that I have different objects within me—a liver that looks separate and distinct from a spleen, lungs that look separate and distinct from skeletal bones—yet all these "separate and distinct" physical structures combine to make up "Jeff," and in sum total, from your general point of view, are considered to be one and the same. Medical doctors, of all people, know how these inner structures all work together in tandem, and even give rise to one another. Do you see how our perceptions can be broken down when we turn away from perceived discrimination outside the body to look more closely at our own "inner selves"?

And so, do you now see how even your walls and television, your furniture and knick-knacks, can be just as valid a "part of you" as your own large intestines? You may have thought that simply because your organs are shrink-wrapped in flesh, to go beyond the shrink-wrap is to be "outside" yourself. Yet, if you are able to "feel" a connection with that wall and that tree, then the visual input to your eyes and brain that informs you of your "disconnection" from them (via the space between them and your shrink-wrapped flesh) is an illusion! If this is the case, the question arises yet again: Where do you reside as a Soul?

"Now wait a minute!" you say. "Things outside in my environment change, move, and operate without my consent—as if they are happening *to* me. How can that be my body? Are you saying that these same types of things happen inside me?"

Absolutely. If you have a sense of helplessness, or feel that events happen *to* you outside the body, then you would also not be surprised to learn the same *perceived* lack of control is going on inside you. Do you ever get sick? Ever get sore muscles? A wart? A stomachache? A headache? Or better yet, indigestion? Even in the course of a "regular" day, a number of different things can manifest within the body. If you were to live in a "perfect world on the inside," you would never allow things like these to happen. But these things do happen, revealing your inner environment to be really no different than the outside. When these inner events happen, you declare that your body has an "issue," but you still acknowledge your body as being your own. On the other hand, when you're functioning "outside of yourself" in your environment, you may often play the role of "victim" in the much larger body of your life and experience, insisting that events are outside of your control, or outside yourself. Do you consider yourself a victim with indigestion? What about cancer? When something like cancer hits, our mind does give us a perception of being a "victim" (or at least, that's how we've been taught to react), yet *it is still our inner cells that are doing the creating of that which would make us ill.* And then, the very same cells that you claimed ownership of previously effectively get "disowned" because of the nasty changes. "I would never have given myself cancer on purpose," you might say. "This had to have happened outside my control."

Let's switch gears for a minute. Do you claim your house as your own? Your stuff is there. Is that stuff not a part of you? It is representative of you, therefore it must be a part of you on some level. Is not your house a larger "expression" of you? Could not the items in your house also be seen as the different organs in your body? Then how is your beating heart—a distinct, physical object—any different than a light bulb over your head—also a distinct, physical object? That your heart beats is an expression of your life force. That the light glows is an expression of you giving light to the darkness when you flip the switch. The heart pumps blood, sending nutrients (and information, too, via blood cells) to create and sustain life in the body. The light emits light waves, sending energy that turns darkness into light and gives us a clearer view (or expression) of the world, and allowing us to continue the work we do within it (as the cells would do for us).

How much thought do you give to a small scratch healing on the back of your hand? Do you dwell on it? Stress over it? Probably not. For the most part, you ignore it and go on about your day. Yet inside your body, so many miraculous processes are going on to create new skin and heal the area completely—restoring damaged tissue, clotting the blood, transforming the clot into new skin, and weaving new tissue. You pay very little attention to it, yet it happens anyway. So let's return to the Atlantic Ocean for a moment. Why do you not "feel" the Atlantic Ocean when you are near the Pacific, if it is just as much a part of your larger body, and if the Soul exists everywhere at once? For the same reason you don't pay attention to the healing of the scratch on your hand—it's not your focus! It's not that such phenomena don't exist—you acknowledge they DO exist—do you deny the effortless healing of a cut or bruise? You just don't focus on it, giving yourself a one-degree "sense" of separation. You can ignore the scratch on your hand, but you still claim that hand as part of you. In the same way, you can take no notice of the Atlantic Ocean if you are near the Pacific. Just know that once you put your thought toward it, the Atlantic becomes your hand, and your hand the Atlantic.

Let's ask the question one more time: Where does the Soul reside?

The answer: Wherever you wish it to. Wherever your focus resides. Since you have the ability to feel and focus in so many places at once—from the earth to the moon, and even beyond—your Soul, the "I"-ness of you, is really everywhere. You simply have to "feel" where you want to be.

Sense now just how grand you really are.

NOTE

1. From the book *Limitless Mind.* Copyright ©2004 by Russell Targ and Jane Katra, Ph.D. Reprinted with permission of New World Library, Novato, California. www.newworldlibrary.com. See p. 42.

Chapter Seven

GETTING IN TOUCH
WITH YOUR SOUL, PART III

THE VOICE(S) OF THE SOUL

The one tiny voice—we all have it. It's that dark little sound in the corner of your head when you're thinking about what you could be doing. It's that small enigma that pops in when you're considering your options, such as meeting that cute guy or girl at the counter at a singles' club (if you're single, that is), or going for a drive to the country, or considering a purchase. It's important that we take some time to get acquainted with this voice, for it has provided the answers to all our queries surrounding our possibilities (up until now, that is), and it can sometimes serve as the barrier between our conscious minds and achieving access to the greater portions of our Soul.

The voice usually speaks to us with a nagging tone. It's a voice of indelible negativity, often screaming out, "Are you sure you want to do that? Because if you do, [insert event] just might happen!" To which, all you can do is look at the said event and think to yourself, "My gosh, do I really want *that* to happen?"

This has been the voice we have relegated our experiences to for most of our lives. We have leaned upon its opinions time and time again, without stopping to think, "Hey, wait a minute, how do I know that's true? And second, who made you the All-Knowing?" (It's *really important* to ask this question!)

This voice has cowed us with its viewpoints and images, making us think and feel that its predictions for the future will come to pass—and usually, its predictions are gloomy. When you've responded to the imagery, the *imagined* imagery, you responded as if it were the only outcome available—"Do I really want that outcome to happen?" You probably didn't consider, even for a fraction of a second, that perhaps—though the little voice may have had the best of intentions—it wasn't the only reality capable of occurring. For me, this little voice has been a personal demon, all too often draining me of my power, preventing me from "going for it" and accomplishing my goals and dreams. I imagine, too, that many people experience the same.

I believe that each us has the potential to tackle this problem once and for all, for doubt and fear keep us from feeling the nature of the unbounded creativity inherent within the Soul itself. If we are to grasp and experience the totality of our spiritual foundation, we must become aware of our thought patterns and determine if certain thoughts are helping us achieve inner union with our true Selves, or hindering us. This requires brutal honesty and in-depth inquiry into the darkest corners of our minds to uncover our innermost secrets. It demands that we open ourselves to the possibility of unseen skeletons we've been hiding—not from others, but from ourselves. It requires us to be an observer of our own ways of being.

Let's face it—the voice in our heads is a byproduct of our imagination. It's a counterbalance and a flag waver, making sure you're checking your common-sense barometer. That, in itself, is not a bad thing. But too often, we allow its cry to be our only focus.

The tone of the voice is instilled in us when we're young and often takes the role of protector, as our parents did—"Be sure to look both ways before crossing the street." However, as we age, we develop our own protective device, and it runs the same way. This voice has its uses, as it is meant to keep us from a variety of dangers. That being said, we must acknowledge that, since it comes *from* us, it is also a part of our Soul's voice. And after hearing the warnings of the voice and being rescued by it a number of times, you've come to trust it and, in turn, ignore everything else—essentially cutting yourself off from the rest of your magnificent Being.

The trust we've bestowed upon the little voice has come with a heavy price: the understanding of our true personal power and our multidimensional freedom—the biological and spiritual heritage of our eternal Selves. You've given the cautionary voice totalitarian control over the rest of your mental and spiritual prowess. Nowadays, when you're faced with a choice, and the voice speaks its mind, you listen *only* to it, because, yes—it did save you one time before. You've awarded it the rank of General. You have also turned your egoic mind over to the details of the past, instead of directing it to the point of power in the present—this is its modus operandi. The voice pulls you out of the Now moment, where all your options exist.

We have to be realistic: The little voice isn't always going to be right. It's only one choice of many.

It's also a voice of distrust.

The voice often offers you the perspective of negativity, because on some level, you've learned not to trust yourself or the other "voices" chattering inside your head. As a result, you've turned any and all decision-making control over to IT. Think about it. Take a moment and ponder its way of speaking to you. Since you, yourself, gave rise to this voice (much as we'd like to think so, it's not coming from anybody else), you must admit that on some level, on the basis of its style, you do not trust or love yourself to a certain degree. You are suspicious of ties and chances for success.

e a moment to remember that you are an invisible Soul, and that the structure of this little voice is also invisible.

It has no form.

It uses the images of the past and imagined future outcomes to keep you out of the present.

It has distracted you into a state of fear, which brings it the ability to control you, in the interest of self-preservation (usually against other negative, invisible beliefs you are harboring about the nature of reality, relationships, and expectations). Once you realize that this voice is a self-made creation, however, the next realization is that you have the power to change it.

Take it back. The voice in your head is not all of who You are. It is simply an expression, an outgrowth, that you've identified yourself with. It is a creation of your ego; therefore, managing it also falls under your control.

Think of it this way: In your head is a team of people, all sitting around a table, and on the table is where you put your thoughts and your desires. For example, you want to go meet that cute guy over at the counter at the singles' club. You present the idea to the panel sitting around the table. Immediately, the negative voice screams out, "You might be rejected!" To which your imagination responds by immediately beginning to conjure up that horrible moment.

As soon as you've imagined the thought, you've glossed over the eternal moment of Now, with all its possibilities, and instead leapt into an imagined future where you're feeling the pain of such a disastrous rejection—yet in reality, this has not happened at all! It is but a nightmarish dream that you allow yourself to get swept up in.

But WAIT—you have a team here, remember? The other members at the table have opinions on the matter, too. When you ignore them, you also dishonor them and their own personal wisdom, and in doing so, you dishonor yourself. By devaluing them, you devalue yourself.

Aren't you more than just negativity?

Aren't you, by your own definition, a good, worthwhile human being?

Then why all the negativity?

What about the other guy on your panel, who says, "He may find that you have a quality he's has been looking for in a woman for a long time." Or the other guy on the panel, who says "Look at how you treat other people. You treat them like gold! You never put anyone down and actually do your best at lifting them up! Knowing and being that, you have a better chance of being accepted, rather than rejected!" Or how about the other voice that speaks up and says, "He's just as nervous as you, and can't think of how to break the ice! You going over there may be just what he needs!" And then another voice chimes in: "Maybe his own voices are telling him he'll be rejected, which is why he hasn't reached out to you!" Can you see all the different variations playing on a single thought here? Is the one really big, bad negative voice necessarily the right one? Have you given it the most authority and power in the matter, despite the viewpoints of all the other voices?

Most people want to be accepted. The truth is, most people wouldn't mind a simple, "Hey, I saw you from across the room and just wanted to come over and say hello. My name is so-and-so." (And if they do, for some reason, object to a friendly greeting such as this, you probably don't want to know them anyway.) Furthermore, if you threw in a little honesty about your own nervousness, they might appreciate your introduction even more. "I'm not used to doing this—meeting new people—so I'm a bit nervous. I'm trying to expand my horizons."

There is an axiom in metaphysics that states the universe always supports what we're thinking and doing, whether it be positive or negative (we can all agree, it doesn't discriminate). So if you inform the universe that you are expanding your horizons for positive growth, you know what? The universe will support that, and bring you those exciting and positive experiences you seek. We'll delve further into how the universe accomplishes this a little later. You may balk at such an idea right now, but in time, you'll come to see how it all fits.

Now, back to the voice. When you listen to the advice of the voice alone, without recognizing all the other options available to you, you will never recognize the freedom of choice you truly have; you will constantly predispose yourself to accept less. This, by definition, is aberrant in the face of the Soul's design.

The good news is that the voice can be silenced by remaining focused in the Now. Usually this voice retains its life in your head by bringing up negative experiences of the past or by projecting negative experiences in the future. This doesn't work in the present. Attention to the present silences the voice. To do this, you must be able to take a one-degree step *away* from your mind and become a third-party witness to your thoughts. Don't judge them, just watch. Notice how often the focus goes to either the past or the future, but not the Now. Then notice the emotion tied up with these not-right-Now thoughts. By living in the turmoil of the past or the fear of the future, your mind is not allowing you to live fully in the true moment of eternity, the Present. Once you open yourself to the point of power in the present and all its options, this negative voice will no longer be able to use the diversion of the past or the future to deter you.

As stated previously, this negative voice is not entirely without merit. If you find it hard to keep focused in the present moment, you can still work with this subpersonality you've latched onto. Give him a place on your "mental panel." *The trick is to keep him at the same level of importance as the other members.* Naturally, we are creatures that are in the habit of trying to avoid pain, but we should also be creatures that are in the habit of enjoying the bliss of our lives as we are living it Right Now. We have that option. We have that right. *Our brains are hardwired for positive experiences—therefore, we are meant to have them.*

We can live with a sense of freedom in choosing and achieving our goals for the future if we give ourselves that option. The trick is to listen to the voice, acknowledge it, and then admit the truth: It's only a single possibility. If it's of the past, leave it there. You are not living in that past moment, you are living in the Now. Feel the emotions, let them flow through you—don't deny or bury them. Instead, become that one-degree-away witness, like a parent witnessing with love an event involving their child. In this case, you are the eternal You, witnessing the mental psychical energies of your own child, your ego. Acknowledge those feelings, but once they have passed, recognize where you are truly living—in the eternal Now.

If you envision your personal "mental panel" as having as few as three members, how much input does the voice have? He's got 33% of the vote. The perspectives of the other two are equally valid, are they not? If your panel has more than three, the power of the negative voice diminishes further.

You are presenting yourself with possibilities, which could then be potential probabilities in terms of expanding your experiences.

Once you have made a choice, make it an intention for the Now, then allow each moment to unfold naturally. Learn to place your faith and trust not in the single voice of negativity, but in the other members of your panel, as well. This may take some time, but as it took only one or two negative events mirroring the advice of your negative voice to create your subsequent dependence on it, it will only take one or two positive events mirroring the counsel of your positive voice to swing the pendulum the other way.

Why this discussion? Why this need to build awareness of these "other voices"?

Because life is a series of probabilities, analogous to the probabilities of an electron in quantum physics. Quantum physicists now know that an electron can exist in any number of probable states at the same time, until consciousness steps in and collapses those multitudinous possibilities into one actuality. Your brain is literally a quantum computer, considering a variety of possibilities that it ultimately collapses into a single actuality by sparking synapses and exploding quantum particles all throughout its tissue.

What does this mean?

That the myriad probabilities available to an electron also exist for you. Your mental attitude and expectations play a huge role in how reality will play out for you, and becoming aware of this fact will enable you to flex a newfound power in your experience that will amaze you.

Consciousness collapses quantum waves of possibilities into particles, and how it does that is based on energy frequencies—informational properties "written" into the energies of the conscious observer. If you are always predisposed toward the negative outcome, guess what your energy is "telling" the nature of reality to become for you. If all of reality is the body of your Soul, and you are believing in and expecting negative outcomes, what are you telling your Soul (and hence all of reality) to be like?

Try giving yourself more options than only negative ones, for indeed, those options truly exist. They exist in the Now, on the basis of the vibration of the energy pulsing within you. Don't put your dreams off into the future by shooting them down as being impossible in the Now. They are a viable possibility in the Now, if you believe they can be. By focusing on what you want in the Now, you will be guided to the doors that will open for you on the basis of the energy of the intention. So long as you keep saying, "So-and-so hasn't happened yet," you are telling your consciousness you do not have what you want, that it is somewhere outside the Now, in the future. You cannot experience any of your possibilities in the Now if you do not even make them potentialities within the very quantum structure of your own brain in the present moment.

So how do you know if the decision that your mental panel has suggested is right or wrong? At what point do you become foolish and naïve? First you must ask—who is determining what is right or wrong? Yourself, or something you have credited as being outside yourself?

As simple as it sounds, let your heart be the final judge. Listen to the voice that speaks in the moment of the present tense, not one that reminds you of a dreamy past or an illusory future. The voice that speaks of the moment will have a different feeling than your imagined voice of negativity. Sometimes, the other members of your "mental panel" will be in agreement with the negative voice, and that's definitely a cue worth considering. Contemplate the possibilities. *Be brutally honest with yourself about what you think and feel.* Ask if you're being hasty and impatient, if it's something you feel you absolutely need to do right now. Do the other voices agree? Are you perceiving your options from a place of being truly centered in the present?

I have come to learn that my voice is wrong in terms of the type of person I am. I know I treat others well and have good intentions in my dealings with them, as opposed to always "letting others down" or "not being good enough" in this area. Chances are, this is a voice of the past that I have unconsciously identified with and hung onto, and I suspect it is probably the same for you. Many of us have both allowed our egos to be chained to the past, instead of living freely in the present.

Why should you not give yourself the same kudos you would give others? Do you not give others the benefit of the doubt? Do you not believe that other people have their own greatness and special place of being—a sense of magnificence and multidimensionality—within themselves, even if they, for whatever reason, do not acknowledge it and instead suppress it?

Take a moment and check in with that voice of yours. While you're there, check in (possibly for the first time) with the other voices on your quantum brainwave panel. Get to know them—you'll know them by how they feel. Then look beyond them to that other portion of your self—the Silent Observer. The one that is just behind your ego. *That's the voice that can help keep you in the Now.*

The negative voice is sometimes needed for caution, and caution is a sense of wisdom. However, demote him to be a true member of the team, and no longer the overlord. The voice knows it needs to be tamed and is welcome to it. It says, "thank you for putting me in my place." It at least agrees that your life *deserves* to be rich and successful. All the voices on your mental panel will toast to that intention, and give you love and thanks for checking in on them to make sure balance among the panel prevails.

Start spending time with the other members. When you are in a position of offering up a thought, place it on the table, and instead of focusing strictly on Mr. Negative, say, "Thank you, Mr. Negative, but today I'd like to hear more from Mr. Potentially Positive, or from Mr. Positive Growth, and then I'd like to hear them contrast their opinions with yours, if possible."

Make it a discussion, not a battle.

Love yourself. Love your panel. And they'll love you back. Your life may just change with the love and respect you introduce among the members of the table in your own mind. Love Mr. Negative, too. Don't ignore him, because you might inadvertently create an event that proves to you just how valuable he is. Better yet, simply disarm him by reminding him that he's looking back to the past or creating an imagined future and is not living in the power point of the present.

Acknowledge your panel members equally, and you'll find that your life has taken a turn into a whole new and welcome direction. As a quantum particle can exist in all possible states prior to an observation, so, too, do all the possibilities of your own existence. This is the magic of the Soul—all options are available to You. And like the observer in the quantum laboratory, You are the observer in the quantum psychic lab of your mind. Give yourself the options you so richly deserve. Then follow me into the next chapter, where we'll discover how those possibilities can be turned into bona fide reality.

Chapter Eight

MANIFESTING REALITY: A PRIMER

Here we have a subject that came into popular vogue around 2006, with the smash-hit book and movie, *The Secret*. Ever since then, new authors have come out of the woodwork in an attempt to gain a piece of the pie, saying "I have the secret they never told you about on *The Secret*," or suggesting they have some sort of "missing link" that guarantees the manifestation of all your desires. The fact of the matter is, *The Secret* and its message is not new; it has been known for literally thousands of years, told from many different viewpoints all leading in the same direction. *The Secret* itself was inspired by a book written in the early 1900s by Wallace Wattles, a man who gathered his own manifestational experiences and concocted a philosophy around the process, titling his work, *Financial Success: The Science of Getting Rich*. In 1938, *The Science of Mind*, by Ernest Holmes, also laid out the process, of which *The Secret* is but a retelling. The first big-time success book on the matter was Napoleon Hill's *Think and Grow Rich*, inspired by Hill's relationship with Dale Carnegie. Others in the modern world, such as Dr. Deepak Chopra and Wayne W. Dyer, have been teaching the concepts in their own way for decades. On the metaphysical side, Jerry and Esther Hicks have made their mark by channeling the information through an alleged entity named "Abraham." Prior to Abraham, Jane Roberts and "Seth" dictated eleven volumes of highly intricate and detailed information about how one interacts with and creates reality—some of it touching upon processes in quantum physics. In ancient times, the philosophy and technique was referred to as "high incantation." All the holy books speak the axiom, "Ask and ye shall receive," and "As you sow, so shall you reap." Very early on, this was the philosophy that my guides were teaching me, and they pointed me in many different directions, to learn from direct experience.

For some people, much of this philosophy is not necessarily based on the outcome of scientific experiments, but on the perceived result of actual living and having extraordinary experiences that are far too perfect to allow being labeled as "coincidence." This was one of the first things I was instructed by my guides to observe. They directed me to notice how my thoughts felt, and then consider how the "coincidences" that occurred thereafter mirrored my previous thinking patterns and feelings. Think about all the times you've experienced a thought or desire, and then boom—somehow, things magically fell into place, and there it was before you.

For the most part, prior to the sensationalism of *The Secret*, most people dismissed the notion of creating your own reality as outlandish, absurd, nonscientific, and utter nonsense (and maybe even went to church to pray for God to intervene in their lives and create reality the way they wanted it). For the naysayers, if there *were* events that unfolded after seemingly thinking about them, they were dismissed as coincidence or a nice happenstance. Thought wasn't given to the possibility that perhaps one could influence matter and move events into existence. Life, it seemed, was purely a random act, where events and circumstances happened *to* you, as if by the roll of a die. You were either lucky, or, worse, a victim of Murphy's Law.

As an interesting aside, there have been numerous tests regarding the rolling of dice, and if we are to teeter on the notion that experience is an outcome on a lucky toss, then one will find these results fascinating and perhaps a bit startling. The dice-tossing experiments are considered the simplest test of all in researching the effects of "psi theory" (powers of the mind), or psychokinesis, and are totally relevant to the possibility that we do, in fact, influence reality. These tests were conducted by psi researchers for more than half a century. The experiments required the participants to choose a particular face on the die and then try to make that face appear on each toss. Overall, it seemed the effects were too small to say with certainty whether control of the dice was actually occurring. In 1989, however, Dean Radin, chief scientist for the Institute of Noetic Sciences, along with psychologist Diane Ferrari, scoured more than 50 years of research on dice-tossing experiments. They found 73 relevant publications cataloging the experiments, representing the efforts of 52 investigators. In the end, they looked at the results of 2.6 million dice throws by more than 2,500 people in 148 different experiments against 150,000 dice throws in 321 control studies. The total number of dice tossed per study ranged from 60 to 240,000, and the number of dice tossed in one throw ranged from 1 to 96. While the overall effect of psychokinesis was considered small, the meta-analysis yielded that it wasn't strictly dumb luck. The odds that the outcome of the dice was due to chance alone turned out to be 10^{96} to 1 (that's 1 with 96 zeroes after it!). By contrast, the results of the control experiments were well within the chance expectation.[1] So to think that your life is merely the fate of a roll of the dice, remember those early experiments which showed a measurable effect on controlling the outcome.

Dice-throwing experiments were only the tip of the iceberg. Digging deeper into the power of affecting reality, forty years of RNG research has clearly demonstrated the abilities of both humans and animals to influence outcomes. I touched on these experiments earlier.

Now, before we get into the steps of manifestation as I have learned from my own experiences and the teachings of my guides (as well as numerous other individuals), I invite you to think about those events and objects in your life that you feel you consciously created. Take a few moments to review past successes in receiving a situation or thing that was a result of conscious intention. If you cannot think of anything, but have recollections of past things you had wished for and the universe magically provided through perceived happenstance or coincidence, note those items. In either case, write down as many memories as you can. Ideally, shoot for at least five to ten different times when you sent an intention or made a decision that eventually resulted in the manifestation of your desire (if you can think of much more, that's even better). If you can't think of that many, that's fine. Ultimately, at least *one* will do—and no doubt you have had at least one experience that meets the criteria (even if it was as small as wishing for that up-front parking space at the shopping center, and then finding it waiting for you). Having this list will help serve as a reminder that you *do* know how to create reality and that you have successfully done it in the past. Even if you feel a bit dubious about the subject at the moment, just follow along with an open mind. Things will seem clearer to you soon.

Up to now, you might have had only a vague understanding or intuitive sense that you had a hand in the circumstances surrounding your life. As has been taught to me from the Other Side and my experiences with ghosts and my own personally created intentions, when it comes to the consummate fabric of your existence, you do have incredible control over your life in terms of creation. Unfortunately, we often allow ourselves to run on autopilot and let go of the wheel, to be driven by what appears to be outside of us instead of realizing our own power within.

A note of caution here: The ability to manifest desires into physical events and things can end up turning into a quagmire if you are attempting to control the thoughts, behaviors, and actions of others. Each person is his or her own valid, multidimensional Soul, with all the same capabilities and freedoms as you. Your ability to impress reality is no lesser or greater than someone else's. The bottom line here is that you do not have the ability to control other people by using forced intention. I see this sort of thing come up in dysfunctional families during readings. "Why can't I make so-and-so do this?" Because that person doesn't want to. Others create their own realities in accordance with the vibrations of their own Soul. As you will soon see, forced intention is more akin to a tuning fork that is a part of You; meaning, forced intention works in relation to You on multiple levels—which can, in some ways, affect your relationships with others—but does not give you power over another person's ability to choose his or her own actions or destiny.

To first understand how manifestation works, it's worth acknowledging the law that the universe doesn't play favorites. Everyone creates reality, and the universe doesn't judge what reality someone manifests. Manifestations can be either positive or negative in terms of experience. All the universe is doing is playing back the information that an individual has transmitted about the nature of his or her own life—beliefs, mental attitudes, feelings, and expectations, for it is these ingredients that are used to *define* the nature of your personal experience. What we are dealing with here is a process—a process of how thoughts and feelings are translated and replayed back to us as events and objects in the course of our lives. In other words, manifestation is a natural law of the universe, much like gravity or the changing of the seasons. Like other natural laws, there is no judgment; everyone experiences them. And like any law in nature, certain conditions need to be met for processes to move forward, or for quantum waves to collapse into particles, and then atoms, molecules, and full-blown manifestation.

Just as the planet shifting on its axis in relation to the sun creates the changing of the seasons, only certain types of thoughts will make way into physical form. Not just any old thought will do, despite what some people have previously written or said regarding this matter. Random thoughts do not have the power to produce reality, as they flutter in and out of our consciousness without much energy-backing to support materialization. However, since we are thinking all the time, and much of that time is an unconscious, back-and-forth ranting and raving that builds upon our inner selves emotionally, which then results in a sense of expectation (often fearful expectation at that), it's no wonder that our experiences appear disjointed and chaotic. Once someone learns how to *focus, feel,* and *project into the current Now moment,* another great magical aspect of the Soul is revealed: natural, creative living.

In an attempt to uncover the truest process of manifestation, I have reviewed my own history of successes, returned to the points taught by my guides, scoured over the metaphysical philosophies of dozens of authors, considered instructions given by various channeled entities, and looked at published scientific results of real tests on the effects of forced intention. After studying all the sources, a roadmap appeared that was simple, elegant, and incredibly *realistic.* I have synthesized this roadmap into a common-sense approach that should be understandable to everyone.

As is the universal rule, consciousness is the creator, so there is no variable for consciousness because consciousness makes all possibilities available. You cannot pin consciousness down in the equation into a single finite form, because consciousness, by its own definition, is infinite and is what decides the form itself. When I say consciousness, I mean You—your Soul. By the time you finish reading this book, you will see that You are a magical Soul, the true driver of your experience, and this roadmap is simply one interpretation. I can only speak from my own experiences, but this is what has worked for me and what I have discovered after nearly twenty-five years of research.

First of all, reality is a reflection of you, much like your house. For instance, when you go into someone's home, you can tell by the arrangement of the furniture, the style of the décor, and the color of paint on the walls just how a person chooses to see him- or herself. You can get a very good sense of the inner nature of someone's life by examining the surroundings they choose to live in. Similarly, a person's life experiences and objective reality are much the same way—they are a direct reflection of a person's inner workings. As the old adage goes, "As above, so below." In this case, it is, "As within, so with-out." The events and objects that surround you are direct physical mirrors to your inner processes—your thoughts, beliefs, emotions, and mental attitudes. You might as well have placed a hand inside your body and pulled out your exterior reality, for energetically, that is what your reality is.

So, how did you go about creating it? Or better yet, how can you go about changing it?

We'll get into the physical theory of how it all works as we progress, but first, let's address the key steps. The number one rule to remember is this: The point of power is always in the present.[2] Being present in the Now is the only Time that contains the power to change events and circumstances. You cannot physically go backward into the past and change things that have already physically been observed to have happened, so immediately declare to stop dwelling on things that happened before. All that is left from the past is *energy*, and that you definitely can change. Likewise, you cannot physically shoot forward into the future, you are *physically rooted* in the Now, so it doesn't pay to be fearful about something that you are not physically experiencing at this very moment.

It's only NOW that matters. NOW. NOW. NOW.

Why this insistence? Because *Now is the only Time you have to work in.* When we get into the chapter on Time, you'll see just how powerful this present moment is. Suffice it to say, though you physically cannot travel backward or forward in Time, your energy and that of quantum particles *do.* This can have a measured effect in the power point of the present for your consciousness and your overall creative experience in manifesting reality.

As discussed in the previous chapter, staying in the power point of the present releases you from the vices of the past and keeps the future open for every possibility. Too often, we remain prisoners to the reliving of past events and emotions, locking them into the present, continuing to *feel* them, and then fearing these same events and emotions in the future—expecting them—and wondering why things don't change! (Are you starting to see a pattern here on how you create reality?) *The present moment is the only time you are actually physically active and alive in your perception of experience.* Once each moment fades into the past, it is no longer a physical reality that you are experiencing, so whatever *emotions* and *ideas* you wish to carry over into your current, present state—the only one where you are truly physically alive and experiencing life—is completely up to you. This doesn't mean you should carelessly disregard something once a moment has passed. Just be aware that the present moment is the only one that you are physically experiencing and working in, where all other events are but *energetic possibilities*—including the past that was a physical reality only a nanosecond before—and where the future is out of your physical reach.

Once you have grounded yourself into the power point of the present, the next step in manifesting reality is identifying the subject of your desire and defining its probability. Yes, you could wish for and even intend to win the lottery, but when you think such a thought, how does it really *feel* on the inside? Realistic? Possible? Now, I'm not here to squash anybody's intentions—for all things are possible with the Soul—but the fact of the matter is, is such an intention realistic *to you?* You have the freedom to think about and desire anything in the world (and also have the innate ability to achieve it), but you are also working within a psychic (mental) framework that has been the foundation of your experience your entire life. Your life, to date, has been built around decades of a particular psychic structure that, in some cases, will not support a major life-changing intention without first addressing the issues that will keep such a possibility from becoming reality: your beliefs.

Beliefs are the first thing that will inform you whether your intention will ever make it to physical manifestation. If you have always believed money is evil or out of reach, or that winning lotteries would be "out of this world," then you have already set yourself up to fail. You must first address the ideas and notions you hold within your consciousness that create the framework for how you orient your expectation of life's experiences. This goes with any area that you are wishing to improve.

If you are lonely, go inside and listen to the messages you keep telling yourself. Do you constantly berate your appearance? Do you give yourself reasons why you can't go out and meet people and why you would be rejected? Do you replay old filmstrips of when you were picked on as a child? Or an old break-up that left you in ruins? If you are sick, do you keep reminding yourself how ill you are? Do you keep telling yourself your body is poisoned and going downhill, without giving any consideration to your immune system? Do you *distrust* your body? Do you feel that the medical establishment cannot be trusted, and they just want to poison you more? Or that, as you get older, you are *supposed* to lose a healthy body to one of aches, pains, and disease?

Whatever the case may be, if you are in a place of lack or you are uncomfortable with your current set of circumstances, by having the courage to go inside your mind and uncover your deepest thoughts, you will find a belief lurking. That belief may only be the tip of the iceberg, as it may be connected to other beliefs (mini-beliefs, as I call them) until you can uncover the core belief. The core belief is what will need to be changed if you are to accept a major life-changing intention as being possible.

If you cannot find the belief, pay attention to your *attitude*. This will be a dead giveaway and lead you into the direction of the belief. Do you distrust people you consider wealthy? Then why would you ever want to win the lottery? Is there something about healthy people you admire, but you can't seem to find that object of admiration within yourself? If you are lonely, what would you have to give up to feel loved? Do you find that in some strange way, you enjoy feeling sorry for yourself?

Mental attitudes and beliefs lead to emotions—the river of energy inside the body. They are all connected. Follow each one of them to uncover what you may be hiding from yourself if you feel you are getting blocked when it comes to realizing a desire. *The emotions create the energetic vibration—the "tuning fork"—that speaks to the cooperative energies of creation within the universal Soul and personal experience.* Please go back and re-read that sentence. It is of vital importance to realize that the "feeling" of your reality, hence its makeup and design, is directly correlated with your emotions—your inner feelings surrounding the conditions you are experiencing. Consider the beliefs that one entertains when it comes to troublesome conditions or circumstances. What are the emotions entangled with those beliefs? Take a look at some of the limiting beliefs I mentioned previously. Obviously, the corresponding emotions attached to the beliefs would be negative, and continued feeling of that negative emotion would naturally create expectations that are going to create a corresponding reality. By contrast, consider an area in your own life where things are going well—that oftentimes requires no effort—and what are the feelings you associate with there? Within emotions lies the frequency variance that speaks to the nature of thoughts and *expectations* of the individual and, thus, *the energy matrix of personal creation.*

Taking baby steps is the preferred method when it comes to deliberate creation. This helps build a foundation, as well as experience and solid proof to a skeptical egoic mind. When it comes to manifesting reality, start out small and work up to the larger things. Remember that list I asked you to write? Remind yourself of your past successes, and that, too, will also help you make greater strides in creating manifested change in your experience. Check in with how you *feel* when it comes to creating intentions. Yes, everything is possible, *but not everything is probable, on the basis of your belief system.*

Believe it or not, this goes even for those who have died.

One of the things I do at a ghost investigation is set up tennis balls. The balls are marked with a number and grid lines and are focused on by a camera in case they happen to move. During one particular investigation, my brother asked an entity to move a ball. At the time, the homeowner's complaint had been that the ghost would flush the toilet—quite a feat—but that it hadn't happened in a few months after she yelled, "Quit flushing the toilet!" My brother and I figured that if the entity could flush the toilet, it should have no problem moving the tennis ball. On the recording of the investigation, my brother asks me to hand him the tennis ball in preparation for the test. The ghost must have known what we were up to, because he clearly stated on the audio, "Have you lost your mind?"

Here we had an entity that either thought we were nuts by asking him to perform such a test, or he didn't believe he could do it. Considering the other things that happened during the investigation (such as pulling a computer out of sleep mode three times at our request, with an EVP of the ghost saying, "Nothing to it"), that this particular spirit was evidently unwilling to try to move the tennis ball suggested that he didn't believe he was capable of doing it. Why not move the tennis ball, if the spirit was so willing to play with the computer? Had this been the same spirit, it wouldn't have presented a problem at all, and he would have probably tossed the ball and said something like, "easy squeezy." As for flushing the toilet, we uncovered at least two other ghosts in the house, meaning that this was quite the hot spot for ghostly gatherings. Whomever it was that the homeowner screamed at to quit flushing the toilet simply stopped doing it. The spirit may have even left the house!

We have been on several investigations where ghosts have been able to communicate with us by one particular device and not another. Why, in some cases, will a ghost easily talk via the use of the dowsing rods and others won't? Or manipulate the lights on the K2 meter, but find themselves unable to create a simple tap on the wall? In many cases, a ghost will admit they "can't" do something, when, on other investigations in different locations, we certainly have seen other ghosts that can! Again, this all comes down to belief: *an invisible psychic structure that has a definite role in creating barriers to physical reality.* Associated with the belief is a negative vibrational feeling—frustration, anger, guilt, etcetera, which acts like a prison cell in the mind's willingness to achieve success.

So here's what we have so far in starting the process of manifestation:

1. **The present point of power is Now.**

2. **Everything is possible, but not everything is probable, on the basis of your current set of beliefs and/ or attitudes.**

3. **Emotions are the vibrational frequency that "magnetizes" possibilities into manifestation. Emotions reveal the "can" or "cannot" expectations, and hence how the environment will respond, with regard to achieving intentioned success.**

The next important step in this mixture is your perception of how you connect with everything else in the world.

Do you feel that you and the universe are one gigantic field of energy?

Or do you feel isolated from everything and everyone?

If the latter, you must learn that the only separation that exists between you and everything else is what you perceive in your mind. In actuality, like I mentioned in the last chapter, every molecule and cell of your being is popping in and out of existence from within a field of energy that spans the entire cosmos, coined the Zero Point Field.[3] This field pervades everything, including you. It's like an ocean, from which every particle rises out of and disappears back into. Think of everything in the material world as being akin to a fish in the sea, where the fish materializes out of the water it swims in, and then dematerializes back into in death—and yet doesn't even realize it's in the water at all! Since the field is everywhere, just like the ocean exists all around the fish, and the fish is part of the ocean, scientists don't even bother to include it in their physics equations—yet they estimate that the energy of this nothingness exceeds all matter in the universe by a factor of 10^{40}, or 10 followed by 40 zeroes![4] Think about that. All the matter in the universe pales to the energy within the vacuum, and this ocean is where all life originated from, including you! Hal Puthoff and his colleagues once proved that this constant energy exchange between all matter within the Zero Point Field accounted for the stability of the hydrogen atom, and, by implication, the stability of all matter.[5] In other words, if you were to remove the Zero Point Field, all matter would collapse in on itself. He also demonstrated that Zero Point energy could account for two basic properties of mass: inertia and gravity.[6] Richard Feynman, the celebrated physicist, remarked that the energy in a cubic meter of space was enough to boil all the oceans of the world.[7] This energy exists inside you.

So, realize that the atoms and particles of your body are engaged with the field *right now*, and that this field pervades the universe, and by association, so do you. Again, this concept of enmeshment with the field is also confirmed by quantum mechanics through the concept of entanglement and, by implication, through psi experiments in remote viewing, which suggests entanglement of the person performing the remote viewing with the environment he is seeing.

Why this emphasis on connectivity?

Because if you believe that you are separated from everything and everyone else, then you will also, by default, perceive and feel yourself to be separated from your intended desire energetically. The truth of the matter is, you want to *feel* and think *in union* with your desire; that the two of you are one together. In that union, you want to *feel* all the emotions of that entanglement—the joy, the peace, whatever the good feelings are. You want to live within your consciousness the experience of the intention in all its glory, from the clear perspective of what it is you want. If not, you will never be in the mode of receiving your desire. In fact, if your desire were to come knocking on your door, you wouldn't be able to meet it, because you are not a visual and feeling equivalent with it—especially if you consider yourself separate from all else. The truth of your intention lies in the realization that you are being enveloped by the object of your desire, that you and the desire are wedded together in the Now moment, and that you can feel that oneness in all its majesty, which is the very next step in the process.

4. Visualize and feel yourself in possession of your desire in the Now moment.

You must feel your desire in all its splendor, as if it were happening right now. Cognitive studies have shown that when a person is imagining a scenario, all the synapses fire and all the muscle groups react as if the image were a real situation. All the same endorphins and chemicals are generated, too. Olympic athletes often rehearse their trials first in the mind before going into competition, and statistics have shown that they come out with the winning edge. So imagine yourself in possession of your desire, down to the greatest detail. Experience it happening right here and now, with all the emotions and synapses firing. It is real, in this moment.

Do not think of it as something that will happen in the future.

Thinking about it in the future will keep it outside your conscious reference of the Now experience—where you truly want the possession to belong and where you are truly experiencing it inside. Neurologically (and energetically, as we will discuss in the next chapter), you *are* in possession of the desired reality at that moment. So think it, feel it, experience it, and acknowledge that it is happening *right now*. Swim inside the emotions and the excitement of actually having your desire, and then tell yourself, "This is my intention happening right now. I and the [state desire here] are one united being. There is no separation."

It is very important that while you are in this state of union, you let go of your ego. Make absolutely no judgment calls of good or bad surrounding the vision and intention. If you do, your emotions will coincide, thereby screwing up your "tuning fork" mechanism. Additionally, when it comes to the act of intention, doing it from an ego standpoint keeps the energy close to your body and in your egoic mind, which is *not* where it needs to be. The egoic mind focuses on self-centeredness and self-preservation, yet your intention needs to enter into the universal mind, which knows no ego. The mind of the universe doesn't judge and doesn't work from the selfishness of an ego, and it is this universal energy which you must match and "toss" your intention into in order to start the process—like dropping a coin into a fountain.

This, by far, in my opinion, is one of the most important reasons why forced intention sometimes fails. The intention isn't allowed to go beyond the egoic mind to truly meld with the universal particulars that will bring it back to the individual. Shamans, monks, renowned energy healers, Qigong masters, and others who are considered "masters of intention" all say that they cannot adequately perform the work of intending without first letting go of the self and entering an altered state of consciousness. Some reach these altered states through mindful meditation, listening to music, chanting, or drumming. Either way, not just any old way of thinking will do—it must be one with no ego attached. And when the ego is surpassed, there's a bonus that adds to the tuning fork of emotions—no negative emotions are present. Love, the pervading force of the universe, coupled with gratitude, becomes the common ground. The universe, acting on principle, moves in accordance with those positive emotions (just as it would equally with the negative).

Take a moment to reconsider some of your past intentions that became reality. How much of your thinking surrounding the desire was self-centered, and you felt a feeling of selfishness at the time you made the real act of intending? You may have had self-serving motives (as we all do when it comes to desires), but when push came to shove, you were able to set your ego aside to connect with the powers of creation. Also note the emotions you were experiencing—that you were exuding like smoke from an exhaust pipe. Artists of all genres admit that their best work comes when they let themselves go and simply let the energy flow—in essence, they swim in mental and emotional bliss, unhindered by thoughts and feelings of negativity or lack. *Feel* your intention as existing beyond or *in place of* the ego.

5. **You must experience the intention without egoic attachment. Let the *feeling* of the intention *replace* your ego.**

Letting go of the ego is also letting go of the outcome. Being attached to outcomes means you are worried that your intention may not come to pass. Along with the worry comes the emotions of fear, frustration, and anger, hence the tuning fork being out of whack. When you ask from an egoic standpoint and hold onto that attachment, you are trying to *push push push* the universe into creating reality. What you are really saying is, "I am still focused on my current situation and believe (as well as feel) it will continue!" In doing so, you are indeed keeping the energy of the current situation—the one that you are desiring to change—energetically and firmly in place. The focus really isn't the intention at that point, but rather that of your undesired state.

If you actually had your desire, you wouldn't be dwelling on it with the same energy of anxiety, would you?

Being attached to the outcome says that you do not trust the process of creation and feel you are doomed to your current reality. At that point, you are simply working against yourself and expending a lot of energy doing it! Remember, the universe doesn't judge one way or the other—positive or negative—it will match whatever thought and feeling meets its energetic criteria in the invisible law of manifestation. A desire coming from the ego, entrenched with associated negative emotions, keeps the energy swirling around inside you, held captive within the egoic mind and negative emotional psychic body. To be in the realm of the ego and associated negative feelings informs the universe exactly what you are expecting for your reality—so it's no wonder you keep experiencing it in the same old way it's always been. You are not in connection with the *positive* forces or energies of the universe—the very things needed to create a new *positive* reality. Being attached to the outcome, by contrast, is not the same as positive expectations, either. Attached to the outcome is *dwelling* and *hoping*. Expectation is a feeling built upon *faith* and *trust*, knowing that your desire *will* come to pass and not just *hoping* it will. You must transcend the ego and enter the realm where all things are connected, where love is the foundation of all being. The experience of reality is a dance of many players coming together in a new display of unity that you are a part of, which leads us to the next rule of manifestation:

6. Never doubt the ability to manifest.

To doubt the ability is to inject the energetic matrix of creation with lethal poison. Doubt is energy that pulls the impetus back and stifles manifestation. You can readily see this with anybody who doubts their own abilities. A doubter never offers enough effort to create any-thing—effort is only ever partially applied. Why give 100%, when it's more than likely going to fail? That is the logic of such a pessimist. Pessimism, doubt, and fear all close doors and stop the flow of energy cold. Again, it's a negative emotion, forcing your tuning-fork Soul to tune in a certain direction. Basically, all negative thoughts and their corresponding emotions are their own energy in wave mechanics. Negative thoughts which generate negative feelings and expectations would be akin to a trough in the energetic wave that cancels out the peak intensity—the positive thoughts and feelings—within the inten-tion's oscillations.

Now, it's easy to formulate doubt when it appears your desire isn't manifesting fast enough. Again, this speaks to the notion of hanging onto outcomes and the feelings associated with such thinking. As we'll see in the chapter on Time, your desire is already manifest in the quan-tum realm. As long as you allow the original energy of the intention to be free and unencumbered, it will continue to vibrate and continue on its way to physical realization in a Now moment. *When you continue to believe in its manifestation, that energy of belief coupled with positive emotions adds to the foundation in the quantum waves of possibility, and also, theoretically, in the Zero Point Field.*

Learning to let go of the outcome can be one of the hardest things to do. But when you understand how the process works, you come to realize that your desire must manifest according to natural law. And laws do what they do, independent of other outside forces. So under-stand that the energy of doubt, fear, and pessimism filters through the exact same law of actualization as does your intention.

Which do you choose to believe and resonate with the most? Your doubts, or the surety of your manifestational intentions? It's the exact same process either way.

Surrender to the process. Let go of the ego, join with the thoughts and feelings of your intention in the Now moment, and allow yourself to merge with the greater consciousness of the universe. The energy of your positive emotions and positive expectations is the guiding force, not your pessimistic and skeptical ego. Let go of your sense of control, which usually comes with a feeling and expectation of negative conditions or circumstances needing to be "wrestled with," and allow the energy to flow out from you uninhibited.

In another sense, having doubt also suggests you are fearing the future—a future where your intention has failed to materialize (or even fear of what might happen when your intention does materialize!). Again, I remind you that *the point of power is always the present.* You can only exist physically in this Now moment. Your thoughts, feelings, beliefs, and mental attitudes will condition your perception of how the *next* Now moment in your life is to be received. If you doubt, you are conditioning yourself to receive a future Now moment with the results of that attitude enveloping you. Your thoughts and attitude create an energetic key that fits into one particular lock matching that key's design, and it will reveal itself as your next moment.

You are the Key Master. You always have been, and always will be. Your thoughts, beliefs, emotions, and mental attitudes create an energetic vibration—the key—that finds the corresponding lock to the reality that matches your vibration. Like attracts like. We all know that universal rule. You are the one that informs your inner world how you perceive your relationship and existence in the outer, thereby informing how the exterior world of possibilities will be turned into probabilities and, ultimately, your experience.

You can continue to add to the intention by following the next step:

7. Act as if you already have, or perform an action that is in alignment with having the intention materialize.

Movement generates energy—literally. This was discovered by a physicist named Elmer Green, a pioneer of biofeedback. He was interested in testing whether or not the hands of remote healers sent out more electrical charge than usual while in the process of healing. He constructed a room with four walls and a ceiling that were made entirely of copper and were attached to microvolt electroencephalogram (EEG) amplifiers—the kind used to measure the electrical activity in the brain. EEG amplifiers are extraordinarily sensitive, capable of picking up even one-millionth of a volt of electricity. Green attached the EEG amplifiers to the copper wall—in essence, creating a gigantic antenna—that would allow him to detect any electricity emitted from the healers from five directions. However, he was soon faced with an enormous problem. Whenever a healer so much as wriggled a finger, patterns got recorded on an EEG amplifier.[8] This revealed just how much "punch" movement can have, even when it is a seemingly miniscule one!

Medical science has proven that all living tissue generates an electrical charge. When you place this electrical charge in three-dimensional space, it creates an electromagnetic field that travels at the speed of light.[9] From these tests, and others like them, we can now see that everyone, healer or not, generates an electrical charge that exceeds the boundaries of the body. Healers are able to project that energy to a client and assist with the rejuvenation of one's condition. You send that charge into the realm of the energetic matrix to create reality. So imagine what *movement* plus the *thought of focused attention* can accomplish.

To make movement, and in particular movement toward the objective of the intention, creates quantum leaps in the actuality of the desire. Again, detach yourself from the ego and let the energy of movement act as a power pack to energize the field of possibilities. The best movement would be to do something that is directly related to the desire (and thus in alignment with it). For instance, if you are lonely, you could walk into a bookstore, mall, or lounge (whatever is your style), and simply say "hi" to a stranger. In this way, you are affirming within the psychic structure of your Soul your commitment to the desire. You are reinforcing it and backing it up. This will build more energy in a shorter length of time.

If you feel that you are poor (tuning-fork Soul on the emotional end of negativity), take stock of everything you own. Now, imbue this list with a pure sense of gratitude (the feeling part of the equation that will set your tuning-fork Soul in the other direction), and realize how abundant you truly are. *Feel* that sense of abundance fill you up. Then go to a store and buy something that is five to ten cents more expensive than what you would normally purchase for a similar item. Be sure your emotions are positive at the moment of purchase, as well as after. When you get home, add that new item to the list and *fill yourself with the sensation of abundance and gratitude.* Affirm your abundance in the Now. Feel it in the present moment. Do this exercise often, and you will discover more abundance finding its way to you. You will see how much more abundant you are. Why? Because your positive emotions and expectations are outweighing the old negative ones. Never tell yourself you don't have enough—always affirm your wealth. If things don't appear to be changing, double-check your beliefs to find out if there are any holding you back or keeping you stubbornly averse to having more wealth and take stock of the emotional charge associated with it. Take baby steps, and you will continue to influence the direction of matter into manifesting your desires.

Ultimately, this taking action is working to recondition the psychic structure of your mind and emotions into being receptive of the unity of yourself with your intention. Let's face it, sometimes when you asked for something, it seemed to fall into your lap without effort. Other times, it seemed like you were Sisyphus, having to push a gigantic boulder up a hill. The only difference between the two is your own mental structure and your Soul's corresponding emotions. For the "simple" stuff, you had no mental blocks in seeing yourself unified with the desire—you imagined it, and the emotions were pleasantly entangled with the thought. Our perspective about the "larger" stuff, on the other hand, is quite different. Admittedly, whenever we apply the tag "larger" to the creation, we have revealed our own inner belief system that suggests the intention "is not going to be easy and will require some work." Along with that thought follows a *feeling*, and hence the law of manifestation follows suit!

Taking action helps to "break up" the mental habits and move beliefs into new energetic possibilities—a journey that moves a potential probability into greater chances of actuality.

As alluded to earlier, the amount of pure concentrated energy that it takes to affect physical reality is, astonishingly, quite small. Using the large TM and TM-Sidhi groups that were tested in affecting major population centers to reduce crime, it was calculated that the size of the TM groups only needed to be the square root of 1% of the geographic population to make the power of the intentions prevail. That is, if you have a city of two million people, you would only need 141 people focusing their intentions with the TM method to effect change. This was termed the "Maharishi effect," in honor of Maharishi Mahesh Yogi, who introduced transcendental meditation back in the late 1950s.

Now, you may not practice TM or any other kind of meditative practice, but what this finding suggests is that the amount of energy needed to create change is not at all overwhelming or intimidating. In truth, you have been creating reality your whole life already, so this isn't earth-shattering news—just a nice affirmation to that which you already know. The more focus you can place on manifesting in the Now moment through movement and action, the more you solidify within your consciousness the reality of the intention's existence in your current reality, and thus provide more thoughts and feelings—the energy needed within your psychic structure—to move it into physical reality.

Current reality is simply an *effect* of previous thoughts, feelings, and intentions (whether those intentions were conscious or not). The act of conscious intention is to reshape the environment, with the understanding that it is all energy and that you supply the architectural design for its construction. Every second, atoms come into existence and pop out of existence. Everything is blinking in this on-and-off dance of energy, and the only thing that keeps the forms in a state of perceived solidarity is what our thoughts, feelings, and expectations give value and credence to, holding the energy in place. To change reality, to create a new reality, is the work of restructuring our inner psychic (mental) reality and the tuning fork of your Soul's emotions to be the blueprint of what we wish to experience physically and emotionally. That blueprint is energetic, magnetic, and cohesive.

Now, this isn't to say that if we stop believing that a chair exists, the chair will disappear. This is about vibration and magnetizing *toward* a particular frequency. If you wish to intend a *different* chair, then don't be surprised if you find one, and the old one falls apart sooner than expected. If we keep telling ourselves that what came before must continue (or if we fear such reality will go on), we keep those events and objects rooted in each successive Now moment. Only when we realize that what is before our eyes is an *effect* of our conscious perceptions—the psychic framework of our held beliefs, expectations, and attitudes—it is then that we see the matrix of creation and become the true captains of our destinies.

If certain aspects of your reality do not meet your needs, credit yourself for the act of its creation—it is simply mirroring back what you have thought and felt into it—then turn it 180 degrees the other direction. Detail the change, feel how that change would be radically different from what you are currently feeling; focus on the new images and internal sensations, and put them in the Now moment, as if it has already happened. Incorporate them into your psychic framework—your mental blueprint of existence.

Now, it is important to realize that being the creator of your own reality is not about blaming or victimizing yourself. It is about being more aware of your thoughts and your inner energies. Being more aware will open up the realization within you of the other possibilities available to choose from, versus running on autopilot. Consult your list of successes from the beginning of this chapter and rejoice in the wonderful things you have already created. Realize that your life has its positive aspects, and you had just as great a hand in creating them with your thoughts and energies as you did those things you are not happy about. You have documented proof of times when you have created positive outcomes in the past, and now you are going to add another item to that list with your next intention.

Here I have detailed the commonalities found in the manifestation literature, along with some findings of scientific studies and input from my own experiences and education.

1. **The present point of power is Now.**

2. **Everything is possible, but not everything is probable, on the basis of your current set of beliefs and/or attitudes.**

3. **Emotions are the vibrational frequency that "magnetizes" possibilities into manifestation. Emotions reveal the "can" or "cannot" expectations, and hence how the environment will respond, with regard to achieving intentioned success.**

4. **Visualize and feel yourself in possession of your desire in the Now moment.**

5. **You must experience the intention without egoic**

attachment. Let the *feeling* of the intention *replace* your ego.

6. **Never doubt the ability to manifest.**

7. **Act as if you already have, or perform an action that is in alignment with having the intention materialize.**

Now let's take a closer look at how this law of cause and effect actually works.

NOTES

1. Reprinted with permission of Pocket Books, a division of Simon & Schuster, Inc., from *Entangled Minds* by Dean Radin. Copyright ©2006 by Dean Radin Ph.D. All rights reserved. See p. 149.

2. This phrase was repeated many times by Seth, as channeled through Jane Roberts. It is an axiom that is particularly powerful when it comes to manifesting reality.

3. A term made popular by the excellent book, *The Field*, by Lynne McTaggart (New York: Quill, 2002). Copyright ©2002 by Lynne MeTaggart, reprinted with permission of HarperCollins Publishers.

4. Ibid., p. 23.

5. Lynne McTaggart, *The Intention Experiment* (New York: Free Press Books, a division of Simon & Schuster, 2007), p.13. Used with permission.

6. Ibid.

7. Ibid.

8. Ibid., p. 21.

9. Ibid., p. 22.

Chapter Nine

MANIFESTING REALITY: THE NUTS AND BOLTS

S o far, we have dealt with some very good theory, combined
with scientific discoveries, and seasoned with sound reason based on experienced results. Still, we are left with our
head cocked to one side wondering: Just what is really going on? How
do my intentions go from being inside my head to becoming my outer
experiences?

I have spent about every waking hour for the past twenty-five
years studying this phenomenon and have tried to dissect every bit of
it. What I have uncovered is nothing more than a person's own magical
abilities, given to everyone equally at birth. You are a fountainhead of
creation. All this comes from your Soul, that which you *are*, and is not
something separate from you. What makes you individual and unique
is your personality and how you use your capabilities to enhance the
value and the lessons of your life experience.

The technique for making reality is the same for everyone—no
one has any more energy or power than anyone else. Yes, there might
be those that have a better understanding of the process and can seem

to create reality with ease, but the technique and method are the same for each and every human being. Again, we are dealing with a natural law of the universe, and the law works the same for everyone.

When you have a thought, that thought is energy. This energy vibrates as emotion and expectations, and thus has electromagnetic properties (we'll get more into this as we go). The vibrational energy strikes a chord with the "lowest" level of particlization—the smallest bit of quantum wavelength that then sends a ripple throughout the field to mold energy into a physical "something." In other words, the energy of your intention takes what was once perceived as a static environment—ordinary energetic reality as it exists at that very moment—and shakes it up a bit, moving random and chaotic patterns within the quantum energetic fields and providing the impetus to move prematter waves into potential material particles. Your intention transmits a wave of thought-energy, much like a radio station transmits its music into invisible airwaves.

The frequency of the thought, emotion, and expectation includes the particulars that make up the desired outcome.

For instance, let's say your desire is to have a piece of pie. The frequency carries within it the type of pie you want—let's say cherry. If you were imagining and desiring a cherry pie, that thought carries the information within the frequency, "the pie must be cherry." Again, this is not so different from a radio station tuned to 98.6 FM, playing rock music where the particulars of the song—drum beat, guitar, vocals, intricate background stylings—are all there, flying around in empty space and able to be heard in digital surround sound. The information within the frequency wave of your thoughts and feelings travels "beneath" normal Time and Space, as it appears that all quantum processes do. Distance doesn't matter. Time doesn't hinder it.

The Electromagnetic Spectrum
the field of energy in which we reside

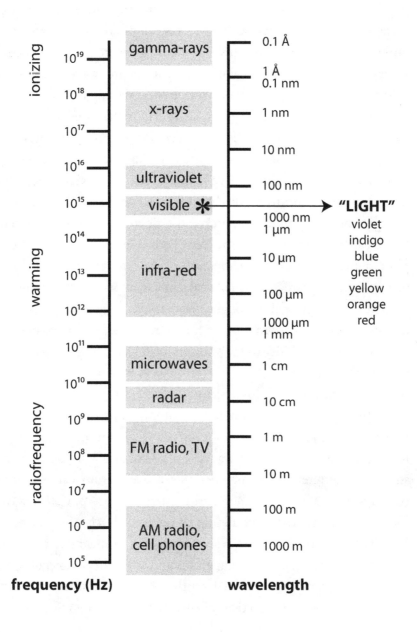

Immediately, the desire is manifested in a nonphysical level of reality. That is, it is a real, valid experience and phenomenon, but it has yet to reach the level of your physical senses and hence *perceived* physical reality. Remember, your senses are only attuned to a short wave band of frequencies, so these filters can often give you a sense of nothing there, when there truly *is* something before you. If you could see the entire spectrum, you would find your desire as a real experience, existing just outside the level of your physical sensing filters.

Your thought at this point is similar to the seed of a flower. Contained within the seed is the realization of the entire flower in bloom—all its components are existent within the seed. The thought and corresponding feelings of your intention are the seed placed into the ground of quantum reality. Out of the sea of possibilities (in terms of experience), the mind has plucked this desire and planted it into the fertile earth, which is fed by the Zero Point Field a few degrees below physical manifestation. Since the roots of the sprout take hold in quantum reality, they are very small and almost imperceptible. However, though the energy of the thought may *seem* imperceptible (remember, it only takes the square root of 1%), it does not negate the existence of the energy and its ability to move and inform how energy is to organize in relation to the intention. To negate this energy would be to negate the seed of the future-realized plant.

Through magnetic influence resulting from the vibration, the thought and corresponding emotions move energy in wavelike patterns, combining with other waves of a like nature, and creating constructive interference. (Remember this concept from earlier? When two cresting waves meet, they create a larger, more powerful wave.) This allows the thought to build up through the levels of wavelengths, little by little. This ascension results in a series of magnetic bondings, pushing particles into becoming atoms and atoms into molecules, and instructing polarities to shift, which then coalesces into synchronistic events based on the magnetism of this rising and changing symmetry of the environment.

"Now wait," you may say. "Not every desire I have comes to pass. What are you talking about?"

We touched on this in the last chapter, but it bears repeating: Every possibility is open to you, but not every possibility will become a probability, on the basis of your beliefs. The universe indeed says "Yes" to your every wish, but in the end do you? Accordingly, do your emotions support your wishes, as well?

You can think and feel a desire, but if you also think and feel it is not coming to you, or that it won't happen, or that the world (or worse, God) is against you, then you put an energetic barrier up that says "No" to you being able to physically experience the intention. You can think powerful initial intentional thoughts, but if you immediately put barriers up to experiencing them, those barriers inhibit the growing process. You might as well put a box around your head!

So, you have an intention. You "seed" it in your consciousness.

Just leave it at that.

You are not seeding it outside of yourself, for there is no-thing outside. You are part and parcel of *all* your reality. Remember, your view and experience of reality is unique to You; your body is the reality you live and experience. Your intention, therefore, can only fit within the makeup of your own unique perception of existence. In other words, don't start judging your intention against the lives of your peers. Again, the intention is not "outside" you for some other-dimensional being to either accept or reject, since you are constructing it as a part of your experiential design through the makeup of thoughts and emotions.

You are the Source.

You are the Creator.

You provide the energy that the Law uses to turn the thought into physical manifestation.

Now, it may appear that other forces, people, even the weather, serve to assist you. Indeed, all things are connected and One. Again, you are a cresting wave on an immense sea of consciousness. Your intention acts like a current in the water. Those that are of a similar frequency and/or who are able to receive the call to action (either consciously or unconsciously) will accept the current flowing through them that your intention created. In that act of acceptance, they will become players on your journey of fulfillment in the desire. They may not perceive their role in your reality as you perceive them, nor, in most cases, will you perceive your role in relation to their intentions. Again, all things are connected, but not all individuals are aware of this union. Nevertheless, everyone will be riding a similar frequency in their own lives and will quite unknowingly harmonize to others' intentions and lend a hand. Again, all of this is not outside of you, as you are connected to everything and everyone else, and everything and everyone are connected to you. As your body calls upon the perceived singular organs to help process the fluids, toxins, and other chemicals throughout your body, so, too, do these perceived "separate" entities—people, weather, etcetera—respond to the call of those intentions from others that are magnetized at similar frequencies in the body of your experiences.

There has been a lot of talk in manifesting circles about being "in vibrational alignment" with your intention, that you and your desire must be a vibrational "match" for it to manifest. "What does this mean, exactly?" I wondered.

Since the intention itself sprang from you, *then the vibration for that intention had to also be birthed by you.* To have the thought, to think of the intention, is in itself the vibration—otherwise, you would not have had the thought to begin with!

The current instruction in this resonating paradigm makes it sound like the desire is outside of you, vibrating at a certain frequency that you may or may not be matching. This disparate gap between you and your intention keeps it from forming, and the hope is that you can find a way to *feel* better on an emotional scale, and that by feeling better you may better free up resistance that you might have to receiving the intention.

Since each of us creates a unique reality unto ourselves, the idea that the intention is on its own frequency outside of you that you must resonate with to "close the gap" just doesn't make sense. The idea is that as your vibration matches that of the intention, the tuning fork experience occurs: Like energies will attract like energies, and boom! There's your desire coming to meet you across Time and Space.

On the surface, this appears to make sound, logical sense. However, as I said, I have problems with this viewpoint.

Your desire comes from you, and you create your own unique reality in relation to your psychical structure. Therefore, the intention *can only be yours*, not outside yourself, existing in some other part of the universe after you have thought it. That thought might *represent* and *vibrate at* a different frequency than one at which you normally resonate. That is to say, the information coded in the intention—the specifics of the desire—may be of a different energetic frequency and vibration than those of your current state of being. It's like twisting a radio dial and finding the rock station instead of jazz, and then having the radio suddenly jump back to static because it's not calibrated (tuned) to receive that particular station for any length of time. Though the radio does not provide the rock music station in itself (it's only receiving the signal), *you do* provide the desire. Therefore, it is not something outside of you, floating around the ethers. It is within you. This should be a great comfort, because if you know that the intention and specifics come from within your being, then you also know the vibrational frequency as well! The desire contained the frequency, and that, too, comes from You. The key to how you should resonate is provided by the desire and its corresponding feelings at the time of its initial inception.

So here you are, focusing on your intention. You're following each and every step accordingly. But what's really going on behind the scenes? Are you raising the vibration of energy throughout your whole being?

No. You are recalibrating. Some may consider this a mere change of phrase or semantics, but it's not necessarily about raising or lowering your frequency as much as it is about recalibrating and retuning. You are dialing your energies to pick up the station the intention resides on. The station itself, mind you, is not outside you—but it is a result of this calibration of energy that your idea gave impetus to. Oftentimes, you are probably swaying back and forth between positive feelings/expectations and negative ones, eventually recalibrating your soul to the more positive end of the frequency rather than your usual state.

The reason it's so important to focus on the reality of your intention already having arrived is to foster the physical events necessary to reach that conclusion through this process of recalibration.

What do I mean by this?

In thinking and feeling that the intention has already manifested, inherent within that manifestation (and its vibration) are the steps that were taken to get there. It's as if the completed reality from a future Now moment links itself backward to the present Now, with all the steps imbedded in between. This may sound outlandish at first, until we realize there have been some scientific tests showing that, indeed, this may actually be occurring.

In 1988, Helmut Schmidt and Marilyn Schlitz announced the results of their unique course of study with RNGs at the Annual Convention of the Parapsychological Foundation. They discovered that the mind *can affect the outcome of events that occurred in the past.* In one case, they had used a computerized randomized process to record

1,000 different sequences of sound. Each sequence consisted of 100 tones of varying bursts of noise. They recorded these sounds, and then mailed them to volunteers. While listening to the prerecorded tape, the volunteers were instructed to intentionally increase the duration of the pleasing sounds and decrease the durations of the noise. After the test was completed, Schmidt and Schlitz examined the original sequences and discovered that the recordings the subjects listened to contained significantly longer stretches of pleasing sounds than noise.

In another test, they programmed the computer to produce 100-tone sequences of four notes, playing them in random order. Subjects were asked to try and increase the number of higher-pitched tones after the recordings had been made. Again, remarkably, a retroactive effect was found.[1]

Schmidt also demonstrated that the prerecorded, but unobserved, recorded breathing rates from laboratory volunteers acquired on a previous day could be influenced to either speed up or slow down, according to the intentions of a person listening to the tape at a later time![2]

Additionally, physicists Edwin May and James Spottiswoode took the backward-time notion and put it to the test by hooking volunteers up to machines that would measure one's galvanic skin response. Then they assaulted the listener with randomized noises through earphones. Measurements from more than 100 participants showed that the nervous system "knew" 3 to 5 seconds in advance of when the listener was going to be hit with a disturbing noise.[3]

It gets more interesting than that. In the late 1970s, a neurophysiologist named Ben Libet performed some fascinating experiments with patients who were awake during brain surgery. His findings give credence to the premise that Time is not linear and can be affected by a future event linking backward in time to the present moment. First, he stimulated the patient's little finger and recorded the response in the sensory cortex of the brain. Alternately, he stimulated the sensory cortex to produce the same sensation and asked the patient to respond when they felt it. Libet postulated that when he stimulated the brain directly, the patient should "feel" the stimulation instantly. Conversely, when the finger was stimulated, he surmised that there should be a delay as the notification traveled from the finger to the brain.

What happened was exactly the opposite.

It seemed that there was a delay in reaction when he stimulated the brain directly, but a reaction was instantaneous when he stimulated the finger. What this suggests is that the brain is actually firing *ahead of the stimulus and sending the information backward in time,*[4] and I theorize that this is based on the observed expectation of that sensation within the consciousness of the individual perceiving it in that Now moment.

Similarly, there have been studies that show that it is physiologically impossible for a baseball batter to hit a 100-mile-per-hour fastball pitch. Considering the time needed for recognition, the visual processing of the speed and trajectory of the ball, the time for motor response, reflexes, and synaptic delays, there is not enough time for the batter to actually swing at the ball, let alone hit it. Again, the potential that the information is presented backwards in time within the brain to enable the batter sufficient time to swing is still being seriously considered.[5]

Remember, you are a multidimensional being. Your thoughts and emotions are electrical and follow exacting laws. As quantum particles have been shown to display properties defying both distance (Space) and travel at the speed of light (Time), so, too, does the nature of the energy of your Soul.

So let's consider for a moment that your intention, projected as manifesting in the Now, actually provides the steps necessary for its fulfillment through that "completed" vibration. How would it work?

Remember that piece of cherry pie you wanted? Let's say you are so hungry that you intend to have this pie. You visualize it, taste it, feel how each cherry rests on your tongue and how warm it feels going down your throat and into your stomach. You make the intention at 10 A.M., with gusto. Oddly enough, fifteen minutes later, there's a knock at the door—from your neighbor, who just happens to have baked a pie. This is not so far-fetched. How many times has something similar happened to you?

Yet we all know, pie making takes preparation: from making the crust and combining the ingredients to putting it all together and baking it. There's no way your neighbor could have done all that in fifteen-minutes. Your intention, thrust forth by its corresponding emotions, would've had to go backward in time at least a few hours to provide the inspiration necessary to get your neighbor moving! Or how about this bizarre coincidence: You go out to the mailbox, and there's a flyer from a new bakery up the street, advertising their specialty—cherry pies! Considering the time it takes to prepare flyers and ship them out through the mail, the fact that it conveniently arrives just after you form the intention is proof positive of the magic of your thoughts and feelings! Though this is a fictitious story of events, consider how many times in your life things have come together in a similar way.

Naturally, there will be naysayers who cry, "Coincidence!" To that I say, if you stop and consider the odds against chance that, shortly after forming the intention, the neighbor appears with a pie or you find the flyer advertising pies, you would find that a random coincidence is statistically unlikely (to a marked degree). My challenge to skeptics would be to start looking at "coincidences" in this way and asking, "What are the mathematical odds against chance of this event happening when it did?" It's always easier for a lazy mind to write things off as chance rather than to run it through the machine of self-discovery.

An intention is a thought coupled with an emotion. *That thought and emotion are energy, which envelops your Self.* Many spiritual healers

Energy is not confined, it is spread out. Our thoughts and feelings radiate out from us in auras of wavelike oscillations.

simulated biophotons

and those who can see auras—energy fields emitted by human be-ings—indicate that when someone is sick, the illness is first apparent in the individual's aura before any symptoms occur in the body. Auras are acknowledged in many traditions and by some in the scientific com-munity, on the basis of Kirlian photography.

Kirlian photography refers to a form of photogram made by

using high voltage. It is named after Semyon Kirlian, who in 1939 accidentally discovered that if an object on a photographic plate is connected to a high-voltage source, small corona discharges (created by the strong electric field at the edges of the object) create an image on the photographic plate.[6] Moreover, German physicist Fritz-Albert Popp discovered that all living things, from the smallest single-celled plants to the organs of human beings, emit a tiny stream of photons, which he labeled "biophotons."[7] In other words, your intention is coded and transmitted partially through light—a part of the electromagnetic spectrum. At that point, you transmit the details of the intention across the fluid, moldable fabric of Time and Space through electromagnetic radiation (of which light is a part). You feel it on the inside as having manifested. It is a real creation, and you do not doubt it.

Since energy at the quantum level transcends Time and Space, your intention *in relation to quantum reality* lands somewhere in your perceived future, simultaneously with your Now moment—complete in its manifestation. It also carries a string into the past, connecting the dots to its completion (intersecting with the Zero Point Field). This action across nonlinear Time is a step toward turning possibilities into probabilities.

Now, all possibilities exist until an observer intervenes. What if the observer chooses to make an observation in a future Now moment of something that has already passed, but has previously gone unnoticed—like listening to the previously recorded tapes with random noises? The outcome adjusts itself accordingly.

Waves move through all Time simultaneously, as well as all Space. The intention (thoughts and emotions), therefore, ultimately covers the fabric of eternity, the past, present, and future in terms of Time, and anything and all things in Space, meaning it's nonlocal. Thus, Time and Space are fluid and moldable. It's only our beliefs in the process that make manifestation behave the way it does. Energy at its most minute level is not confined to the Here and Now, it is *spread* _ghts and feelings, too, traverse this energy, radiating out _s in auras of wavelike oscillations.

Our auras are made up of light—a wavelength of light that falls outside the normal frequency range of most people's eyesight. But light (specifically, photons) is the driving force for electromagnetism, as light has no mass and never comes to rest.

Do we know of anything else that has no mass and never comes to rest?

That's right—Your Soul!

You project your intention, and you work toward recalibrating your energy to match the energy of your intention. You are aligning yourself with the particular frequency or wavelength of experiencing an event or receiving an object of your desire. In other words, if you intend to receive an object, it is the *event of receiving it and being in possession of it* that constitutes the frequency or wavelength of the electromagnetic radiation that matches up to it on the nonlinear time scale.

The vibrational match in the process of recalibration is the frequency or wavelength in the Now moment of *feeling wedded to your desire as if you already have it,* coming into coherence with the frequency or wavelength of that real event in the *future* Now moment (which exists simultaneously on the nonlinear scale of energetic Time). Being in coherence—that is, Being at the same oscillations and energy frequency as the target intention—traverses Time to that future Now on the energetic scale. That coherency informs the gap between Present and Future of the steps needed to move in the direction of the realized intention.

Resonating at the frequency of receiving the desire in a Future Now moment simultaneously brings those steps into play. If one were to step back into the framework of Time, it would appear that the

Re-Calibration of Energy to Intended Event/Object

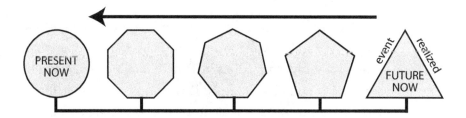

Here, the intention of the Circle was to become a Triangle. On the timeline, it is realized at a simultaneous Future Now Moment. Its energy, having been intended as being completed in the Present Now, allows that completed future to present the steps needed for its transformation backward through Time (so long as the Circle continues to believe and resonate in coherence with the view of the completed event). Since it is not customary for the Circle to be able to see the future outside its current state, it would perceive its transformation as happening in moment-after-moment fashion, when in reality, it already was completed and now the energy is simply re-calibrating to perceive the event/object within its normal frequency range.

future Now reached backward into the past to the Present, and in so doing, the steps needed to be taken to realize the manifestation in the future also presented themselves. One only needs to be aware and watch for these clues to allow those strange "synchronicities" to fall into place.

The mechanics of how thoughts and feelings create reality follows this experience:

1. A thought produces an image and a feeling. So long as the conscious focus of the observer remains on this thought and feels as though it is already manifested, that frequency of realized manifestation radiates from the individual. The

radiation projects via the individual's aura (or some other frequency wavelength along the electromagnetic spectrum). The frequency crisscrosses the universe in nonlocal Space and nonlinear Time through quantum processes.

2. The frequency or wavelength of the focused thought—so long as the individual continues to believe in its manifestation—instantly materializes in Time, though you may not be aware of it consciously. Since it is completed in that future Now moment, the steps taken to complete it are also inherent in the manifestation. They, too, appear simultaneously on the timeline as a result of the electromagnetic wavelength or frequency being transmitted by the Soul as a manifested event.

3. Continued belief in the reality of the desire builds amplitude in the frequency. Subtle energy vibration informs the tiniest subatomic particles, all the way up to larger macroscopic particles, and even waveform dynamics and low-level telepathy within people and other living systems, to rise into coherence between the present Now and a future Now. The arrival of the manifested future in the Present is the coherence being realized by the individual's physical senses, which can then perceive the arrival in relation to the physical apparatus (body).

4. So long as you continue to maintain belief in the intention as being manifest and real and that you are in possession of it and feel this union emotionally, the coherence realized between all systems of reality magnetically materialize the bridge (the events) that take you there. It is because the intention is perceived as being manifest that the steps to its

completion are particlized. Perception is deemed to be the combination of visual thoughts, plus corresponding emotions and expectations. The future informs the past, as well as the past informing the future.

As another example, consider that simple intention of the parking space you want. You are *five minutes away* from the parking lot when you announce your intention. "I want an up-front parking space—right outside the front door!" For someone to finish up shopping, pay for and gather their items, make it out to the car, load it up, and pull out in time for you to get the spot (and keep the spot from being taken by somebody else), your intention would have to inform reality from a time frame *longer* than the five minutes it takes you to reach your destination. The person who needs to release the space to you would have to be "informed" at the right time to be able to get through the check-out line and make it back to the car and pull out. Likewise, you would also be informing yourself of the route to take and navigating any delays along the way, such as stoplights—in some cases, *after* you had already gone through them. In other words, had you not been held up by the two-minute stoplight ten minutes ago, you would be experiencing an entirely different set of circumstances and reality at the time you made the intention. All in all, though you made the announcement five minutes from the parking lot, the energy of the intention *reached backward into the past* to orchestrate the details necessary to deliver your desired parking spot. It boggles the mind, simply because we do not usually stop to think about the mechanisms in place to bring us the fruits of our desires.

Nothing is coincidence. Scientific research proves the effect of observation on reality, transcending Time and Space. Other research demonstrates the electromagnetic abilities of light, which you emit via your aura. Scientists have established that we have the ability to affect and create reality—down to the smallest atomic and quantum processes, even for an event as minute as securing your ideal parking space. Review your own personal list of manifestations from the last chapter to remind yourself just how many times you have deliberately created reality.

You are a divine Soul. A magical Creator. You can be as free as you choose to be. Reality is your playground. Just keep in mind that your psychic framework of beliefs and emotions acts as the referee. You will only go as far as your current set of beliefs allows. Remember, a belief is an *invisible* framework. It is just a thought, and a thought can be changed at any time.

The first step is realizing that the details of your life are orchestrated by *you,* and you alone. You are constructing your life through your quantum brain and feeling its effects in your multidimensional body—therefore, the only intelligence in your existence is your own. It is not related to your neighbor's—your neighbor has his own life, intelligence, and emotional makeup. You are the one that provides all the perceptions—thoughts, feelings, and expectations—surrounding your life. You either accept or deny viewpoints and feelings. There is no such thing as "outside forces" working either for or against you. The process of thought leading to physical manifestation doesn't judge, because it is simply *a process,* just as your body doesn't judge the process of digestion. The intelligence backing the events and circumstances of your life is your own. Do not question your ability to turn thoughts into reality, for you have already proven that you can and do. It is your natural way of Being.

The Universe is one cooperative mind. It is like one big electron, able to exist in various states simultaneously, yet it is interconnected and perpetually passes information within itself, no matter what state it is in. The process of thoughts to physical manifestation only becomes garbled when you yourself become garbled about whether the desire is possible and plausible *within the context of your own existence.* You can have any desire, and you can see it as possible and plausible with other people, but perhaps not for yourself. Or, if you can't see "how" a desire will manifest (that is, you are unable to predict rationally how such a thought can come to pass), then you are simply short-circuiting yourself. On one hand, you have your desire, but on the other, because you cannot follow the course of events through to its fruition mentally, you project doubt and stunt the availability of its occurrence. This is why it is so valuable to look to your past successes, for they remind you that you do not always need to know the *how* or see the steps of an intention unfolding—just be rest assured that it *is* happening.

So why should any future desire be any different than these other ones on your list? They are not. That is why you must tell yourself, "I am building on my past successes. *I am putting another notch on my belt, and I can feel this to be true.*" To think otherwise simply reveals that you have a different attitude and corresponding emotion in your own consciousness. And your consciousness is the Universal consciousness—it is part and parcel with it—so you are feeding the energy to manifest totally in compliance with the nature of the process, on the basis of your Soul's being.

Thoughts and feelings are like sunlight. As the sun fuels life on earth and compels it to move in mysterious ways (from a distance of many millions of miles, no less), so do your thoughts and feelings affect particles even smaller than quanta, which then affect how energy manipulates quanta, which in turn clumps atoms and molecules together. This can happen no matter where you are on earth, like the sun providing the energy to allow life. All of these thought/feeling particles carry information, like little DNA. This information "informs" reality, like the sun informing the inner atoms and molecules of the plants, causing them to grow in a certain direction. So do your thoughts and feelings energetically inform the movement of particles in and out of reality, which informs reality how to Organize.

You are the Great Organizer of your life. As you think, "Pick up pencil," your body orchestrates thousands of movements to make it happen, yet you don't fully comprehend how. As your thoughts have the ability to move seemingly distinct and separate entities inside your body (muscles, blood, tissue, tendons, organs, etc), so too do they perform the organization and movement of things in your "outer" body known as physical experience. The two only *appear* separate, but you affect your external experience as equally as you do your internal one— you just usually fail to give yourself the credit (until now). You have proven that you do affect outer reality, through reviewing your past successes. You may not *consciously* understand the how, but you have proven that somewhere in your Being, you absolutely do.

If a desire does not seem to be manifesting, then examine your thoughts. You will find that, at some level, you are not believing it is possible within the framework of your current existence. You are most likely holding back because of *fear*. For example, "How would my life change by having the desire?" Check for that "nagging voice," because, chances are, that's what it's saying. That's what is stopping you.

Those desires that have very little impact in terms of change are always quick to manifest—there's nothing to lose, and they are easy to *feel* "locked into place." On the other hand, those "larger ones" that do present risk, or radical change, may upset you. Again, this is why it is important to look at your past and say, "I am building on these prior successes." That you have survived and moved on from the previous ones, and proven that your thoughts create your present and future reality, indicates that you can deal with what happens down the road.

Use these past successes as your foundation, like a house. When you pour the foundation of a house, you don't leave it behind to build the walls somewhere else on the property. No, you build the floor and walls *on the foundation*. So use your previous successes as a way of reminding that "nagging voice" of just how scientific and absolutely true it is that your desire *will manifest as physical reality*.

Now go and create your life.

NOTES

1. Michael Talbot, *The Holographic Universe* (New York: HarperCollins Publishers, 1991), p. 226. Used with permission.

2. From the book *Limitless Mind.* Copyright ©2004 by Russell Targ and Jane Katra, Ph.D. Reprinted with permission of New World Library, Novato, California. www.newworldlibrary.com. See p. 89.

3. Ibid., p. 87.

4. Fred Alan Wolf, *The Yoga of Time Travel* (Wheaton, Illinois: Quest Books, 2004), p. 65, 158. Used with permission.

5. Ibid., p. 66.

6. Wikipedia. Available at: *http://en.wikipedia.org/wiki/Kirlian_photography.*

7. Lynne McTaggart, *The Intention Experiment* (New York: Free Press Books, a division of Simon & Schuster, 2007), p. 27. Used with permission.

Chapter Ten

THE SOUL WITHIN
THE CONTEXT OF TIME

Have you ever been focused on a task and then glanced at your watch to see the hand ticking off the seconds hesitate? This happens to me all the time. I will look at the watch and feel I am waiting longer than one second to see that hand snap into the next moment. Every time this happens, I exclaim, "That was longer than one second!" This is not an uncommon occurrence, because of the simple fact that Time is an effect of consciousness.

Take an inventory of Time in your life from the standpoint of a single day. You will oftentimes sense time moving either quickly or slowly, but it is always in relation to your focus. If you are bored, time drags. If you are having a great time, the moments whiz by.

Also notice that Time moves much differently in your dream state. You can take a fifteen-minute nap and dream of events that would take an hour or more to accomplish if you were awake. You may think, "Nonsense. Sixty seconds always equals one minute, no matter where you are in the universe." Indeed, for centuries, that was the prevailing belief. Then Einstein's theory of relativity smashed that notion to pieces.

Einstein created a thought experiment by using a large locomotive to make his point that Time is relative to the observer, in terms of physics and the study of physical reality (consciousness, as we will see, can take it step further). Imagine an observer standing midway inside a rapidly moving train car and another observer standing on a platform as the train zips by. Let's say the guy inside the train flips on a strobe light at the exact moment that he and the man on the platform pass each other. The gentleman on the train can see the front and rear of the car at fixed distances from the light source—so since he is standing midway inside the car, he would see the light flash reaching the front and back of the car at the same time. The observer on the platform, however, would see the back of the train car catching up toward the point at which the flash burst and the front of the train as moving away from it, based entirely on where he was standing. The speed of light is finite (186,000 miles per second) in all directions for all observers, but from his point of view, the light heading for the back of the train will have less distance to cover than the light headed for the front. His view is completely unlike the view of the gentleman in the car itself, hence the phrase, "relative position."

Einstein also theorized (and was later proven) that gravity affects Time. This came as a result of the discovery that light waves "bend" around the gravitational waves of the sun during a solar eclipse. This bending of light creates a time dilation effect that slows down the movement of light, creating a change outside the old Newtonian belief system that 60 seconds equals one minute. In other words, Time is not fixed.

Quantum mechanics also supports Einstein's experiments. Teensy-weensy particles called *muons* strike our planet in the form of cosmic rays, usually at very high altitudes in the mountains. The average lifespan of these particles is about 2 microseconds (a little over 2 millionths of a second). Some die a little younger, some a little older—at around 6.3 microseconds. These miniature particles can be counted by using a device called a *scintillation counter*, which can also track the particles' life spans and what happens to them when they die and decay.

In one experiment, physicists ascended a mountain 6,300 feet above sea level. Using their scintillation counters, they discovered that 568 muons passed into their devices each hour. The particles traveled down a short vertical tube, where they came to rest and decayed near a second scintillation counter. Around 30 particles made it to ripe old age of 6.3 microseconds. The experiment indicated to these scientists that the particles moved at near the speed of light.[1]

Next, they took their counters to the seashore. They anticipated that if a muon traveled at near light-speed, it could travel the 6,300 feet down to sea level in about 6 microseconds. Given that most of them don't live that long, however, they didn't expect to find very many that would survive the journey. Astoundingly, they found that 412 had survived the trip!

How did this happen?

Einstein's relativity theory states that Time does not function the same way for a moving object as it does for one standing still. Moving objects experience a slowing down of Time, so that while the rest of the world passes through a given time period, the moving object passes through in a shorter amount of time. In this case, the average lifespan of a muon, because it was moving and not stationary, was extended to nine times its expected length.[2]

Here, we see that Time is not something fixed, but rather something that is quite flexible. In the last chapter, we saw how people could influence the past by intending observations from the Present. Other psi studies have shown that we also have an effect going the other direction, into the future.

Forced-choice experiments are tests where any number of possible outcomes are available from a pool of standardized options, and it is up to a participant to try and "force" the future outcome before it is selected. This is like offering a series of colored lights—say blue, red, and green—with a computer making a random color selection on Tuesday, yet a person will try and force it to choose the green light on Friday the week beforehand. In the earliest studies, decks of cards were shuffled by hand with a declaration of what card (number and suit) would be pulled from the stack after it was shuffled. In later studies, RNGs were used to see if participants could force what random numbers and fluctuations would occur in the machines weeks or sometimes months ahead of the experiments—meaning that at a future date, either more 1's would be produced in a given experiment, or more 0's. Indeed, forced-choice experiments could be perceived at best as lab-generated intention tests, or as possible proof of precognition (if in fact the participant wasn't forcing but possibly trying to "see ahead" the outcome of the events).

In 1989, Charles Honorton and Diane Ferrari published the results of a meta-analysis of these kinds of experiments conducted between 1935 and 1987. Out of 309 studies reported in 113 published articles, contributed by 62 different investigators, they had a database of nearly 2 million trials by more than 50,000 subjects. The study designs ranged from the use of ESP cards to computer-generated, randomly presented symbols. The time interval between the perceived future outcome and the generation of the future targets ranged from milliseconds to as long as a year. The combined results of the 309 studies produced odds against chance of 10^{23} to one, favoring precognitive choice![3] Of course, the question arises: Is it choice, or are these people "looking into" the future? Either way, such experiments demonstrate that if one is seeing into the future, then that moment of Time is not independent of the Present and is, in fact, somehow accessible to and wrapped up with it. With forced choice, it shows that the future can be accessed from the present and indelibly impacted.

Similar precognitive studies were also performed at SRI's remote-viewing program. These tests were designed to be different from the standard remote-viewing tests, like those I described earlier with Pat

Price and the Palo Alto pool. Those original remote-viewing tests were designed to simply describe the location at the time it was felt the target team had arrived at the site. In these new trials, the experiment was to remote-view the location *before it had even been chosen* from a pool of potential locales. In 1975, Russell Targ and his colleagues carried out a series of four deliberate precognitive trials with Hella Hammid. All four of her remote-viewing descriptions, according to Targ, correctly matched the targets ahead of time, before they were chosen at random. In one case, she described a location with "manicured trees and shrubs...a formal garden." She then went on to describe a path leading to a balcony and steps. After the target team returned from the location some time later, they revealed the site as being the Stanford University Hospital, the grounds of which matched her description in uncanny detail.[4]

Robert Jahn, Brenda Dunne, and Roger Nelson of the PEAR group conducted 227 formal experiments in which a viewer was asked to describe where one of the researchers would be hiding at some pre-selected later time. They discovered that the accuracy of the description given by the viewer was the same, whether the viewer had to look hours, days, or even weeks into the future. The overall statistical significance of chance was determined to be 1 in 100 billion![5]

The ability to somehow "see" into the future typically falls into the domain of psychic readings. During one of my groups, a sitter had asked me where her son, who had just entered the Navy, was going to be stationed. She didn't give me multiple-choice answers, but allowed me to interpret what the energy indicated. After taking a breath, I could feel myself getting pulled across the Pacific and landing in Japan. The sitter was aghast, for she didn't believe he could be stationed so far from home. (After all, her husband was also in the Navy, and she had hoped that he could use his authority to sway the powers-that-be to station their son closer to home.) Nevertheless, several weeks later he received his commission...to go to Japan.

We have all heard stories of how people, whether considered psychic or not, have been able to somehow see the future and avoid disasters. There are nineteen documented cases of people who had precognitive glimpses of the sinking of the *Titanic*[6]—in one case, a novelist, Morgan Robertson, wrote about it *fourteen years earlier* in a fictional tale called *Futility.* In his book, a down-on-his-luck sailor boards a ship that eerily matches the design of the *Titanic*—its size, propellers, masts, gross tonnage, and capacity of people. This fictional vessel also collides with an iceberg in the Northern Atlantic and sinks, with a great loss of life. The most astounding part is that he called his fictional ship "Titan."

The outcome of all these scientific experiments and cataloged details seems to indicate that we have tapped into nothing less than the perimeter of eternity itself. We are discovering that Time, like Space, is something that is not defined as a linear progression. Moreover, with the inclusion of Einstein's work showing that Time is relative to the observer, and our own experience with Time appearing "slow" or "fast" within our own lives, it appears to be something that is not "outside" us, but rather exists inside our consciousness. It is something that can clearly be accessed by our consciousness—and that I propose is *created by* our consciousness.

We are the ones who have sliced up Time by defining its passage through the clicking off of a series of seconds into a minute, and by tallying a certain number of minutes as an hour. However convenient this is for synchronizing meetings and events between people, the fact of the matter is, the only moment that is real is not the one that just ticked off the clock one second ago, or the tick of a future moment one or two seconds ahead. Instead, the real moment of experience is Now—the present moment, in all its fluidity to the past and future. We can never physically experience the past or the future, although we may be able to tap into them in our minds. We can only *physically* experience Now.

To drive this point home and have you glean some experiential knowledge of this quagmire, lift your hand and point your index finger as if you were shooting an imaginary gun. Curl your finger around the trigger and squeeze off an invisible shot. Once you have done that, point your finger again, then try to physically go backward in Time two seconds and *not* pull the trigger that you just pulled. Go ahead. Point your finger and try to change what you did in the past. You can't. That moment is physically gone and out of physical reach. By way of comparison, jump ahead two seconds into the future and pull the trigger. If you curled your finger and pulled, you did it in error. You didn't jump ahead two seconds into the future—you did it Now.

You see, all you ever *physically* have to work with is Now. You physically *only* exist *Now*. Yet we know from scientific studies that you can *affect* the past and the future. The trick is, you can only *experience* those outcomes in a present Now moment. That is, the future and the past are not physical realities. The past and the future, like quantum particles, are nothing more than a field of *energetic possibilities*. These possibilities can be molded and defined into probabilities (and those probabilities, on the basis of their energy, could be labeled as certainties), but they will never be physically experienced until an observation is made in the Now moment. Until that precise moment of observation, past and future are simply unmanifested potential possibilities. It is the focus of consciousness that determines how that energy will be particalized from probability into physical reality in a Now moment. It is *consciousness* that changes the energy into concrete experience.

Since past and future are potential energies affected by the focus of mind-energy from the present Now, that focus of mind spreads out across the continuum of Time. In other words, Time can be perceived as a field of synchronization, where past, present, and future all exist side by side. Which means that the past and future occur *simultaneously* with the present.

This may seem hard to grasp at first, but here is a way of

understanding such an astounding concept: Consider this moment, right now, on earth. Our earth has forty different time zones, all happening at once. In America, if you are on the West Coast and it is 1 P.M. on a Tuesday, at that very same moment on the East Coast, it

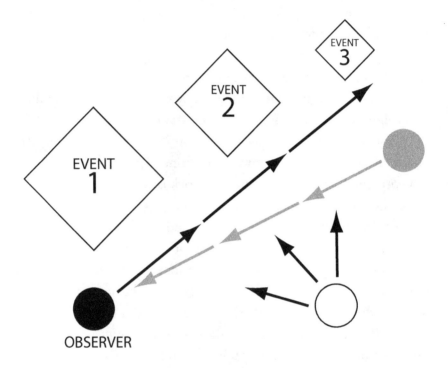

Here we have an observer (circle) in three different areas, showing three different views of Time. On the left, he sees an event as happening in a 1, 2, 3 fashion; yet if he were standing on the other end witnessing the same event, due to his relative position, things would be seen as happening in a 3, 2, 1 sequence. Finally, if he were to be standing in the middle, all events occur simultaneously. This is why three different observers to a car crash can have three different stories as to what happened first, second and third during the accident. [Spatial left, right, and middle are not to be taken literally, but rather are representations for the variety of human perspectives and cognition.]

is perceived to be 4 P.M. On the opposite side of the planet in some foreign outland, it may be perceived as 3 A.M. on Wednesday. Yet if you were to be an astronaut in space looking down on our blue-green orb, this apparent Time differentiation is occurring *all at once*. It is simultaneous from the astronaut's point of view.

And so, Time is all a matter of perception in relation to consciousness. We often like to think of events happening in a 1-2-3 fashion. Yet physics acknowledges, by way of the observer, that one person may see the particulars of an event in a 3-2-1 pattern, while another sees it as a 1-2-3 pattern *at the same time*. Pretty wacky, huh? For instance, if someone were to witness a car crashing into a light pole while people are crossing the street just out of the car's path, some people would see the people reaching the other side of the street before the car hit, while others—because of their relative position—would see the car crash a few seconds before the people reached their destined sidewalk. Remember our strobe light in the train car from earlier? That is also a good example.

Again, the observer is the key.

Spiritually within the Soul, Time is something we create to provide a framework for our experiences on an individual basis. There is no physical past, and no physical future—there is only the perception of such. Experiential Time exists as Now, and has always existed as Now. The nexus of eternity is from this moment of the Present, where our consciousness emerges into physical experience. As we have demonstrated, our thoughts can affect the *perceived* past and the *perceived* future. The impetus for those effects comes from our present point—a Now moment. These effects shooting backward or forward in Time also cannot be experienced, except within the Now moment. The Now, the present point, is the nexus of power and the realization of eternity. Your Soul covers this expanse. That you can affect the perceived past and future with your own intentions reveals your multidimensionality and your own eternal validity across all Time.

FREEDOM FROM STRESS AND ANXIETY

With the point of power being the present moment, you no longer need to remain tied to stress, guilt, remorse, or regret about the past, nor anxiety and fear of the future. In this very moment, where your flesh and experience materialize out of eternity, you are free from both past and future events in terms of their emotional and psychological hold on you, especially since you can affect both from this eternal Now moment. All that there is, is Now. The past and future, again, are unmanifest energy that has no physical recurring effect on you in the Now. Any effect you might feel is on the inside, held in place by your conscious mind. The past and the future, like anything, are only a perception. Yes, you may have accidentally wounded yourself yesterday (or, worse, got into a car crash), but those events themselves are no longer real in terms of physical reality, for they have collapsed back into the field of energy and potential. In this type of scenario, though you cannot physically go back and keep yourself from getting wounded or being in the crash, you can lessen the emotional and psychological impact, as well as speed up the recovery time of healing. By consciously intending the wound or the crash to have less energetic impact, you take creative control over the probabilities of both past and future to mold reality in a way that is multidimensional versus linear. (Keep in mind, too, that on some level, you energetically created the incident in your consciousness in the first place—whether this was deliberate or not. Sad, but true. Still, you have power to lessen past impacts by changing up their energetic potentials and reimagining them).

This is not to say you should ignore the past or the future, but don't give either more power than that in the moment you are actually experiencing—the Now moment. Past and future, being unmanifest energy, have no physical effect on the Now, for they are strictly potential possibilities. The past, though we have concretized it in our mind and essentially collapsed particles into a previous Now experience, once that experience has passed, unseen variables not observed can still be affected from the present point (Our egocentric consciousness filters out much experience, leaving many variables untouched). In addition, variables that were collapsed in the past, like all things, do not stay the same, and can therefore also be altered by the present, within the context of observed reality. For instance, you may not be able to go back and change the moment you broke your leg in the car crash, but you can still lessen the impact and speed the process of healing in the Now, and, in some cases, by reimagining the accident (and without consciously knowing it), save yourself from breaking an arm, too (which then usually results in a memory of a policeman who saw the incident saying, "That impact should have broken your arm, as well." Nevertheless, such reimagining can considerably speed up healing time both physically and mentally). On the surface, this may sound kind of absurd. I grant you that. But when it comes to energy and reality, just ask a scientist how the quantum field behaves. You know what he'll say? "It's absurd."

The past and the future cannot hurt you, spite you, ruin you, degrade you, build you up, make you stronger, or give you a million dollars. None of that can be *physically experienced* in the past or the future. The only moment in which any of that can happen is *Now*.

This is not a license to be careless. Your energy travels through a continuum that speaks to all Time occurring simultaneously, and each moment is but a snapshot of your energy in eternity. That is to say, you can't go out and hurt others, and then when the moment has passed declare that it never happened. You and all things (including other people) are connected and One, and the observation of each creates reality. If you hurt another, you are hurting yourself via your own eternal, nonseparate connection.

Remember, everyone is multidimensional. It's how you choose to manage the energy you focus on in the Now that determines your state at any given moment. Do you remain in guilt, regret, or fear? Do you remain terrified of what *might* come in the future?

Don't. You're not living the future. You are living the present.

Remind yourself where your experience is being played out. Point your finger and pull the imaginary trigger as we did before, then try and go back into the past and create a different outcome, or jump into the future. You can't do it physically. Now is the moment that defines you. And yet it has already dissolved into another Now moment.

The past is only a memory—again, it is not physical. As soon as the Now moment leaves physical expression, it is gone. A good analogy is the expression, "Ashes to ashes, dust to dust." Invisible, unmanifest particles assume physical properties, and then return to invisibility again. Ask a dozen eyewitnesses about an event they all experienced yesterday, and you'll get a dozen different viewpoints. It is only *perception* that remains, and that perception is biased by one's psychical framework surrounding the experience. Regardless, the events of the past hold no sway over you, save for what you choose to keep in your consciousness. The physical "hard bed experience"—the actual moment of experiencing it in physical expression and reality—is over. It's done. All you have left are memories (and maybe a memento) of the occasion, but you cannot physically re-experience it as a Now moment again.

This reality of Now is an invitation to free yourself from the prison of psychological Time that may have been holding you captive. When you are feeling anxious, worried, or stressed, ask yourself if you are focusing on something from the past or fearing the future. If so, bring your awareness back to Now. Remind yourself that the past and future are not physically accessible—only Now is. You need not *feel* the physical stresses and anxieties about moments that do not exist within your current active experience. As *unmanifest energy*, the past and future *cannot* harm you.

If you are feeling anxious about an event in the past, realize that the event itself is over. Focus your awareness on what is happening around you in the Now. Acknowledge the validity and reality of what is really going on Now.

If you are feeling anxious about the future, likewise, return your attention to Now. The future cannot harm you any more than the past. It is true that we attach more importance (and hence apprehension) to what we perceive to be the future—only because we anticipate that it will become a Now moment, and we fear what that moment may bring. But the fact is, the future will always remain outside your reach. The future, like the past, will never materialize as a physical reality. Only Now does. If you fear the future, only by acting in the Now do you have the ability to change it.

Take a second and examine this moment you are living in.

Are you safe? No one is threatening to kill you or otherwise destroy you at this very moment, are they? Then, yes, you are safe.

Are you secure? If you are sitting down or perhaps reclining as you read this book, then yes—in this Now moment, you are secure.

You are safe and secure in this moment. Remind yourself of this fact if you find yourself stressing about the past or the future. Immerse yourself in the moment. Place your consciousness squarely in the present, and identify all that is around you. Feel yourself locked into everything surrounding you, as if you were a puzzle piece completing a picture. If the environment is quiet, feel that silence create a sense of stillness in your Being, and allow it to calm you. If it is a cacophony of noise, try to identify each sound as if it were an instrument in an orchestra. Notice the variations of color in all the objects before you. Focus on the Now, and only the Now. Realize your relationship to it. Define what is really happening to you in the moment. Do not exaggerate the truth of the present by focusing on anxieties from the past. Do not rob yourself of the present moment by entertaining fearful thoughts about the future. Simply *Be in the Now*. It is the only moment of physical expression you'll ever have in this lifetime.

TIME IN THE CONSTRUCTION OF REALITY

When you have a desire, the energy inherent within that thought has nonlocal properties. That is, the energy is so subtle, so minute, that it works within the realm of quantum mechanics. It defies locality and Time. Remember, coherent quantum particles communicate over any distance—even from earth to Alpha Centauri—without any lag in Time (aka, faster than the speed of light). Your desire is the initial target objective, and You, as the regular vibratory energy of your consciousness, moves into the act of energetic recalibration to materialize the object into manifestation. You are matching your energy to the energy of the desire as a completed thought-outcome.

Since Time is spread out and thus simultaneous, as soon as you form a desire, in nonmanifest Time, that intention is realized. That is, the energy is there, and it does exist in a Time continuum. It is a component of your consciousness. It exists as a Now moment—just not one that is materialized for your current filters to translate. It is simply not a physical experience moment—yet. *Energetically*, it is *real* and *objective*.

Within the great field of infinite possibilities, you have chosen an intention and identified its characteristics. You have thus turned possibility into probability by making this discovery and making the *decision* to go for it. As soon as you decide, you cut yourself off from returning to the normal routine of just "living life." At that point, you begin the process of recalibrating your sense filters to accept the intention as a physical Now reality, and thus your energy shifts into recalibration

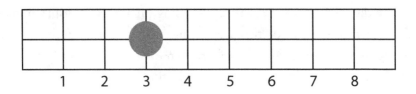

mode. This is where the perception of 1-2-3, this-comes-before-that unfolds. This is the journey toward the manifestation, where you immerse yourself into the magic of its creation.

Let's look at it another way. Let's perceive Time as we would a ruler. Say that in the Now moment, you are standing on the ruler at number 3. Due to the nature of perception, you cannot see ahead to numbers 4, 5, or 6 (just as you cannot see what is physically going to happen tomorrow—unless you have some of that psychic stuff going on). Yet if you could "back out into space," or, in our case, "back out of Time," it's all right there in front of you as unperceived (unmanifest) energy/reality.

So here you are, standing at the number 3. Using our pie analogy from earlier, let's say you crave a delicious cherry tart. That thought, due to its intensity and clarity, creates an energetic wave throughout all Time and Space. In essence, you just tossed the proverbial rock into the pond. Because of the quantum nature of the thought, the frequency of the desire immediately makes the item a reality in nonmanifest Space/Time. Now, also because of the current state of beliefs you hold, the

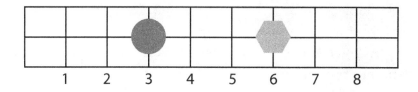

reality of a perceived future physical Now moment with the pie lands on the ruler at number 6. Again, this is all based on the quality of the thought's energy in relation to your psyche's beliefs in the likelihood of receiving it.

In a nutshell, as soon as you had the thought while standing at number 3, it materialized on number 6 on the basis of its frequency in relation to your standard vibration. Unfortunately, because you cannot physically see beyond the moment you are standing in (number 3), you do not see it on the ruler at number 6. Only until you physically march ahead and land on number 6 will you physically be one with the intention.

At any rate, let's say the desire for the pie was an intense one. Remember how it created a wave of energy? A ripple effect? Not only

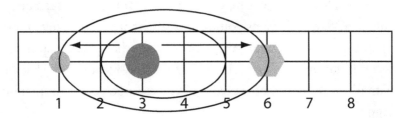

did the frequency come into reality on the number 6, but its intensity also traveled *backward* to number 1.

This is where your neighbor comes in.

Remember how your neighbor loved to bake? She was energetically "in tune" with the wave of your thought. On a level of consciousness beneath awakened awareness, she picked up on your energetic wave and rode it like a surfer, declaring, "I'm going to make a pie!" Little did she know that the desire was yours (or maybe some of it was hers; either way, resonance of energy was there).

As you continue to think about the pie, and you send out more electromagnetic quantum-thought waves, your neighbor takes the steps required to deliver the pie to you. Still in tune with the vibration of your frequency, the building of the quantum wave rises to such a degree that your smiling face pops into your neighbor's mind. She begins to wonder if her fabulous neighbor (you) would like a slice.

The process of energy building creates movement that is materialized as the journey to fulfillment, both on your part and that of your neighbor. This is true with any manifestation. The process of recalibration has results that appear to be a journey of 1 to 2 to 3, and so on. Living with yourself, it is downright difficult to see these changes as anything other than a gradual, step-by-step process. But if you were to be an outside observer and only witness yourself in increments—say, five minutes every two or three days for a larger manifestation goal—you would have a better perception of seeing the changes as quantum leaps—distinctive changes in actions and energy across stages of evolution.

In continuing our example, the evolution of the coherent energy of thought to the target goal of eating the pie lands you on number 5.9 of our imaginary ruler of Time. This is when the neighbor knocks on your door and offers you a piece. When you take a bite and all your senses burst the way they did in your original thought—voila! You just reached position 6 on the ruler, where the receipt of the pie had materialized energetically, having made the journey starting from number 3. This is simultaneous Time in action, as perceived through the filters of consciousness.

As I mentioned earlier, Time, like Space, is an *effect*. When it comes to realizing intentions, the effect of Time is created by the dissonance between the energy of the goal and your current vibratory state. The closer the two energies are in harmonic coherence, the quicker the manifestation. The further apart, naturally, the wider the gap that must be traversed. This is why those "smaller," less obtrusive goals seem to happen with so much ease, as opposed to the larger ones.

This does not mean you are unable to change your energy and beliefs within a single moment, thereby altering the trajectory of manifestation. If your thought landed on number 6 of our imaginary ruler, you have every ability to uncover limiting beliefs, change them, and do some pretty amazing work to rematerialize the intended goal on number 4—thus making the journey to realization quicker.

It's all about energy and frequency.

There is no defined "length" to Time. Only the perception of consciousness creates such an illusion. This is part of the great mystery of the Soul.

TIME AND THE PSYCHIC EYE

Everyone wants to know something about their future, so they can prepare for what is to come. Having been a practicing psychic medium for over a decade, I can tell you that just about everyone wants to hear something regarding the road ahead. When questions are specific, such as, "Will my boyfriend and I get married?" usually I will get an answer. It will consist of an image of a calendar year, separated as twelve blocks for each month. One of the blocks will glow in comparison to the others and will "pull" itself out ahead of the rest. A line circling the calendar will denote how many annual rotations will occur until the particular month comes into play. If the line rolled completely around the calendar once then stopped on the third block during the second go-around, lighting up the third block, then my answer would be, "In two years—the month of March of the second year."

For most people who believe in psychics and frequent their services, whenever a prediction is made, the client makes the mistake of turning the prediction to a prophecy of fate—something that is guaranteed to happen. This isn't always the case (as any real psychic will tell you). However, in many cases the predictions do come true, even if they seem outlandish at first.

How does this happen?

It's all based on the client's energy. Again, we are dealing with frequencies. When a psychic tunes in to the client, the subtle vibration of the sitter's energy opens up a field within the psychic's senses. This field can show a multitude of possible futures. The client's frequency will cause a certain future scenario to stand out amongst all the others, and this will be the one the psychic focuses on. From the standpoint of Time, the psychic is given that view of the entire "ruler" (or in my case, calendar years) and can gauge—on the basis of the sitter's current frequency—what is *probably* going to happen surrounding a certain situation and at what time. The energy informs the psychic sense what

probabilities are most likely to be experienced and those '
rently in play.

On some occasions, I have been able to predict a particular outcome, but not necessarily the time frame. This could be because the
client's energy is too "jumpy" or transitory. That is, the energy shifts
with such rapidity, the times of manifestation are not fixed and could
be experienced at any number of possible moments. There have been
other times when the client's own spirit guide blatantly says, "she is not
to know when." This suggests that there are certain things to be done in
route that could be missed if the client knew exactly when something
was energetically and probabilistically going to happen.

The reason psychic predictions have a habit of coming true may
be a three-fold answer. On one hand, the client never shifts her energy,
beliefs, or attitudes, and thus there is no reason why she wouldn't fulfill
the prediction. In other words, her energy that informed the psychic
never shifted or altered after the reading, so she walks right into where
the energy told the psychic she would go.

A second possibility is that the psychic was able to pick up the
energy of the future as it traveled backward into the past. Since we
know the future can inform the past, this certainly cannot be ignored.
Indeed, with the nineteen reported predictions of the fate of the *Titanic*, it is just as likely that the event of that tragic April night sparked
a wave into the past that gave rise to such perceived premonitions.

On the other hand, there's always the possibility that the psychic
may have inadvertently planted the idea of what the client's future *could*
be, and the client simply believed it and made it happen. This suggests
the psychic may also be a good hypnotist, which I do not doubt is possible. If a client were to elevate the validity of the psychic in her mind
as being something of a person with authority or other "higher" connections, that viewpoint could create an erroneous belief that facilitates
the absorption of the psychic's prediction as a matter of fate.

The future, I believe, is never written in stone. It is all based on the frequency of energy. Could the *Titanic* disaster been avoided? I believe the answer is yes. I caution every client who receives a precognitive reading that as soon as they walk out the door, they can shift the energy of their reality by a mere thought and prove me wrong about the future. In some instances, this has been the case. In many, however, it is not (and unfortunately, I think the same holds true for the *Titanic*). For someone who can be given a glimpse of the future, it still takes effort and energy to create change—to alter the standard vibration of their Soul into something different. If one has a belief that reality is a brick wall, well...sometimes, people let the wall win. For those who do not realize their own power or do not believe the future can be foreseen, then, sadly, by default, they allow the energy of their consciousness to act in an almost deterministic fashion and absolve themselves of free will.

In the realm of Time and psychic prediction, there is always a question of fate. If it's fate, where does that leave free will?

Free will is always available and intact. It becomes a question of whether or not the client chooses to exercise it. Every Soul creates his or her life on the most intimate of levels. No one has any power to steer someone out of bounds, unless the client somehow gives away her power and validity through an erroneous belief. Everyone is on a level playing field in terms of attributes and the ability to create reality, Time, and Space. It's a matter of realizing one's own stumbling blocks—the beliefs, attitudes, and emotions that may be holding one back. You are your own jailor. Remember, as a Soul, you are physically less than a mist. But you have the ability to create physical life and reality around your invisible Self. You are an incredible power, and nothing can take that power—your identity and attributes—away from you.

TIME IN RELATION TO HAUNTINGS

With the passing of Time being an effect of consciousness, what a strange thing it must be to hang around a location for decades or centuries. To you and me, it would be a long, solitary confinement. However, to an entity that has discarded its physical fabric, it may not necessarily be so.

As I mentioned earlier, a pair of EVP questions I always ask at every investigation is, "Are you affected by the passing of Time? Do you perceive the movement of Time?" On several occasions, I have received the answer audibly on my recording, as "No." The most astounding, as I said, was the claim, "It's all wrapped up." To me, this suggests something similar to our analogy of the ruler.

Time is something that is spread out, and a ghost (depending on the point of view) may also be "spread out," to a certain degree, with it. That is, the decades and centuries that pass away may not be perceived by a ghost as lasting year after year. If Time is "all wrapped up," then the entity would have access to projecting or inserting his consciousness anywhere within the Time continuum. Here, I am referring to an active intelligent haunting, and not a residual haunting. (A residual haunting is when the energy from an emotional and oftentimes traumatic event saturates the environment to such a degree that the location replays the events in a clockwork fashion—the same time, the same day, doing the same things, ad infinitum. It by no means suggests a disembodied spirit of the dead is hanging around—only the aftereffect of the event has lingered. Here again, we have an example of how our thoughts and emotions can traverse Time through the experience of residual hauntings.)

If we were to perceive Time as a wheel, then a ghost would be at its hub. From there, the ability to touch any part of eternity would be at arm's length. Conversely, eternity would spin around the ghost, and if he were not aware of it, the physical world would pass by almost without notice. Centuries would zip along without any sense of mo-ment-to-moment Time. This is what I theorize happens to those ghosts who continue to remain wrapped up in their own mental prisons and disturb the living with their psychosis. Such was the case with the ghost of the young girl I mentioned in chapter two. She believed she was still having epileptic seizures. Her distress caused dishes in the kitchen—one room away—to shake and clang together. Only after my teammates and I were able to convince her that she was dead and the seizures were her own illusions did she finally decide to move on. Being wrapped up in Time, she may not have been aware of how long her confusion had persisted in our perceived view of years. From her perspective, it may have seemed like no time at all. Yet her experience lasted through waves of Time to that final day when we she finally left, free at last.

Many people report hauntings when they are in the process of remodeling their homes. They will report that prior to reconstruction, the location was quiet and gave no clues of spooks. They believe that because they are rearranging a ghost's once beloved home that the spirit has become unsettled and now wishes to reveal his disapproval. This may partially be the case, but I always wonder: Why remain quiet beforehand? If a ghost always inhabits a location, why wait for remodeling to make himself known?

The reason may simply be that he had always been there, but the homeowners didn't see the clues until they started paying attention to the environment they were looking to change. Another explanation may be that if a ghost is wrapped up in Time, he wasn't in the house prior to remodeling at all. But, once things started to change—walls coming down, paint coming off the walls, whatever—he could see or feel or otherwise sense the change in the location coming from somewhere within the field of Time. At that point, he was able to focus himself into the environment—the actual Time and Space—and thus set out to begin his ghostly shenanigans.

If Time is, indeed, an effect of consciousness, this doesn't mean that a person may fully understand the why's or the how's of a phenomenon—but certainly, things change when moving from this dimension to the next.

Modern science posits that Time is entangled with Space. That being the case, upon leaving our dimensional universe, these items might seem nonexistent or otherwise break down. Quantum mechanics, by contrast, shows Time and Space as being something other than what we have believed it to be in the first place. As Einstein pointed out, the perception of Time is relative to the observer. If that observer happens to live "outside" the typical realm of measured Time (as a disembodied entity would)—by nature of the individual's nonphysical consciousness, he would undoubtedly have a far different perspective of Time than we would.

That a ghost can insert himself so specifically within a particular place and Time while it appears eternity is wrapped around him just goes to show how incredible the Soul is. We oftentimes lament the idea of a ghost—how lonely a lost spirit must be—it gives us a sense of abandonment by the angels and the cosmos. Yet, these earthbound spirits give some tantalizing clues as to the wondrous, magical, and indeed *eternal* nature of our beings.

TIME IN RELATION TO THE SOUL AND REINCARNATION

Everyone agrees the Soul is timeless and eternal, but have you ever stopped to think just what that means? If such a thing as reincarnation exists, how does that work with Time being illusory and simultaneous?

Now, I'm not here to discuss the merits or try to prove reincarnation, but it is a widely believed universal theme. It was even included in the Bible up until 532, when Constantine had such passages stricken because he felt that if people believed they lived multiples lives, they wouldn't live their current life to the fullest. Some say the change was made in 552 with the fifth Ecumenical Council.

Aside from the myriad religions that believe in reincarnation, Hinduism and Buddhism leading the way, there has been current research with children who can give accurate details of previous lives—and these claims have been validated. Most of this work was pioneered by Ian Stevenson, who traveled the world for decades to study claims of reincarnation in children. Many of these youngsters were able to recall names, cities, and accounts of a deceased person's life (which were subsequently verified)—even describing how they died before incarnating into a new body. Several of these children also displayed odd birthmarks that resembled deathblows experienced by the previous personality. In several cases, the stories were frightening to the child's new parents, because of how eerie and accurate the information was. Nature itself suggests the theme, as the changing of the seasons each year brings the death of the leaves of a tree, which rejuvenate again in the springtime.

Now, reincarnationalists often use the concept of prior existences to burden themselves in their current lives. Whenever a certain condition inhibits experience, oftentimes you'll hear a person say, "The condition comes from a previous life." But when all Time is simultaneous, how does this happen? And just how many burdens does one carry if existence is linear, carried over from a previous life? It begs the question: The more lives I live, do I not invite more problems in future lives by the baggage I build up in my past? Will not this successive weight cripple me down the road? What a horrible existence it would be to carry the weight of so many past lives on your shoulders!

You have to change your thinking.

If all Time is simultaneous, your lives are not successive; you have just as many in the future lying ahead of you as you do in the past. That being said, you don't hear anyone saying, "Your negative condition is the result of a future life." Yet, at least in the realm of the quantum, such reality theoretically exists. I declare it is because we have oriented our consciousness in this realm to a linear experience of past-to-present, without direct conscious knowledge of the future. That orientation "closes off" future experience from reaching our conscious mind. Yet—we have all heard stories of people having premonitions, such as in the case of the *Titanic*. So, how does this apply to your individual Soul?

As you exist right now, You are a singular personality, taken root in a particular time frame for experience. This time frame, on average for most, can run anywhere from seventy to eighty years, or more. Now, each time frame comes with its own set of beliefs, values, and frameworks for the development of your consciousness, which then gets compounded within the greatness of your Higher Self, also called the "Oversoul."

Your one single personality is but one of many, like fingers on a hand. Imagine that your fingers represent five different personalities, and the entire hand the Oversoul—the collective experience of the fingers. Yet, the hand also has the ability to move about upon the wrist in a gesture of making its own decisions. On a linear scale of perception, you would be the thumb first, the index finger represents a second personality, and so on. But once you step outside of linear time, you see the whole hand—including your pinky (which would represent a future self). This means all lives are occurring *simultaneously*.

You are part of a much larger entity, psychically connected amongst the multiple personalities. This psychic connection, when filtered through the perception of linear time, is what contributes to the past-life observation.

Another example would be a light prism.

When you shine pure white light through a prism, the light separates into an array of individual colors. These colors, like multiple selves, appear distinct but also "bleed" into one another. In our case, the white light is the Oversoul, which then "shines through" the prism of Time. The different colors of light would be seen as the different personalities, each taking up a different place on a Time scale continuum that is ultimately simultaneous.

How does this solve the "issues from a past life" phenomenon? Because the multiple personalities are a part of this larger entity, to which the experiences of the various personalities are shared, in particular a personality's powerfully charged emotional events. Such high-intensity emotions carry a radical electrical charge that transcends the filtering of Time and Space to reach all the various personalities, much like when you stub your toe, the pain also goes up your leg. The charge is encoded with the experience of the single personality—the details of the events (objects, inciting incident, and corresponding emotions). This information is then called up by a different personality existing in another Time and Space when she (or he) is in a similar energetic situation, vibrating at the frequency where the simultaneous personality's experience resides. This other self "reads" the energy and reencapsulates it within the mental psychical framework he/she has developed, and voila!—receives what appears to be a past-life "memory." Since the personality is a part of the same Oversoul as the original personality, one could easily make the claim, "It happened to *me*."

All past-life crutches disappear when one considers the power point of the Present, in the power of Now. However, since we build our lives from a moment-on-top-of-moment belief (and this belief directs our perceptions), this becomes problematic. It's at these junctions where past-life regression therapy can indeed help with curing phobias and other carryovers from simultaneous personalities.

We as a species have conditioned ourselves to bury "the past" within our consciousness, even the immediate past. We know that some adult conditions result from childhood traumas in this current life. We hold onto the emotions, or bury them beneath our normal waking consciousness, which can then result in physical ailments. We hold to a belief in the structure of the past and allow it to inform the present, without fully acknowledging the incredible power of the present moment and its ability to free us from such chains. By holding onto the past, we also hold on to the charged energies from those previous moments, which can then stew inside our physical tissues and emerge later as illnesses.

Again, you must understand that the only moment in existence is Now.

That being said, since nearly everyone throughout Time views reality through the framework of past-informing-the-present and glosses over the Now potential, when it comes to reincarnational dramas, events in simultaneous personalities can be so traumatic that the energy is felt and/or experienced by other simultaneous selves—however, I would stipulate that the information of such trauma is examined or "filtered" by each individual consciousness before inclusion into one's experience. In other words, the individual consciousness of each personality accepts or rejects the inclusion of the trauma, on the basis of the individual's own "life profile" and "objectives," vibrational frequencies, and relative mental frameworks. That is, if a personality believes his present is a result of the past and does not accept the power point of Now, that personality will feel the energy of the personality perceived "in the past" (and accept it as a past-life incident) versus a secondary personality, who chooses to leave "the past to the past" and look solely to the future or remain focused in the present.

The free will of each personality is observed as paramount. We are constantly filtering with our psyches, on the basis of our own invisible framework of beliefs that are totally unique to our beings. Much of this uniqueness in filtering comes as a result of the beliefs we build up that are distinctive to each time period, as thoughts, values, and other perceptions vary from era to era.

As an arm is a part of you, yet you designate the arm as its own appendage, the same can be said of your simultaneous selves. These "appendages" are a part of a larger body, and that larger body is the Oversoul. At this point, I can only speculate that the information of each personality's experiences gets incorporated into the Oversoul for its journey of life, fulfillment, expression, and growth—much like the information from your nerve endings in each finger informs your brain and you make a decision to either grasp with all your fingers, or to pull completely away.

Information moves through all the selves in a similar fashion to the way information moves through your current body. Remember how we talked about the way you can "feel your hands and feet" simultaneously? The information gets passed through your cells at lightning speed. The same can be said of life-psychical experiences. Remember, being less than a mist, your multiple personalities are invisible minds

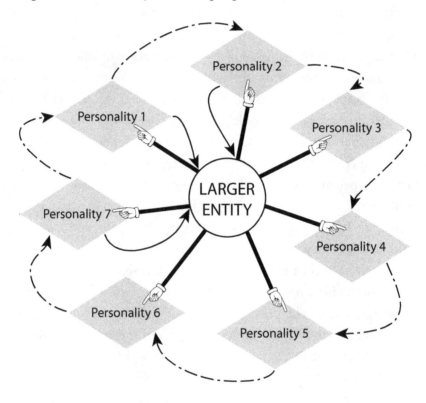

Simultaneous Selves in the Field of Simultaneous Time. The selves orbit and are connected to the larger entity, like your fingers connected to your hand, connecting up to your brain. The outer arrows represent high-intensity emotional events that get carried by psychic channels (frequencies) amongst the personalities. The inner arrows going back to the larger entity represent the totality of the individual's personality connecting to the larger body of your "Oversoul." All are interconnected and exist wholly yet separately through experiences and the filtration of Time and Space.

(psychical structures) creating and filtering experiences to appear in a Time and Space fashion, yet they also exist beyond the dimension, and, therefore, such knowledge of events and feelings becomes accessible to the entire choir. Each personality chooses in the psyche how it filters and views objective reality, as well as the information translated across the psychic domains. In essence, the Oversoul is again like an electron—existing in multiple states at once. However, each state is its own observation and reality.

Think of the multiple simultaneous personalities like radio stations. Each personality is its own station—one plays rock, another rap, another country. Each is transmitting simultaneously. Now, these personalities not only transmit, they also have the ability to receive—they're now two-way radios. But due to the nature of the internal mechanics (the psyche), the tuning-knob is calibrated to receive only certain types of stations from the cornucopia of transmissions, on the basis of each individual's mental framework. As a radio can sometimes pick out a "ghost voice" amidst static, we too as personalities can pick up "ghost voices" from other personalities through the fabric of Time, including our own personality, which gives us an unusual event of "precognition" and déjà vu. The difference between us and a radio is that, with a little mental conditioning of the psyche, we have the right to choose which "station" we want in terms of experience and the ability to change the inner mechanics to find the others. It all occurs simultaneously. But remember—it can only be experienced in the Now. It is both tantalizing and mind-boggling.

In the end, what does all of this mean to you?

It means that Time is under your control.

If you believe in reincarnation, it means you belong to a greater family of personalities and to an even larger Oversoul. You also have direct access to eternity through Now, being free from the past and the future. This Now moment of eternity gives you access to all possibilities and all your other simultaneous selves, with their knowledge and experiences psychically connected—if you practice and allow that framework to be a part of you. With the appropriate mental orientation (beliefs), you can access any one of these simultaneous personalities on a more conscious level, to where you can gain more knowledge or assistance with issues in your current life that may have already been worked out or easily handled in another.

It also means that your existence is unique unto itself—that you are not burdened by past-life incidents (this also relates to karma, as well). It also shows that you have incredible powers at your disposal, as you are already engaged in filtering Time and Space for you own expression and experience. In addition, being that you are part of a greater Oversoul, let that knowledge provide comfort in the fact that you are here *on purpose*—that your life has meaning and absolute validity in its existence on this planet. Imagine how handicapped you'd be if you were to live without your thumbs. Imagine how awful it would be for your Oversoul to exist without You. And this is just one tiny level with regard to the validity of your existence.

You are a magical Soul. You are beyond Time and Space. You are a blessing every-*where* and every-*when*.

NOTES

1. Fred Alan Wolf, *The Yoga of Time Travel* (Wheaton, Illinois: Quest Books, 2004), p. 7. Used with permission.

2. Ibid., p. 8.

3. Reprinted with permission of Pocket Books, a division of Simon & Schuster, Inc., from *Entangled Minds* by Dean Radin. Copyright ©2006 by Dean Radin Ph.D. All rights reserved. See p. 162.

4. From the book *Miracles of Mind.* Copyright ©1998, 1999 by Russell Targ and Jane Katra, Ph.D. Reprinted with permission of New World Library, Novato, California. www.newworldlibrary.com. See p. 126

5. Ibid.

6. Michael Talbot, *The Holographic Universe* (New York: HarperCollins Publishers, 1991), p. 211. Used with permission.

Chapter Eleven

THE SOUL/BODY/MIND CONNECTION

Your thoughts create your outside physical reality by how they resonate and how your emotions vibrate within the quantum universe and organize particles and patterns into events and circumstances through the conscious effects of Time and Space. The first level of bursting into that outer realm is through your physical body. Here your spirit, the ghost in the machine, has its most intimate connection with the world of matter through the enmeshment of flesh. Your energy fills the bio-body suit and energizes it into motion.

Now, in using the term "ghost in the machine," it would be easy to confuse that phrase as if I were saying You are separate from your body. Here you have a ghost (You), and it slips into a costume (the body) that is divisible from you, and oftentimes operates independently of your perceived spirit.

However, from what I've learned in studying science, as well as those messages received from the Other Side, this is not the case.

The body, like everything else in your life, is a product of your creation. It is not separate from you, but another extension, your most immediate and intimate creation—the first creation.

For those readers who are suffering from a debilitating illness, or who were born with a physical deformity, or someone who just gets sick an awful lot, I know that what I am saying sounds incredulous. "Why would I do this to myself?" you ask. There may be any number of explanations possible. For instance, certain modes of experience could only be available through such hardship – if that is what your condition creates for you – which benefits the overall Soul in its sense of fulfillment, value, and worth. You are performing an incredibly valuable part on behalf of your overall spiritual being, beyond the egoic mind, at that point. Also, thinking and believing limiting thoughts may result in the limiting physical conditions; running strictly on autopilot and not paying attention may have resulted in such painful manifestations. Perhaps such a condition has helped you to understand, through compassion, what other people in similar experiences go through. Maybe your circumstances will provide the impetus for others to change, who are inspired by your condition. Or, it could be any combination of these (as well as some others I might not have thought of).

Remember, reality is created through the mode of observation and perception as filtered through your invisible psychic structure. The Soul understands this intimately. It, and You (there really is no separation), know on many levels that physical experience is only one mode of operation, and not the only reality that exists—and that life here transitions to many other realities. I am tempted to say that this physical reality is all illusion, for to a certain degree it is, because it is all a matter of interpretation by psychic and mental filters, meaning each person perceives everything uniquely unto himself. But the fact of the matter is, the illusion has its purposes and is therefore quite real and quite valid as an environment from which to derive experience and expression. To call it all illusion is to undermine and invalidate the experiences of all life here on this plane.

"Why would someone do that to himself?" When it comes to debilitating illnesses or harrowing physical conditions, it is indeed an interesting question. I find myself asking that when I see advertisements for gory horror films. "Why do people choose to go see that??" They are, to a certain degree, looking to engage in those moments of horror and terror—otherwise, why pay the money to see it? They are not terribly different from those who create lives of physical suffering, for on some level the condition has been accepted as a route of experience.

It is important to note, however, that I am not justifying the victim mentality. That is, it is not necessary to blame one's Self for any negative condition, even if you consider yourself the cause. It is well enough to simply acknowledge that it exists, then realize the point of power is in the present and that you have the ability to change it, alter its characteristics, and take steps in that direction. To dwell on victimization of one's Self while one has every power to influence reality to effect change is a waste of energy, effort, and mental resources. As you will soon see, it is obvious that we have more control over our bodies than we ever imagined. This goes beyond taking our vitamins and exercising daily—this goes straight into how our thoughts and feelings affect our cells, tissues, and organs.

As an example—and a wonderful way to kick off this excursion into the wonderful effects of your Soul—Dr. O. Carl Simonton, a radiation oncologist and one-time medical director of the Cancer Counseling and Research Center in Dallas, Texas, saw a sixty-one-year-old patient afflicted with a fatal form of throat cancer. The patient, we'll call him Jack, was not expected to live. He had lost nearly a quarter of his body weight and was barely able to breathe, much less swallow his own saliva. In a rare experiment, Dr. Simonton suggested that Jack could influence his recovery.

Within a mere two months, Jack had completely regained his weight, and there was no sign of the cancer that medical science claimed had a 97% chance of killing him.

How did he beat it?

Dr. Simonton taught him how to relax and use mental imagery techniques.

Three times a day, Jack, in the course of the standard radiation therapy, imagined the bombardment of radiation as being millions of tiny bullets shooting down the dreaded cancer cells. In addition, he visualized the cells as being weak and confused, making it impossible for them to repair the damage they sustained. For all intents and purposes, he was waging a war inside his body. Moreover, he turned his white blood cells into immune system soldiers, swarming the dead cancer cells and hauling them out of his body through the liver and kidneys.

The results were indeed magical.

Jack experienced almost no negative side effects that would normally occur with radiation therapy, such as damage to skin and mucous membranes. The results were so dramatic that Dr. Simonton did further tests with more subjects. For a pool of 159 cancer patients considered incurable, with a death expectancy of within twelve months, he taught these people the same techniques he had with Jack. Four years later, 63 of them were still alive. Within that group, 14 showed no evidence of the disease, the cancers were regressing in 12, and in 17, the disease was stable. The overall survival time of the group was twice as long as the national norm.[1]

Though these findings became extremely controversial, therapeutic imagery is now one of the most widely used forms of healing techniques for many conditions. It is one of the first things we turn to when using thought to create reality, embedding these images with a feeling and sense of completeness.

All avenues are available to you in your experience, even with regard to the health of your body. You can use your imagination, your mind, your beliefs, and your emotions to cure yourself of even a deadly cancer.

THE PLACEBO EFFECT

Prepare to be astounded. Everyone knows what a placebo is, right? A placebo is a sugar pill (or similar substance) given to a patient in lieu of an actual drug, even though the patient thinks he is receiving actual treatment (in double-blind tests, the doctors are also unaware of which patients have been given the phony pills). Then tests are run to see if the patients receive the same benefits from the placebo as they would from the drug.

The results are astounding.

Placebos in the past have cured people of such conditions as migraine headaches, warts, clinical depression, asthma, rheumatoid and degenerative arthritis, diabetes, multiple sclerosis, cancer, and other conditions. The placebo generally performs successfully an average of 35% of the time, and even as much as 50%, depending on given circumstances. In six double-blind studies, placebos were found to be 56% as effective as morphine in relieving pain![2]

In 2001, University of Connecticut psychology professor Irving Kirsch, using the Freedom of Information Act, received information on clinical trials surrounding top antidepressants. The data revealed that in more than half the trials for the six leading antidepressant drugs, the placebo pill actually *outperformed the drugs themselves,* the difference being less than two points on average, on a clinical scale of 50 to 60 points. "The difference," Kirsch says, "is clinically meaningless."[3]

The placebo effect goes even beyond pills.

In 2002, in a study published in the *New England Journal of Medicine,* Dr. Bruce Moseley conducted tests to see how a placebo would affect patients undergoing surgery. His test group was a group of patients suffering from debilitating knee pain. He divided the patients into three groups. In one group, he shaved the damaged cartilage of their knees. In the second, he flushed the joint, removing the material thought to be causing the inflammatory effect. He performed these surgeries the way they would normally be performed for this kind of condition.

The third group got the placebo—no surgery whatsoever. In this group, the patient was sedated, three standard incisions were made, but nothing more was done. In fact, the doctor simply pretended to do the surgery, even splashing water to simulate the sound of the knee-washing procedure. After forty minutes, Dr. Moseley sewed up the incisions as he normally would, then prescribed the same postoperative care as he did for the other two groups.

The results? The first two groups improved as expected.

The placebo group? They improved just as much as the other two groups! In a video clip that ran on the news, one of the patients was seen playing basketball with his grandchildren, something he couldn't do before the surgery. In fact, the patient had to use a cane prior to surgery because he was in so much pain. He simply couldn't believe that no surgery had actually been performed on him, which he was informed of two years after the mock surgery.[4]

One of the most astounding placebo effects occurred with a California interior designer, Janis Schonfeld. In 1997, she participated in a clinical trial of the medication Effexor, for depression. The condition had arrested her life for nearly thirty years. However, instead of receiving the drug, she was given a placebo. The results of the sugar pill not only cured her of the depression, it revealed that her prefrontal cortex was greatly enhanced, as evidenced by brain scans obtained during the trial. She even experienced the side effects of Effexor, as if she were taking the actual drug. When she was told that she was given was a placebo, she couldn't believe it. She insisted that the researchers double-check their records to make sure.[5]

These kinds of effects clearly show the massive power of our minds and the energy within our Souls in creating our reality, down to the tissue level. Dr. Bruce Lipton, in his amazing book, *The Biology of Belief*, makes a persuasive argument that our beliefs even change our

DNA. He posits that we are not controlled by our genes, because genetic changes occurring within a cell must be stimulated from outside the cell, from its environment. That environment is influenced by our thoughts and emotions. It's these subtle agents that affect cellular biology, division, and gene activation. As patients recovering from illnesses and diseases by taking a sugar pill have repeatedly shown, this is the absolute truth.

Does everyone who receives a sugar pill experience the same effects as the real drug? No, but does everyone who takes the real drug always improve? No. There are always side-effects and other conditions that may occur, or there may be no discernable effects at all. Not every drug is 100% effective, because not everyone believes in any one treatment method. Again, this all comes down to conscious variables too numerous to pinpoint, but it is guaranteed that they are laced with beliefs, mental attitudes, and emotions.

Often negative ones.

Dr. Lipton relates a story of patient who had cancer of the esophagus. The patient was treated, but everyone in the medical community "knew" that the cancer would return. Of course, no one was surprised when the patient died a few weeks after receiving a diagnosis.

The real shock came during the autopsy.

There were a couple of cancerous spots on his liver and one in his lung—but no trace of the esophageal cancer everyone thought had killed him. "He died with cancer, but not from cancer," physician Clifton Meador told the Discovery Health Channel. He emphasized that the amount of cancer found within the patient was too little to be the actual cause of death. This, Dr. Lipton says, is the Nocebo effect, the power of Negative Beliefs.[6]

Our connection as a Soul to the body is so intertwined that our susceptibility to believe information from noted health "authorities" affects us to our detriment, at times. Since our thoughts create our reality all the way down into the tissue level, we often don't realize that doctors themselves in the act of "prescribing health care" are promoting such ill effects. It's no wonder why we spend billions of dollars a year on drugs for physical and psychological ailments. It's also no wonder why drug companies continue to rake in such massive profits, while trying to downplay research on understanding the placebo effect. If the mind can truly alter our bodily chemistry, all the way down to ridding ourselves of terminal cancers (or even benign tumors—imagine the cellular and biological complexity of a wart, which is one of the most commonly removed tumors via placebo), then it's definitely not in the best interest of giant chemical conglomerates to study and encourage "self-help" remedies.

Yet, this is exactly what needs to be done.

The downside of chemical drugs is obvious. We are a holistic body, living in a holistic universe. One thing invariably affects the other (again, there is no real separation between body and environment). These drugs, which are designed to alleviate a specific condition never do just that—they affect other parts of the body as well. Just listen to the laundry list of possible side-effects on the television commercials. Yet experiments have shown that when it comes to mental imagery, belief, and further study of the placebo phenomenon, we have the ability to end the reign of nasty side-effects altogether. With the proper guidance, a patient has the ability to cure himself, without the needless ingestion of pills to mask the real condition, while upsetting more of the body and its functions. Many a physician will cry "heresy" at such a statement as this, but study after study has proven it to be so. I am not telling you, "don't go to the doctor," especially since that is a major belief system in our culture. What I *am* promoting is that perhaps medical science isn't all it's cracked up to be.

MORE MENTAL MADNESS

Spontaneous cures for diabetes. Unimaginable strength within mere seconds.

These things you can't get with placebos. But you can if you have a split personality. Studies on individuals with multiple personality disorders have shown that when some patients move from one personality to another, startling physiological changes occur. Dr. Bennett Braun, of the International Society for the Study of Multiple Personality in Chicago, has documented a case in which a patient's subpersonalities exhibited allergic reactions to orange juice all except one. In another case, he recorded a multiple personality of one of his patients that responded differently to drugs than the others. One personality was easily affected by 5 milligrams of diazepam (a tranquilizer), while another was hardly affected by as much as 100 milligrams.[7]

Other amazing feats are exhibited by the body of a person with multiple personality disorder, such as one personality being left-handed and another right-handed. Eyesight can also differ between personalities, forcing a person to carry alternate prescriptions of eyeglasses to accommodate each subpersonality. Moreover, one personality could be color-blind, while another is not. Brain scans obtained in patients with multiple personality disorder have shown that brainwave activity actually changes when a person switches personalities.

What does all this mean?

In essence, it demonstrates that the body is quite capable of creating rapid, effectual change. All too often, we dwell on our physical condition, keeping it in place, not giving our cells the chance to change. It is a known fact that every cell in the body will have died and been replaced within seven years, meaning that the cells that make up your body seven years from now are not the same ones that you are carrying with you at this very moment. The cells within you now will be completely washed away and replaced. If that's the case, then why do so many conditions continue to stay the same—or worse, advance? Especially when the body is replaced by new and different cells?

Some people would argue it's cellular memory. I disagree. Again, the activity of a cell and its functions are greatly influenced by the environment around them, and according to Dr. Lipton, the complexity of certain conditions goes far beyond the simple cell's memory banks.

Certain conditions do not change because we do not empower them to change.

Once you are told you have diabetes, for instance, you are certain you have diabetes. Yet there have been cases of multiple personality disorders in which diabetes has completely disappeared between one personality and another. This means that the insulin production of the body does not necessarily operate independently of your whims, and that you can control it. It just requires your attention, a change in energy, frequency, and vibration. Of course, you have to believe 100% this can work in order for it to occur and imbue yourself with the feeling that it has occurred. Too often we're taught how to live within a certain disease or illness, as if there were no cure or possibility for change, when it's very possible that the exact opposite may be just as plausible. Again, when you're taught to live within the structures of disease, those structures act as the prison walls in which you are held captive. Until you believe you can make an escape, you will remain behind bars.

I'm reminded of a story I once read about Michel de Nostradamus. Most people know him as the 16th century seer who could supposedly foretell the future through his ambiguous quatrains. What other people don't know is that Nostradamus was also a physician during the time of the bubonic plague. His wife died from it. He went throughout the French countryside, helping those afflicted by the deadly disease. Where hundreds of people were dying daily, Nostradamus treaded courageously. When asked why he did this, why he chose to go where everyone else was fleeing from, he replied that he simply didn't believe he could get the disease. Could it be that this belief alone kept him immune to bubonic plague? Nostradamus believed so. Although he was afflicted by gout later in life, he was not afflicted by the plague, true to his beliefs.

You are an amazing creation of energy, rising in and out of the Field of all creation. You are part and parcel of the force that's been around since the beginning of this universe—14 billion years, and possibly longer. The makeup of your body dances in concert with your consciousness, and the ailments you perceive are the ones you've allowed into your body. You've allowed energy cysts to swell and turn into physical maladies.

"But I can't change all on my own," you say. "I still don't necessarily believe I have the power."

Fine. If you're someone that oftentimes berates your magnificence, your health still doesn't have to suffer. All things come from a magnificent Source, including your neighbor, who was happy to help you fill your empty stomach earlier. She may be able to help you again.

INTENTIONED HEALING

The use of the hands has been a source of healing for thousands of years, extending back before even biblical times. Today, there are many different variations, such as Reiki and Shiatsu, as well as therapeutic massage. I'm not necessarily talking about psychic-faith healing, where the physician magically dips his hand into your guts and wriggles around your entrails, as can sometimes be found in third-world countries (and in many cases, with patients claiming resounding success). However, there are sources of hands-on healing that are indeed magical.

In her landmark book, *Hands of Light,* Barbara Brennan talks about her own experiences as a hands-on healer. With a background in physics and an affiliation with NASA, it's fascinating to learn about her journey in healing patients through what she terms the Human Energy Field. More or less, she is talking about the aura. And her track record has been amazing. Her hands-on healing has cured people of a range of illnesses, even cancer. What's interesting (with regard to our research here about creating your own reality) is that Brennan has said that illnesses appear in the Human Energy Field *before* they show up in the body. "Most diseases are initiated in the energy fields and are then, through time and living habits, transmitted to the body, becoming a serious illness. Many times the source or initiating cause of this process is associated with psychological or physical trauma, or a combination of the two."[8]

Brennan further relates that illness has a deeper meaning than what we see on the surface. She says that illness is "a message from the body that says 'Wait a minute; something is wrong. You are not listening to your whole self; you are ignoring something very important to you. What is it?'"[9]

Through her hands-on healing, she is able to see—via a person's energy field—information relating to the illness and how to cure it. Usually the cure requires a change of living habit, or a change of mind. Again, everything being a frequency of vibration in the universe, if you're thinking and feeling a certain way, those energies will reflect upon your body, meaning you will be either healthy or not so healthy. All options are available to you, and it's your choice.

Hands-on healing, like most things, may not work on the first try. You may experience some temporary relief, but like a piano being tuned for the first time, you're going to need additional sessions and you'll have to do the homework prescribed to turn the new energy, the new frequency, the new tune, into something that once wasn't normal but then becomes the norm. Change your habits, change your energy, change your thinking, and you will change your life. Hands-on healers can provide clues and open doors, but in the end, it's your life, and you are still responsible for it. Your body will respond to whatever thoughts and emotions you choose to walk around with.

What if there's not a hands-on healer around? What if you can't find someone who has experience in, and knowledge of, hands-on healing?

Since we are all part of the quantum field, then we can also take advantage of the field's values of nonlocality. In other words, you can receive help from people who don't even live in your city, your state, or even your country.

LONG-DISTANCE HEALING

Yes, there is some evidence of the phenomenon of long distance healing, as well. Stories abound of people who heal miraculously as a result of prayer or long-distance intention. In his 2001 book, *Spiritual Healing*, psychiatrist Daniel Benor examined more than 120 studies from around the world to show that, yes, psychic, mental, and spiritual healing efforts *do* have an effect.

In December of 1998, an article was published in the *Western Journal of Medicine* that detailed research conducted at the California Pacific Medical Center on the positive therapeutic effects of distant healing on men with advanced AIDS. This research was heralded by Fred Sicher and psychiatrist Elisabeth Targ (daughter of Russell Targ, one of the founders of remote viewing). In this test, men with AIDS were gathered in the San Francisco Bay Area. Each was told he had a 50/50 chance of being in the treatment group or the control group. The doctors themselves had no idea which man fell into what group, as Elisabeth and Fred—the project leaders—wanted to keep it as "blind" as possible. These patients were selected to have a similar age, T-cell count, and number of AIDS-defining illnesses between groups. At enrollment, their individual conditions were assessed, as they were six months later, when physicians reviewed their medical charts.

The healers selected for this study came from all walks of life, all different faiths, in all different parts of the country. The only thing they had in common was that they had at least five years of practice in their particular form of healing. Their backgrounds included Christian, Jewish, Buddhist, Native American, and shamanic traditions, as well as a few others. Each patient in the healing group was treated by ten different healers, on a rotating schedule. The healers were asked to focus their healing on their assigned patient for one hour, for six consecutive days. None of the patients with AIDS had ever met the healers, nor were they aware they were in the focus group. That's right, none of the patients knew if they were the ones being prayed for or not.

In the end, the results were amazing. Some of the patients were even able to tell that they had been a part of the focus group, on the basis of their level of good health, in comparison to some of the other patients—with significant odds against chance of realizing this. The outcome was as follows:

The group receiving healing treatments experienced significantly better medical and quality-of-life results by the odds of 100 to 1. They had fewer outpatient doctor visits (185 vs. 260); fewer days of hospitalization (10 vs. 68); less severe illnesses acquired during the study, as measured by illness severity scores (16 vs. 43); and less emotional distress. In her summary, Elisabeth Targ concluded, "Decreased hospital visits, fewer new severe diseases, and greatly improved subjective health, support the hypothesis of positive therapeutic effects of distant healing."[10]

This is just one study out of myriad healthcare trials. There have been case studies of distant healing performed on cardiac patients, with results showing success significantly beyond the realm of chance. In the *Annals of Internal Medicine,* John Astin published a study about the examination of prayer and distant healing in sixteen double-blind trials, which yielded results showing the positive effects of prayer and healing with an overall significance of 1 in 10,000 for 2,139 patients![11]

Again, this all speaks to the magic and wonder of each consciousness alive on the planet. We have the ability to help not only ourselves, but everyone else, as well. Our thoughts—the energy of our Souls—traverse the physical landscape into the realm of quantum nonlocality, to be picked up by the quantum biological bodies and minds of our brethren, no matter where they live. Once received, one can either accept change (consciously or unconsciously) or not.

Whatever you focus on, getting healthier or remaining sick, will determine what energies you accept, what possibilities you collapse, and what material reality you will experience. How do you choose to *observe* yourself and your condition?

Love the life you have, and love your body, because it works so hard for you. Remember, you are a Soul, come here to this plane to grow through experiences and expression. You couldn't fully accomplish all that without the cooperation of millions of cells and a splattering of organs. They work tirelessly to sustain you, as they have a vested interest in your evolution, and you in theirs. It's an enormous cooperative effort, keeping you here in this dimension for the Soul's life and expression.

Take a moment to sit and feel your body. You can feel it, even on the inside, can't you? While feeling it, send it love. Consciously offer love from that nexus area, where your Soul meets with the physical inner workings of your body. You may not even know where this nexus is, but just imagine it. In imagining it, you may feel it. Tell your body how much you love and appreciate it. Tell it how grateful you are for its continuing efforts in keeping you alive, healthy, and mobile.

Your body will respond.

It will love you back. You can build a rapport, a trust, between your Soul and your body. You may actually be able to use the rapport as a guide to loving and trusting your own outer relationships with friends, coworkers, and mates. If you can learn to trust your body, you can also learn to love someone else.

Your body, like your environment outside of you, is a manifestation—and a highly cooperative one—of your expression of being. You know you create your body by the cooperation of molecules and atoms coming together to create the intricate workings of the vehicle. You provide the impetus, the energy, the power, to magnetize and become a cohesive unit. Maybe you didn't know this before. Perhaps you believed the body was provided for you to inhabit. But as mentioned earlier, consciousness is the base, the start, and so it is with your body as well. It is a magical, living expression of your immutable power and being.

You thought about living here in this Space and Time before your birth, and your desire was so strong that your energy was able to vibrate all the particulars into place and manifest the body you now inhabit. This may sound fantastic at first, but it is a metaphysical truth. *Your body would not have come into existence without your desire to be here.*

The communication between your molecules directly mirrors your most intimate thoughts about yourself. As I said earlier, your body is the manifestation of the most intimate connection between your spirit and this dimension. Your energy drives it! Therefore, your energy affects it.

Love your body, and you'll love yourself.

Love deeply—and how deeply you will be loved.

All options are available to you.

You create your health.

You create your disease.

You create your life.

You create your reality.

Make it a good one.

NOTES

1. Michael Talbot, *The Holographic Universe* (New York: HarperCollins Publishers, 1991), pp. 82-83. Used with permission.

2. Ibid., p. 91.

3. Bruce Lipton, *The Biology of Belief* (Carlsbad, California: Hay House, Inc., 2006, p. 141. Used with permission.

4. Ibid., pp. 139-140.

5. Ibid., p. 141.

6. Ibid., p. 142.

7. Michael Talbot, *The Holographic Universe* (New York: HarperCollins Publishers, 1991), pp. 98-99. Used with permission.

8. Barbara Ann Brennan, *Hands of Light* (New York: Random House Inc., 1987), p. 7.

9. Ibid.

10. From the book *Limitless Mind*. Copyright ©2004 by Russell Targ and Jane Katra, Ph.D. Reprinted with permission of New World Library, Novato, California. www.newworldlibrary.com. See pp. 146-148.

11. Ibid., p. 140.

Chapter Twelve

THE SOUL AND MASS EVENTS

arlier, we talked about experiments conducted by the
Global Consciousness Project, using RNGs throughout
the world to verify that human consciousness can have an
effect on perceived random processes. We also saw documentation of
what can happen within large geographical areas when only the square
root of 1% of the population focuses on a single outcome. We have
talked about how ghosts can stay locked in their own solitary states on
the basis of their own limiting belief systems. We have discovered how
the energy of our thoughts moves through the law of energy transfer
into physical manifestation with a dissonance we create, called Time.

The further we peer into this microscope of metaphysics, the
more we see the fluidity of Time and Space. As the universe first whis-
pers to us of its true nature though the realm of quantum mechanics,
we begin to suspect something that is both extraordinary and perhaps a
bit frightening. As the voice builds, we begin to connect the dots of our
thoughts and emotions as being the seeds for this wondrous garden we
call individual existence. A new revelation dawns that is not only life-
changing, but may be potentially earth-shattering: We may be 100%
responsible for everything that happens to us.

Everything.

Even earthquakes, tornadoes, floods, tsunamis, fires, and hurricanes, which are considered to be catastrophic events. On the surface, this seems like a fantastic declaration, but when you start to factor in all the scientific discoveries of thoughts influencing matter, telepathy, and the reality that thought-energy has electromagnetic properties that spur quantum processes into action (as evidenced within our own bodies), the fantastic begins to take on a much different appearance.

Reality is an individual perception. I may hold up a copy of this book in front of five people, resulting in five different realities and five different books. If one person is color-blind, his book may look different than it does to someone who can see color, therefore his *experience* of it and *reality* of it is unique to him; to another, it will appear to be a thick book that requires too much time to read; while to another it may seem too thin and lacking in substance (I hope not!). We are not, in accordance with our psychic framework of beliefs and perceptions, all looking at the same book. In the realm of quantum mechanics, the experience of the book is independent to each observer; each observer creates his version of the book for himself. What connects all of us is the shared psychic (mental) experience that we can all at least agree that we are experiencing something called a book.

This breakdown of reality also applies to the greater whole. A natural disaster, though it may affect and change the lives of millions, is a unique and distinct event in the life of an individual consciousness. However, due to the number of affected lives, we are also looking at these events as being a shared circumstance for larger meanings within the Soul.

In the case of a natural disaster, the participants may all agree to be experiencing a horrendous (or sometimes a joyous) event; but like the book example, that event will be perceived, processed, and assigned meaning individually. No two people will have the same inner experience with it—though it appears they share the same set of outer circumstances.

If energy attracts like energy, and frequency gives rise to events, then, on some level, the details of an event are just as much a psychic phenomenon as they are a natural one. Energy bonds for any creation begin in miniature and then grow to the macroscopic. This suggests that on some level—mainly unconscious—people who experience major events together have created that unity amongst themselves, along with the event, energetically, before the event's arrival.

This would seem to go against all common notion of reality.

Yet again, if reality is energy based—and it is—and if probabilities are turned into certainties by individual observation, thoughts, emotions, and expectations—which they are—and if conscious telepathy has been demonstrated to exist—which it has—then it becomes almost frighteningly clear the roles each of us may play in contributing to a personal and yet also a collective event, even if it were to come from our own unconscious thoughts, fears, attitudes, and expectations.

Psychic connections exist between all people. This is demonstrated most notably by people who are related to one another. We hear stories of how relatives separated by vast distances (say, several states) will have a sudden urge to connect and make a phone call, usually because something traumatic has occurred to one of them. Likewise, twins are also well known for having a psychical bond to their sibling.

Often, people will have lucid dreams of deceased relatives. Here again is potential proof of psychical connections. More astounding are the "physical" visitations some have had in speaking to a loved one as they were dying in a location miles away.

In his book *Parting Visions,* Dr. Melvin Morse relates his own experience of dreaming about his father. His father was facing him, telling him "Melvin, call your answering service. I have something to tell you." He awoke with a start and made the call. He was told that his mother had been trying to reach him all day with urgent news—his father had died.[1] *Parting Visions* is a cornucopia of incidents detailing people "seeing" deceased relatives before death, and, in some cases, people who remained behind were somehow able to follow a dying loved one through the tunnel to the Other Side—sharing the death experience. I highly recommend it as a book on predeath, psychic, and spiritual experiences as perceived through the work of a medical doctor trained in Western scientific thinking.

The psychic connections between loved ones, especially those that have predeath visions (and, in some cases, those who share the transition), are obviously quite strong—a testament to the emotional bonds that exist between individuals. The love is so powerful that when the desire for communication was aroused, the event of a predeath vision quickly followed. Like quantum particles, psychic connections to our loved ones are macro versions of quantum mechanics entanglement and nonlocal reality, where two particles are joined, but are then separated—however, they can still communicate across any distance in no-Time.

We also send psychic signals not just to our relatives, but to everyone around us.

Remember, we are all wired to be both transmitters *and* receivers. Unlike a deathbed vision that is spurred by the intense love between two people, the psychic signal that is carried through the ethers between groups is a very subtle signal—so subtle that the standard clutter occupying our conscious minds easily blocks it from view. However, that doesn't keep it from connecting with our subconscious mind. Only when the conscious mind relaxes and lets go do some of these messages filter up into a brief glimpse of awareness. This is why so many people experience premonitions during dream states; their normal conscious mind has dipped to a frequency level capable of accepting the incoming transmissions without being filtered out by the usual mental frameworks.

This subtle telepathic communiqué rests within the archetypal "unconscious." That is, if we consider the whole of humanity to be a gigantic ocean and the peaks of the waves as individuals rising from the sea of Being, these psychic signals would be the slow-moving currents running below the surface. The tops of the waves—the conscious mind (personal ego) interacting with the perceived outside world—are hardly affected by them, but the current passes between all the wave crests and minds, gently moving the currents of experiences along.

Here we get into the notion of the collective unconscious, where Carl Jung postulated the existence of archetypes that can be found throughout humanity. Within this collective unconscious, subtle telepathic messages pass between people constantly, informing at minute levels the things "stewing" in everyone's lives and environments. Nearly 99% of it goes completely unnoticed by our conscious brains, because the conscious brain is only considered with individual reality—looking out for Number One. That is to say, the conscious individual mind is the *egoic* mind. It will only pay attention to data that relate directly with its egotistical-self belief systems and frameworks. It is, quite simply, filtering the subtle phenomena out.

Nevertheless, a subtle form of communication *is* going on between entire populations of people—quite likely without them realizing it. Too preoccupied with the visual perception of separation occurring at the bodily level, we easily forget that waves of information are passing by us all the time in the form of radio waves, and television or cell phones signals, ad infinitum. In addition to that, quantum and atomic matter continues to exist without physical barriers in between, sending energy back and forth and interacting with the virtual particles of the Zero Point Field.

The subtle energy of an individual is always on the go, so to speak, like photons of light. When light leaves the sun's surface, it still travels across the galaxy unimpeded, as do a person's subtle energies. Recall that energy never dies—it goes on and on. And that energy can be picked up and read by another's subconscious. This is where the germination of mass events takes place.

As we saw with the TM-Sidhi groups influencing change within large geographical areas, the combination of thought waves and their corresponding frequencies amongst groups of individuals can affect the environment. Since the energy in "everyday life" is so apparently unchanging or static (suggesting that reality is just the status quo of typical thoughts and emotions doing their thing), at first it appears that nothing is happening. But, as mentioned earlier, if a small group begins to think and feel differently (whether ego-conscious about it or not), the new frequency builds, and waves of energy meet similar frequencies and grow into larger waves. At that point, the potential possibilities emerge into physical reality. As this building energy blossoms, the dynamics of its design become available to unconscious awareness; that is, a person's subconscious is aware of what is happening, but the conscious mind isn't. The egoic mind, too preoccupied or blind by its framework, refuses to acknowledge or work in this "lower-energy" domain. All things being connected, the realization of this building frequency becomes available to everyone. The Soul, in its greater wisdom of the overall life of the individual (greater than the egoic mind, that is), acts as the Observer in relation to the ego to determine participation in the upcoming event.

As we've revealed, each person's reality is unique to the perception of the individual. A person may have a number of objectives he or she is unconsciously (or perhaps consciously) working on—in terms of desired experience—that a mass event may fulfill. Here, by using a traumatic event like a hurricane or flood, for example, an individual may be looking for a way to "shock" her system to experience a different kind of awareness. So often, major climactic disruptions move people into psychic avenues they never would have considered possible in everyday life. In these cases—where some kind of deeper meaning is being cried out for in a person's life—a mass event facilitates that.

A common reason for being involved in a disaster is for an individual to experience many layers of experience *all at once*. In today's world, where everything is expected to move with amazing rapidity, it would not be out of the question for whole groups of people looking to experience a dramatic "rush" on so many levels to participate in a mass event that facilitates that outcome. Too many people feel that their lives are down trodden, without purpose, less than perfect, and in need of some sense of validation. To be involved in a major upheaval can bring the kind of experiences needed to fulfill the desire of connection and sense of worth craved by the individuals within their inner experience.

There is also a multidimensional view, as we are more than just our individual selves. Remember how all things are connected and are One?

Mass events bring a union within the collective of cultures and humanity. On many levels, global society begs for some sense of unilateral cooperation and community in contrast to the usual competitive, warlike division often being played out on political and religious stages. Mass events—typically disasters—bring the reality of compassion and union that must transcend the standard geographical and philosophical boundaries. Here, we witness the ascension of consciousness moving out of the state of the ego and into the Soul state of harmony and Oneness.

In any event, Souls accept the roles of being victims and martyrs for the progression of others. On the surface, such an act would appear insane from the relative position of the egoic mind, for it is akin to suicide. Yet the Soul of each individual who accepts the task is aware of a much larger reality to some degree, one that we are all a part of. Some know on an intuitive level the value of their life and sacrifice, and they accept the realization that this reality is but a fragment of a much larger universe. That is, for those who make the ultimate sacrifice in a disaster, the choice is made knowing that:

The act itself is not life-ending, but life-affirming, as the death creates an effect on the survivors and moves them into new awareness and new avenues of experience.

The death itself is not the real death of one's personality, just the Self's journey in this three-dimensional universe. The victim's life continues on—the type of continuation determined by the possibilities inherent within his mental framework (which we will discuss in the next chapter).

Those who participate in mass events, whether as survivors or casualties, each have their own inner reasons for being there. They are fulfilling the realization of psychic energy that corresponds not only with their own personal frameworks, but with the larger psychic structure of the collective whole. It is certainly not linear thinking or living, but quite multidimensional.

Direct participation in a major event provides a unique communion between the Soul and the egoic conscious mind—a richer, deeper creative experience not perceived as possible in everyday living conditions, as believed by the individual. With trauma, the egoic mind calls out for insight or for a miracle within the Soul to ease its suffering and provide validation for one's existence or truth of a greater consciousness. Somewhere within the individual's normal routine, a connection to the Soul has been neglected. But like a child who knows he has lost his way home, he creates circumstances through psychic structure and energy manifestation to bring the home to him. The event's creation is a way of breaking through the barriers of the conscious mind to find union again with the Source. Again, this is all done by choice (going round about the ego) long before the event occurs in physical reality. This yearning for greater expansion by the individual is also indicative of the larger whole, which these events address.

Like individual reality, the frequency of a mass event materializes in simultaneous Time at the point of highest and purest intensity generated by the populace to be involved. This intensity is the focal point of energetic concentration between the psychic communications running amongst the pool of participants. As energy builds and the details of the event become clearer, the group consciousness directs the "event energy" to a specific point in Time. At that moment, participation is pretty much a done deal between survivors, victims, and even rescuers. The myriad of experienced outcomes and purposes unraveled by the event have been agreed upon, in certain terms, long before the crisis happens. That may sound outlandish, until we remember that Time and Space are created in relation to an observer (You) and not by anything else.

As with all group activities, not everyone in the local geographical area will want to participate. Some people, on a deep Soul level, may acknowledge the coming event but choose not to be directly related to its creation or participate in the aftereffects. Here, depending on the egoic conscious mind, these folks will either receive a premonition about the trauma and take heed, or they will unconsciously find ways of avoiding it—such as taking an unexpected trip out of the area moments before the event materializes into the Now moment.

Considering things this way—people choosing to leave and those choosing to stay—reveals the deep layers of experience that we, as conscious beings, are willing to accept into our lives and have the ability to choose from. Neither leaving nor staying is a judgment against any particular Soul; it is only what a Soul believes is going to mirror the desired intentions and goals of the individual personality and the greater masses at that time. Some Souls prefer to learn and experience growth and reality through less traumatic means, while others enjoy the adrenaline or feel it's necessary for some other mode of growth, expression, or experience.

Again, this information is made available to everyone at deep, unconscious levels. As the energy builds, the information rises to where an individual will detect it, decode it, and then decide if it is in his or her best interest to go through the experience or avoid it.

Nothing that happens to anyone occurs by dumb luck or chance. Is it dumb luck to get stopped at a red light and delayed two minutes, only to discover that had the light been green, you would have been a participant in a six-car pile-up two miles down the road? When you factor in how simultaneous Time communicates within our consciousness, and how future events can move backward in Time to inform the present, it becomes more likely that events are perfectly timed and orchestrated, rather than resulting from coincidence.

Energy attracts like energy. If the information of a traumatic event reaches the consciousness of an individual whose energy does not vibrate in sync with the overall "tone" of the event's frequency, then he or she will not be an energetic player in the drama. The energy of the individual will create a different set of circumstances that keeps him or her clear of the tumultuous river of trauma.

THE EVENTS MIRROR THE PSYCHIC CONDITION

Energy and frequency, as distributed by particular types of thoughts, attitudes, and emotions, create the type of mass experience that occurs. In terms of disaster, the kind of psychic turmoil brewing underneath will "inform" the atmosphere and environment of the kind of experience to be played out. For instance, will the mass event be an earthquake? Flood? Tornado? Hurricane? Disease epidemic? These conditions are all tied to certain frequencies and thought conditions.

It may sound like a fantastic concept, until you look at it on a deeper level.

When you start paying attention to mental and emotional climates surrounding geographical areas that experience certain types of disasters, it is an odd thing to realize that a correlation exists between the disaster and the participants' frameworks of experience.

I live in a location where earthquakes are considered common—the Pacific Northwest. However, our earthquake record is not the same as that of Southern California. Southern California is known for the San Andreas fault and the frequent tremblers that give rise to major incidents. If one were to track periods of earthquake activity, either in Southern California or in my own area, one would see a high correlation between emotional competitiveness in industry and personal lives, creating fractures that appear not only in relationships, but also in the earth's crust. Large earthquakes have also occurred in Japan and China, where people compete in much higher degrees and in harsher circumstances than we do in America, impinging upon deep emotional triggers. Suicide rates among men in Japan are much higher than men in America, and this is believed to be a result of such a competitive nature.

What about places like New York and Washington, DC? Aren't they just as competitive and "fractured" as any other geographical locale? It's a valid question. Should they not have devastating earthquakes, as well?

It is a well known fact that people on the East Coast think and behave—in other words, approach the fundamentals of life—from a much different perspective than their West Coast brethren. That song, "New York State of Mind," is applicable to this concept. Very often, East Coast dwellers will talk about "West Coast Thinking," drawing a distinct delineation between the perceptions on living life offered by the population in one location versus another. The psychic energy and frequency of New York and the East Coast are much different than those of Los Angeles. It's like comparing apples to oranges. They might have a similar "shape," but the core of each is unique. Again, it all comes down to the nature of observation. East Coast people observe their realities different than those on the West Coast.

The same can be said of Washington, DC. Without a doubt, the fractures that exist between political parties could have an adverse effect on the environment. Again, it is not within the psychic framework of these politicians to participate in a mass event such as an earthquake. It is also important to remember that many people in Congress don't necessarily live in Washington, DC; they have homes in the states they represent. What would be fascinating is to chart atmospheric disturbances and crime rates during times when Congress is in session versus when it is not. That would make for some interesting science!

In the past few years, we have witnessed two tsunamis—one that killed nearly 100 thousand people in Indonesia, and a second that hit the Samoa Islands. (It's interesting to note that the day after the Samoa tsunami, a massive earthquake hit Southern Sumatra). Tsunamis result from earthquakes in the ocean that displace huge amounts of water. Yet, it is not the event of the quake itself that we are psychically dealing with in terms of the mass event. It is the resulting tsunami, creating some of the worst destruction and loss of life experienced in a natural disaster. Due to the magnitude of the event, there could be any number of individual psychic reasons for its creation. Could there also be a mass-populace reason?

One way of pinning down a possibility is to watch the outcome of the event. Remember, mass events (like individual ones) are designed to mirror a frequency of thought intended to move consciousness in a specific direction. After major tsunamis, you find humanity coming together in a concerted effort of unparalleled compassion and unity to help those in the impact zones. An emotional bond is expressed across the globe. Consider this emotional expression when realizing that water is believed to be the archetypal dream symbol for deep emotions.

Remember how the tsunami of 2004 happened the day after Christmas? Here was an event that required humanity to actually move in the direction of the holiday's spirit: peace on earth and good will. The timing was not at all coincidental. Elsewhere in the world, the Iraq and Afghanistan wars were in full swing. Such major tsunami catastrophes force us to experience the emotional connections lacking in humanity as we blow each other apart in military conflicts. These kinds of large-scale traumatic events balance out war and destruction. With war, so much thought of human disregard is needed to combat the enemy. A clear line of "us versus them" has to be established for a soldier to do his job. Major events such as tsunamis balance out that energy on a global scale.

The human "body consciousness," in an act of balance, will always look for something to enforce the values of compassion and world unity—concepts inherent in the Soul. Unfortunately, this takes an event of incredible impact to seize civilization's attention on the prospects of compassion and well-being. Natural disasters provide this focus in a world of suspicion, distrust, and division, where we are intent on killing one another mercilessly and with immense contempt.

Mass events help in defining a greater identity for a large group. So often we feel ignored or pushed under the rug. Disasters bring awareness and energy where it is needed within the context of accepted delivery. That is, if the evening news were to sensationalize events of positive force and good will, you would see less disaster and more uplifting events.

Alas, this is currently not the case.

People's compassion and thrust to "do good" are not drawn by positive events—rather, they are drawn by negative upheaval, as such energy tests the limits of a person's mind. Now, someone could just as easily say that a positive event could stretch someone's Soul. To this, I would agree. Unfortunately, it is not the overall *accepted belief* among the general populace—thus the reinforcement of negative mass events over the positive.

MORE FREQUENT EVENTS

Without a doubt, you have heard the notion that we are having more frequent large-scale events throughout the world than we did in the past. This may or may not be true when considering that it has only been within the past two decades, with the advent of the Internet and global communication technologies, that we have instant access to news across the globe in almost real time. Prior to the communication revolution, knowledge of mass events in other countries could be better regulated. We may not have heard about some catastrophes simply because certain governments may have chosen not to share inner plights with the outside world. In this sense, there's no way to gauge with any definitiveness if we are experiencing more traumatic mass events than before.

If we are experiencing more large-scale events, it is also hard to tell by what percentage. Again, past data is lacking. Are we experiencing a 1% increase, or 10%? There may be five more traumatic events a year in comparison to what—1950?

On the surface, and maybe perhaps intuitively, it does *appear* that we are having more earthquakes, hurricanes, super-storms, and tsunamis than in the past. And this may be true. If so, I believe we can expect this to increase, on the basis of increasing population figures alone. Right now, nearly 7 billion people are crowding this earth, and that number will continue to grow. With more Souls vying for space, more resources being depleted, and more economic strife and widespread separation occurring through political and religious ideologies, we are going to continue to experience an increase in traumatic mass events.

The psychic energy output of 7 billion people is quite a bit larger than say, 4 billion. Remember, it only takes the square root of 1% of the population to create change, if the intention is strong enough. It makes frightening sense that the more people you have being pulled through man-made mental/emotional/physical strife, the more psychical events will be created in the world environment. People's thoughts do affect reality—again, we have seen this documented in scientific studies. This is why it is so important to start "waking up" and becoming conscious of our thoughts and actions. It's a simple mathematical truth: more people = more events.

But, we do have a choice.

Are those events disasters? Or are they positive transitions through a new creative medium? We have a lot of work to do if we wish for the latter.

THE END TIMES?

Another popular motif we keep hearing these days is that we are living in "the end times," or that humanity has reached a "pivotal point" and that we must make a decision—otherwise, we are doomed to destruction.

My response—from being a psychic and explorer of consciousness—is that no, this is absolutely not happening. We are not in any kind of "end times," and humanity is *always* at a "pivotal point."

Everyone loves to make today out as being far worse than yesterday and graver than the past. Again, it is all relative. It would have been easy for someone being exterminated in a Nazi prison camp during the Holocaust to say they were living in the end times and that humanity was at a crisis point—for it certainly was! In my own opinion, the death and destruction that occurred during World War II have constituted the blackest mark in humanity's consciousness in the past 200 years, and definitely more than anything we have experienced in the last fifty. To my recollection, since then, we haven't tried wiping out a single race or culture the way the Nazis did to the Jews (though some would argue, with validity, that the ethnic cleansings that have occurred in various African nations would constitute such an effort), nor have we released nuclear weapons on people of other nations, the way we did to the Japanese. Today, nuclear holocaust is an imagined threat (yes, it is a possibility), but in 1945, it was *physical reality*. We need to put all this into perspective.

However, like I said, we *are* always at a "pivotal point." Every moment is a moment in which we can choose either to grow in a positive direction or to head closer to the grave. Our Soul, our consciousness, is always in a state of Becoming—that is, becoming more than we were the moment before. This constant change and evolution brings with it a unique set of stresses and crises that force us to continue down the evolutionary path. Each Now moment is different from what came before and is an invitation for development. However, it is not any more or any less climactic than any previous time in humanity's evolutionary consciousness.

Every Now moment is the most important moment, for the very fact that the point of power is *always* in the present. That, by default, makes every Now moment a pivotal point, a crisis point, a decision point. We are always growing, always changing—that is simply the nature of existence. Things are different, yes, as every moment is different. But we are still traveling on the path of Soul expression and experience.

So much today is being said that we need to "make a choice" or we will suffer the consequences. Yet none of the doomsdayers are saying what would happen if we were to select the right choice as an alternative. They just assume we know what a good choice would produce, so they bypass it and continue to focus on the bad. Do they believe we would somehow go back in time to when the stresses of life and conditions were nonexistent or better regulated? We cannot physically move backward into the past, and there will always be some sort of stress as the Now moment pushes and pulls us in the direction of multiple probabilities.

Doomsdayers say we must avoid disaster but fail to give us a glimpse of the wonderful utopia they are hoping for. Do we know what that is? How can we *intend* a better future without first deciding what that future will look and *feel* like? Right now, we are still too focused on the negative and are creating more expectation in that direction than in the one in which we belong. Since we are, as always, at a pivotal point, we need to *decide* what it is we truly want and *direct energy in that direction*, not toward what we should fear.

Currently, as 2012 approaches, the doomsdayers are painting a picture of things marching along relatively normally until December 21, 2012, when—out of the blue—some sort of judgment will be leveled against us because of how the planet is aligned in the cosmos and how the poles shift. Massive earthquakes will allegedly rip apart the earth's crust, the oceans will "fly over" the continents—and life as we know it will end in a variety of unpleasant ways.

What an absurd notion!

If such a thing *were* to happen, since the nature of this alleged end centers around large-scale macroscopic bodies throughout the universe, such as our own sun and the other planets that share our solar system—we would have indicators long before December 21st. There is no way it could happen without adequate warning, as if somebody just "flipped a switch." Aside from that, there is no evidence that any such planetary alignment would produce the kind of interactive field capable of setting off such disastrous events. Any astronomer will tell you that distant stars exert no force capable of creating such a catastrophe. This same nonsense was touted back in the 1980s, when all the planets in our galaxy were going to "line up." Back then, it was believed that all our communication systems were going to shut down and that the planet was going to be besieged by major climactic upheaval.

All this hoopla surrounding 2012 stems from the Mayan calendar. Archeologists have admitted that it doesn't indicate the end of the world, or even the end of the calendar. It addresses only the end of a particular era in the Mayan culture surrounding one of their gods, Bolon Yokte.

The Mayans held the number 13 as being a mystical number and used it as the final number in cyclical events. In 2012, it is the thirteenth era for their god of creation and destruction—hence, the final cycle for this deity. Being masters of astronomy (as all ancient cultures were—they didn't have the Internet and televisions to distract them, so they focused on the stars), they were able to chart the seasons and celestial alignments for centuries to come and choose the winter solstice as the time for the god's end.

However, with every ending comes a new beginning. What the doomsdayers aren't talking about is that the Mayan calendar also eludes to events beyond 2012, one in particular for the year 4772.

Don't worry about 2012. Like the change of the clock at the turn of the millennium, it will come and go, and the consciousness of humanity will continue on its course of evolution.

Now, there are also those who say, "No, it's a shift in conscious awareness. Those who can make the shift will survive, and those that can't, won't"—as if to say, those who don't think alike will somehow be overcome by massive amounts of stress and disease and find themselves dying from such ignorance. Being in the metaphysical community, I've heard this declaration for nearly thirty years. "We are on the edge of a consciousness shift. Level four energy is going to level five, and those who can't make the energetic change will not survive."

Sure they will. In fact, things won't be much different for them than they are right now. Life is an act of consciousness existing in multiple probable states, experiencing multiple probable realities. Variations will always exist, and people will always exist in different states of consciousness across the board, throughout all Time. That is the nature of consciousness and of Being. The Soul is experiencing and expressing itself in all possible states at all possible Times. Level four, five, ten, or twenty-eight—it doesn't matter.

For eons, we have loved to think from our egoic mind that those we perceive as "beneath us" will somehow "get their due" because of their "lack of knowledge" in comparison to "us." This is nonsense. We are connected just as much to the lowly slug as we are to our big toe. This notion of energy and frequency moving to a "higher level" and frying the minds of those who can't make the shift is the New Age way of saying, "If you don't believe in my god, you will burn in Hell." It comes from the ego in an attempt to completely invalidate the individual's unique spiritual path, as well as the immutable power and validity of each person's eternal Soul. No one wins out over anyone else, because we all exist in one big ocean. I might equate it to cutting your own arm off and beating *yourself* with it over a disagreement you have…with yourself. It's just insanity!

We are always approaching a new shift in consciousness. Every day is the experience of that shift, and everybody is going through it. It has been that way since the beginning of man's first breath. Each step in the march of man's progress is the unfolding of that expansion and growth of consciousness—from living in caves to building the pyramids to constructing the Eiffel Tower. That is also the nature of the Soul—to expand and become greater with each moment. Each person will experience it in her own unique way, suitable to her desired speed and method for growth.

"We are living in the end times predicted in the Bible." This is another favorite cry rolling around the Western world. In truth, everyone has thought that ever since the book of Revelation was published, and many cultures that lived prior to the existence of the Bible also declared they were living in the "end times" of humanity and of the world. By the year 53, rumors were already rampant that Christ had returned. The Thessalonians, then being instructed by the apostle Paul, panicked, thinking they had missed the Savior's return. Around 968, a solar eclipse brought immense panic in the German army of Emperor Otto because they believed it was a sign of the apocalypse. The same happened with Halley's comet in 989 and with a supernova in 1006. In 1533, Christ's return was predicted to occur at 8:00 A.M. on October 19th. In 1843, William Miller created his own movement (called Millerism) on the basis of his studies of the Bible, in which he declared that the end times were to happen between 1843 and 1844. In 1925, the Jehovah's Witnesses lost huge amounts of followers because they falsely predicted that the end times were going to happen that year. Having bungled that date, they predicted it again in 1975—only to lose even more members after the date had come and gone. Each era has had their own "signs" believed to correspond with Biblical prophecy, keeping the drama and fascination of "living in end times" alive and well. Every volcanic eruption was a sign; and the black plague outbreaks of the mid-1300s, 1500s, and 1600s were all thought to be a part of the "end times," as well.

Our present is undoubtedly going to be perceived as larger, more complex, and more precarious than the past—hence, a fear of the "end times." It is just the nature of the Now moment. It is also the nature of our ego to be so self-centered. We always want to perceive ourselves as existing on the edge of the abyss; it makes us feel alive and engaged and gives us some sense of responsibility for what must come ahead. With the point of power being in the Present, our feeling of being naturally assumes that emotional and psychological position. However, it doesn't mean the future is going to be a disaster for humanity. We need to be aware of the psychic power we have in numbers and how we can harness that power to influence the environment to create events that affect the world. Our future and reality isn't something that happens to us by forces outside of us—it is created *by us* for specific and definite reasons.

Do not fear the end of the world. Humanity will not go out in a blaze of ruin. Our collective consciousness is always performing a balancing act. Perhaps it becomes precarious when so many people have shifted over to autopilot, unaware of their own freedom and ability to choose reality from a conscious perspective, and when you have those who wish to influence others with "end times" nonsense. But we have always been here and always will be. Remember, we are energy. Energy never dies, it simply transforms. We need to realize that we have absolute choice and free will to determine just what that form can be.

When the last moments of physical breath are exhaled, it is not the end. It is a new beginning.

NOTE

1. Melvin Morse, M.D., and Paul Perry, *Parting Visions* (New York: Harper Paperbacks, 1994), p. 65. Used with permission.

Chapter Thirteen

THE SOUL'S JOURNEY AFTER
PHYSICAL DEATH

The afterlife has been a preoccupation of humanity since the dawn of Time. The Egyptians glorified it; in the Western World, Judaism and Christianity popularized it; and science vilified it for lacking any tangible proof. For our discussion here, let us just say that for right now, science still cannot provide tangible proof for consciousness itself, yet we all can agree we are alive and conscious. Materialist scientists are, at best, skeptics awaiting a standardized model to test for survival after death (which ultimately cannot be accomplished physically to begin with). At worst, they are die-hard materialists who may never see beyond the effects of the consciousness they so ardently deny for lack of physical proof. Death, by its nature, provokes the lack of the physical, so it will be a long time coming for hard-core scientists to procure the answers they require.

The study of the afterlife has taken many roads. Spiritualists credit Kate and Margaret Fox of Hydesville, New York, with the official start of the spiritualist movement in 1848, and the act of communicating with the dead. The Fox sisters claimed they had been contacted by the spirit of a peddler, who communicated with them through rapping noises. On several occasions, onlookers were able to witness this communication in action (though later, there were many counts of fraud wrought by the Fox clan, and the whole thing may have been a hoax). Prior to that, as early as the late 1600s, Emanuel Swedenborg claimed to talk with spirits while awake and provided some of the first writings of the supposed landscape of the spirit world.

Spiritualism took off in the late 1800s and the early 1900s. During this era, a plethora of mediums arose. These early spirit-seekers were more concerned with providing entertainment, defrauding clients, and making money than forming honest connections with the deceased. This was the era of table-tipping and conducting séances in total darkness to keep the sitters from seeing strings, idle hands, and pure trickery. Mediums would employ a "spirit box," which was really no different than a magician's box, made with false doors and curtains to trick audiences. Some mediums would even create ectoplasm during a séance—that slimy, icky film claimed to be the residue of an intense spiritual contact. Like I said, many of these mediums were found to be cheats and hucksters, yet there were a few in the pack that even to this day cannot be explained and may likely have been genuine.

One such medium was Leonora Piper, the Boston housewife who was studied by the American Society for Psychical Research (ASPR) for nearly twenty years, and whom William James, the world-renowned psychologist, declared his "white crow." James affirmed, "In order to disprove the law that all crows are black, it is enough to find one white crow." To many paranormal investigators, Leonora was just that. She never used spirit boxes, table-tipping, or other devices to distract her sitters—she was a different breed of medium, called a trance medium. She would go into trance and then use her voice or automatic writing to transmit information regarding people's relatives and events, usually through an intermediary spirit-guide, referred to as a "control." Leonora's first intermediate claimed to be a French physician named

Phinuit, but he was later replaced by other spirits. She was studied extensively and put through a gamut of tests with tight controls. (In one case, a private investigator was hired to follow her movements to make sure she wasn't doing background research on clients—though in many cases, she never knew ahead of time who the clients would be). Many of the scientists who studied her believed as William James did—Leonora could somehow communicate with the dead, as she could describe specific events, characteristics, and even names of those who were deceased or wishing to address individuals from the other side of the veil.

Scientific investigation into the notion of an afterlife inspired a few sincere-minded individuals. One such scientist was F. W. H. Myers, who cofounded the Society of Psychical Research (SPR) in 1882. He spent decades studying ESP, telepathy, and the survival of life after death. On the basis of his results, he became a firm believer in psychic ability and cross-communication (a term used at the time for communicating with spirits between multiple mediums). It was believed that after he died, he successfully made contact through several mediums, the most notable being Leonora. She was able to give details of Myers' last conversation with a friend, Eleanor Sidgwick.[1] Later, it was believed that he had dictated the contents of an entire book, *The Road to Immortality* (1932), through Geraldine Cummins. Of the work, Sir Oliver Lodge—who knew Myers when he was alive—attested that owing to the style and nature of the material, he had no reason to believe that it wasn't produced by Myers' spirit. "(These) are the kind of ideas which F. W. H. Myers may by this time have been able to form."[2]

Additionally, one of the most bizarre and interesting cases centered around Ms. Piper and three other mediums, Mrs. Verrall and her daughter, Helen, and Mrs. Holland (a pseudonym for Alice Kipling Fleming, sister of Rudyard Kipling), between 1906 and 1917. Each woman, without communicating with one another and living thousands of miles apart (though in a few instances, Leonora was in

England where the Verrall's lived, but was kept under heavy scrutiny), received information that, on its own seemed rather meaningless, but when put together created a singular message that supposedly came from Myers. Recurrent topics such as star, hope, Browning—referring to specific pieces of literature which Myers was quite familiar with—and even anagrams—were transmitted through each medium, some within only days of each other (in one documented case, five hours, traversing thousands of miles), without any of the mediums being aware of the contents passing amongst themselves. It was only later, when members of the SPR were reviewing the recorded documents of each of the medium's messages that the pattern was discovered and the overall meanings identified. In a few cases, the supposed spirit of Myers even mentioned sending a complementary message to one of the other mediums, hoping his overall message would be discovered and the picture of his immortality revealed.

Henry Sidgwick, also one of the founders of the SPR, carried on Myers' tradition after he himself passed away. Similar to his colleague, his messages that were transmitted through the mediums pieced together certain phrases and identifiers from a particular work of classical literature to validate the cross-correspondence phenomenon between the various psychics. For many who followed the SPR, these cross-correspondences provided more than ample proof of life after death. What are the odds of one piece of literature being sliced up and sent to separate mediums, and then recombined to discover the whole picture? In many cases, the literature and passages chosen required advanced knowledge of the classics, which both Myers and Sidgwick had in their lifetimes, but which a few of the mediums did not, notably Mrs. Piper. In some of the cross-correspondences, the chosen work happened to be one of the select favorites of the deceased.

For many students studying life after death, the cross-correspondences were tantalizing—however, many argued that the messages could have resulted from telepathy amongst the mediums, or super-psi—a form of extraordinary mind-reading between people thousands of miles apart (which in itself would be an incredible feat). Considering how complex the correspondences were, to me that seems completely untenable. In the case that started it all, Mrs. Holland (who knew nothing about the SPR in England, as she was in India) was instructed by Myers' spirit to contact the SPR, giving her the direct address, and supplying her with the first piece of the cross-correspondence puzzle. It seems wholly impossible that telepathy from some other medium could have created this. Only Myers himself, with the knowledge of the address, the knowledge of whom to address his dictated letter to, and his knowledge of the classics makes the most sense.

The most famous story about attempting to prove life after death centered around the famous magician, Harry Houdini (1874-1926). He promised his wife that if survival after death was real, he would find a way to communicate with her. Alas, it appeared he never did. Then again, Houdini made it a personal mission to discredit mediums while he was alive, so why would he use one after his death? It would not, in my opinion, have been in the nature of his being—thus, he left only silence when he departed. It may have been too big a blow for his ego to admit from the Other Side the possibility of communication.

Nevertheless, the search for life after the grave has never diminished. It is just as popular today as it was during Houdini's time. Such celebrity mediums as John Edward and James Van Praagh captivate audiences in the thousands, and the media have capitalized on it through movies and television series.

As I mentioned in the first chapter, I became a medium after witnessing the effect of John Edward. Ten years later, I have given thousands of readings and have communicated with spirits living here and on the Other Side. I'll discuss in more detail later how this communication takes place. Here, I want to give a quick overview on life after death, on the basis of my own personal experiences from the multitude of readings and paranormal research I have been involved in. Coupled with this, I will highlight some findings discovered in the cognitive sciences that are quite fascinating.

The final breath of life. It's something we all dread. Once the lungs exhale, what comes next?

What do you think?

Consider the Now moment—this very moment in which you exist. In your life, has there ever been a moment where Now ceased to exist? No! There has always been the Now. Even before your birth, a Now moment was being experienced by everyone else. It is safe to assume the Now will continue after your body dies. All there is, is Now. It is eternal. You have always experienced life in the timeframe of Now, stretching into the past and reaching into the future. Knowing that the past and future are simultaneous with Now, it is impossible to lie in the moment of your death and all of a sudden have Now come to a screeching halt.

Try to imagine Now coming to an end.

Here you are, looking at your surroundings when Now ceases.

What would that look like? The room freezes, like a freeze-frame on a movie still? Or does it turn black? In either case, you would still be alive, for to even have the *perception* required to note these conditions means that you are still experiencing a Now moment in your consciousness! You will always be in the Now.

Now is eternal, and so are you.

This does not necessarily mean that you will occupy a physical body, however.

Recall the first rule of thermodynamics: Energy never dies, it simply transforms. This would apply even to you, as you are energy.

At death, the energy of your animating force transforms. Your frequency shifts to where the electromagnetic bond of your Soul to the cells of your body is broken. Right now, you are vibrating at a frequency that creates a magnetic connection between your invisible spirit and the body. That is, your energy creates mass due to its vibration, giving rise to the body through intent and electromagnetism. At death, your vibration changes, altering that frequency. At that moment, at that alteration of energy, you are able to leave the bio-body suit and move into the other energy realms that correspond to your new frequency.

Out-of-body-experiences (OBEs), also known as astral travel, are not uncommon and provide a glimpse into this natural shift of energy and act of leaving the body. Those who experience intended acts of OBEs describe how they must typically enter a hypnagogic state—that state between waking and sleeping, where indeed the vibration of consciousness shifts from beta into alpha.

At any rate, when the last breath comes, either your energy shifts and releases the magnetic bonds of spirit to the cellular body itself, or the body (through trauma) shifts its energy and releases you. Since your Soul is existent in everything, you are ultimately changing your energetic focus from one location (inside the body) to another (outside the body). What happens next is still something of a mystery, and we can only speculate on the basis of near-death experiences and that which has been received through the psychic readings of myself and others. But it appears you have choices.

"She says she was met by two others. One a sister."

A message like this can sometimes appear during a sitting, letting the sitter know that when a relative died, he or she was immediately greeted by a deceased family member who assisted with the transition. In a few cases, the client's deceased pets are also present. However, in the paranormal ghost cases I have investigated, this approach by other deceased family members either didn't happen, or the newly departed refused their assistance.

In the case of earthbound spirits, I believe the dead entity had at least one person waiting to help him or her. One of the key factors in the NDE experience, as well as in those who relay visions the closer they get to death, is the visitation of a spiritual being to guide the person to the Other Side ("Heaven"). In many cases, it's a relative the dying person knows. In numerous readings, the dead have often communicated that they were assisted in crossing over and that they met up again with lost friends and relatives. However, if a person were to die traumatically and is not yet ready to let go of the environment, unfinished relationships, or other confining mental frameworks, he could easily resist any help in leaving the earth dimension. Free will being paramount, no one—deceased relative, nor angel, nor spirit guide—would have the right to abduct him. The psychological trauma of such an action could end up proving more harmful than healing. Just because someone has died does not mean he is free of emotions or confining psychological frameworks.

In several of the ghost cases I have experienced, the spirit harbored a belief or attitude of fear surrounding the Other Side that kept the individual earthbound. The old adage, "He was a God-fearing man" became a literal truth. So many spirits stay behind for fear of being judged for whatever sins they felt they had committed. At the time of passing, they saw the tunnel and chose not to enter it. They heard voices calling them, but willed themselves to ignore it. Shedding the mortal coil doesn't mean we also rid our minds of toxic beliefs.

In most cases, I believe people's curiosity about what lies ahead carries them forward. Consider that a moment earlier, the dead person was in physical reality, perhaps dreading the end of his life or getting quick glimpses of a potential afterlife. Then his energy feels a "twinge" and he suddenly realizes he is free of his body. In some reported cases of NDEs, the dying report hearing a "buzzing" sound upon exiting the flesh.

What happens next in the unfolding drama would be his emotional and mental reaction to death.

Curiosity? Fear? Expectation? Confusion?

This is why somebody comes to meet him, typically a relative or someone that the dying would trust to facilitate the introduction. If the new arrival acquiesces to his situation and is willing to leave earth behind—whoosh! Up the tunnel he goes.

The tunnel experience is a universal theme in both NDEs and in actually crossing over. The sensation of movement through the shaft, I believe, is a natural by-product—an effect—of a person's energy shifting yet again from one frequency to another. This shift, however, is more like a quantum leap. Instead of changing from, say, 10 Hz to 12 Hz to break the magnetic bonds of spirit to body (these numbers are arbitrary—no one knows what the actual frequency is), the shift from earthbound entity into the next dimension could be as great as 12 Hz to 1200 Hz, for example.

Everything exists on a wavelength along the electromagnetic spectrum, and it is the process of energy recalibration that moves you along the continuum. This frequency movement, filtered through the senses (whether physical or not), could give the sensation of flying or being sucked through a vacuum tube—much like those moments where you are sitting in a parking lot and the person parked beside you pulls out, yet you could swear it was you who was moving. Again, it's all a matter of perception.

Now, scientists have uncovered that by stimulating the right temporal lobe of the brain, similar experiences occur—the sensation of being out of the body, and even zooming down a tunnel. At this point, every materialist in the room may stand up and scream, "See! It's all in the mind!"

Well, yes and no.

When a person has an OBE during temporal lobe stimulation, it appears that he is definitely out of his body. Melvin Morse, M.D., while studying the NDE experiences of children, found an old textbook documenting cases of temporal lobe stimulation performed by Wilder Penfield. Penfield was examining an area just above the right ear, called the Sylvan fissure. His notes record patients exclaiming, "I'm leaving my body now." Or, in some cases, "I'm half in and half out." Other patients claimed they were hearing music, seeing dead friends and relatives, zooming up a tunnel, even having a panoramic life review![3] That a patient can communicate to the doctor what he is perceiving makes it appear that he is still very much inside his body; however, consciousness—again, unable to be defined by science—can travel and exist anywhere in the universe. Remember those remote-viewing trials? Also, remember how two electrons, once separated, can still communicate across vast distances? Here, we may have a macro version of that micro quantum reality. As the patient expresses himself outside the body, the body responds and matches the expression (thus enabling the conversation with the doctor), for the two are *entangled*.

At the very least, science has discovered *where* in the brain these esoteric functions occur. This is natural. The physical body *should* have a physical counterpart that rises out of the invisible nature of consciousness. This doesn't mean the energy of consciousness, nor its experiences, are confined or held prisoner in that tiny physical area of the brain. That physical area simply provides the apparatus for transduction of psychical/nonphysical data into the body's brain for reconstruction in the individual egoic mind.

Once the spirit leaves the physical body, it appears he gains a new body. That is, the dead don't see themselves as invisible or transparent. They speak of having a new kind of physique, one in which they can choose how old they wish to look and that doesn't "break down." Here again, the purpose of this new body would be filtering sensory data out of the environment for egoic mind reconstruction. Its frequency is different than the physical bodies we have right now, but it is still a body nonetheless. As we can obtain different bodies during our dream states—ones that may not reflect a particular injury or disability, leaving us free to walk or fly—so, too, do we obtain yet another type of body for movement and expression in the frequency domain of the next dimension. It seems that bodies are more fluid and moldable than we originally thought!

Let's say we have a gentleman who has just died and has zoomed down the tunnel. Like so many others have reported, he will come to a wondrous field of flowers and butterflies. The field is a common location because it is widely recognized by nearly everyone on earth. That is, most people are familiar with a field of some kind. It is a location that is both recognizable and inviting. Only moments into the afterlife experience, one's emotional and mental condition is still very much taken into account by those sent to initiate "introductions." More or less, the field is a middle ground—a transitory location in which to greet the newcomer and debrief the life experience. If he hasn't already met a spirit guide or a figure who emulates religious reverence, here is where that meeting will take place.

As I said, the mental state of a new arrival is still very fragile. Now that our spirit has realized he has survived death, mental instincts and beliefs take over. If he were indoctrinated in the Christian faith, this would inform him of a certain framework of what the Other Side is supposed to be like. Similarly, if he were a Muslim, that, too, provides a framework of expectation. At first, these beliefs will manifest into the egoic mind to help smooth the transition. To do otherwise would not be at all helpful and would severely debilitate one's inclusion into the "real" afterlife, because the lack of the anticipated protocols would undoubtedly create a sense of fear and dread.

At the start, the spirit sent to welcome the newcomer may appear to be the dead man's vision of Jesus, Mohammed, or even Buddha.

This is as it should be. Imagine the terror and inability to integrate into a new life if you believed you were going to see Jesus, but instead saw Osiris—the original Christ figure from ancient Egypt. You would panic! If you were brought up Mormon—you may be expecting Joseph Smith to greet you. He'd better be there!

The inclusion of this religious-inspired Being makes for much-needed comfort for what is to come next: the life review. It is one of the most common reported traits of the NDE experience, and one that is repeated to me often when I am communicating with a client's deceased relative if the topic of the transition itself comes up.

The life review can take many forms, such as watching a movie, reliving experiences in three dimensions, or fast-forwarding through blurbs. In some cases, the life review takes on a multidimensional perspective—the person can see the events of their entire life in a simultaneous fashion. That is, a person's whole life spreads out before them—again like our ruler of simultaneous Time. Whatever the method of perception, the review has an incredible impact, as it reveals the effects of our choices on the lives of others, whether they be people, animals, or the environment. Many NDEs report that they not only see the results of their thoughts and actions, but also *feel* the emotions of those they affected, both good and bad.

The life review affirms, again, that we are really just One Consciousness branching off into various states of multiple existence, exploring all possibilities at once. To be able to feel the emotions of another—to not simply empathize but essentially *become* the other person's experience in the life review—solidifies this notion. You are, in essence, forced to put aside your own egoic mind and meld with another portion of the greater conscious mind, of which you are an individualized portion, as well as the person you are identifying with.

In those cases where a person's life is spread out in a simultaneous fashion (think of a film strip, where all the frames are there and the movie is complete in the canister, but you have to watch it through a projector to experience it in Time), one can focus on a particular point, and it replays that moment again from history. It is filled with all the thoughts and emotions from all the particulars in the scene. It can be an incredibly emotional and enlightening event for a new arrival.

Here, the inclusion of the religious figure (in some cases, a whole audience) is highly advantageous. Seeing your life from a third-person perspective and feeling the emotions of those in the scenes is unlike anything we can experience here on earth. You see your life in a whole new light, and as is natural, begin to judge yourself on the basis of the recorded actions. The religious figure remains a source of comfort during those dark and traumatic moments of our lives. He is also there to help us better understand our mistakes.

Once the review is finished, it becomes easier to move forward. A sense of closure occurs as a result of the debriefing. Any traumatic incidents that a person may feel as being "unfinished" are acknowledged as being something that can be addressed and worked on once one settles in to the new environment.

In a few incidents, a soul who has lived a rather hard life or is otherwise drained by the life review will receive a "power up." Emotions may have left an arrival's energy spent or even depressed. The religious figure, possibly with an accompaniment of other entities, will channel a fresh range of energy to the consciousness. It is almost like receiving an energy shower that clears the dirt and grime away that had built up from physical life.

When the Soul is ready to finally move on, he is then entered into a "hub," designed to transport new arrivals to their next location. The description of this jumping-off point was first penned by Michael Newton in his groundbreaking book, *Journey of Souls*. Michael, a hypnotherapist, had a client accidentally regress during one of his sessions to a place that left him astounded. The client claimed he was "between lives." Since the book's first printing in 1994, Michael has pioneered life-between-life sessions, culminating in several books (including

Destiny of Souls) describing hundreds of patients' memories as recalled during hypnosis. Though hypnosis is still considered somewhat controversial by mainstream scientists, the fact that so many people without any connection to one another from all parts of the world describe the same types of experiences is remarkable. The details of the hub is one of those experiences. Newton wrote, "When I hear accounts of this particular junction, I visualize myself walking with large numbers of travelers through the central terminal of a metropolitan airport which has the capacity to fly all of us out in any direction." One of his clients described it as "the hub of a great wagon wheel, where we are transported from a center along the spokes to our designated places."[4]

Recently, I was giving a reading for my wife, who had lost a co-worker to cancer. Her friend, Diane, alluded to the hub during the reading, giving me a glimpse of a network of transit tubes where people were being guided along. She commented that it was one of the most amazing things she had seen—that the organization of it all was mind-boggling (though she used her own colorful language to explain it). The correct path in the chaotic multiconnectional hub seemed to have been known by mere intuition—or else some force outside of her was leading her, she couldn't tell which. There wasn't any apparatus or vehicle the person had to use, she said—they just got in line and started moving.

Every once in awhile, a story comes along where someone had an NDE and instead of going to the heavenly field, they encountered a land of unspeakable horror. This is a rare occasion, but one that needs to be addressed.

As stated throughout this book, your thoughts create reality. In the three-dimensional universe, Time is created as an effect of the dissonance between your energy and the frequency of your desire within the framework of matter. Once you step outside the body, however, you are no longer in three-dimensional Space/Time. Spiritual energy moves at a much quicker rate than does the rate of matter. This faster pace makes for an almost instantaneous manifestation of one's psychological mind. Again, outer reality is a reflection of one's inner experience, beliefs, attitudes, and expectations.

At the time of death, if someone were to harbor intense feelings of dread, guilt, and fear, and believed on an inner level that such a hellish experience was his destiny—or, conversely, that he didn't think he was worthy of Heaven—those inner ideas would play out before his eyes. His intense inner expectation informs reality (as it always has) and death, being the great equalizer in some people's psyche, mirrors the inner landscape of attitudes, beliefs, and expectations without the Time dissonance created by slower moving matter.

But fear not, because there are spirit guides, angels, and lost relatives who make their way into these landscapes for the purpose of rescuing those caught within such horrid psychosis.

The actual environment of Hell is not a real place. Rather, it is a stolen landscape of several pre-Christian and pre-Jewish cultural myths, starting with ancient Egypt. The Egyptian Underworld was filled with lakes of fire and hideous demons. The term "Underworld" also describes the visual given to the modern view of Hell, as being "inside the earth" or "down there, underground," indicating the origin of this mythic locale. The phrase "gates of Hell" no doubt refers to the many gates the Egyptians believed they had to pass through on their journey through the afterlife. The climax of this sojourn was to meet up with the beloved slain god Osiris (Jesus) in the Hall of Judgment, where the deceased's heart (Soul) was to be weighed against a feather (Truth). If the heart was heavy, that meant the dead person was full of sin, and his soul was to be devoured (eternal damnation and extinction). If the heart remained balanced, he was accepted into Ra's heavenly barque, a boat that sailed across the sky, and he was permitted to continue his life in a spiritual landscape that was a duplicate version of Egypt, called Rosetjau (Heaven).

The concept of Hell was not only intended to frighten adherents into obeying God's word, it was also a way of converting the pagans by infusing their own myths and legends into the new religious creed. It was an act of homogeny. However, in the grand scheme, the only Hell that exists is one in which the believer participates in the reality of his mind. There is no landscape set aside on the Other Side to torture heretics, nonbelievers, and evildoers.

One of the lessons my guides taught me and that I have seen through the actions of humanity is that the ideas surrounding good and evil are decided by the ego. It is in relation to the ego that actions are weighed. What is good for one person may be perceived as bad by another. It is by group consensus that actions are agreed upon as being bad and turned into prohibitions, crimes, and the like—such as rape or murder. Indeed, such actions are heinous, leaving many people scarred and ruined. However, when one steps back and perceives life as a manifestation of energy and the effects of consciousness, there are no longer victims and aggressors. On some level (and this sounds quite alarming), the energy of the victim and the energy of the aggressor were in coherence, and thus the outcome materialized as a Space/Time event on the basis of the attitudes, expectations, and beliefs of both. What it boils down to is this: Since reality is a manifestation of energy that we inform and create, how ignorant are we of this responsibility, or how knowledgeable? On top of that, if we do understand this phenomenon, how ignorant or knowledgeable are we with regard to the effects?

This is what the landscape of the afterlife triggers and epitomizes within the Soul. It forces one to look inside and acknowledge what they still have yet to learn. Is one ignorant—meaning he simply does not know (but can learn) how his actions and energy offerings have outcomes? Is he knowledgeable of our grand connectedness of Being? Of how our thoughts and emotions vibrate to create reality?

One is never left hanging. On the Other Side there are counselors, teachers, and "universities" to help guide us into living the best life we can, at the speed at which we choose. It isn't about blaming or drowning in guilt, it's about learning to become the most loving and compassionate Soul possible and uncovering the untapped potential of the Soul's eternal capabilities. In this way, we get to experience all the possibilities inherent within us, as well as serve as a source of inspiration and reflection for others.

Reward and punishment in the afterlife, contrary to religious doctrine, is not doled out by angels or by a moody overlord. The nature of consciousness is always about expression and expansion—and that doesn't change on the Other Side. If anything, it is *enhanced*. Since thought manifestation comes more quickly and psychic functioning more easily, a whole new perspective is explored regarding one's abilities, nature, and freedom. The inherent connection to all things is better understood, and a far more enjoyable, inviting, and *loving* experience is lived by everyone.

In the absence of death, punishment and fear become mute. There is no ultimate act of punishment that an exterior force can foist upon an individual, because no one really dies, and the "spirit-body" cannot be harmed.

When this realization is made, threats become meaningless. Love is All There Is.

When you suddenly realize that You can never die and that situations result from your own thinking, energy, and corresponding actions, you are moved into a new position of living from your heart-center, as opposed to living from a place of fear and seeking protection. It becomes important to you to better understand how love, empowerment, and cooperation breed success rather than competition, reservation of resources, and paranoid suspicion. All things being connected and One undivided energy, One cannot divide Itself by Itself.

Now, there are Souls who, after their life review, brand themselves in a very negative light. They view their previous life on earth as representing the height of ignorance—whether this was truly the case or not. By their own sense of guilt and personal resentment (and not by the judgment of any angel or god), they will select for themselves a method of punishment. They may elect to live in timeless isolation—cut-off from others until they can work out the blame and guilt they feel. Others will place themselves in the company of similar Souls, who perceive themselves as "sick." They will take on the appearance of illness and, depending on the extent of their own perceptions, even make themselves look like demons. In this way, they exhibit a realization of their inner struggles. They deny themselves what is good in order to provide a sense of punishment and eventual balance in their consciousness for what they felt they did wrong. They will, in some cases, still perceive themselves as a danger energetically, and remain isolated from the "higher" frequencies. Again, this is by choice—for they cannot lie to themselves about their actual state, nor can it be hidden from the psyche of the One Mind, of which all are a part of and have access to.

Every chance is given for rehabilitation. Education and counseling are always available. Love is the foundation for change. Unfortunately, someone who cannot love himself due to regret and guilt induced by his former actions oftentimes refuses love that is offered. The attitude of "I don't deserve it" or "How can you love me after the horrid things I have done?" is a typical belief harbored by these damaged Souls. The entity must learn inner forgiveness and wish to grasp the next rung in the ladder of knowledge that is available to him.

The afterlife isn't about right and wrong. Moral codes and ethics do not swirl about, with love and hate offered as emotional prizes (or in hate's case, an afterlife penalty). As I have said, it is about knowledge and ignorance. Do you believe in the knowledge that all things are connected and One? Do you act in the knowledge that your thoughts are the thoughts of the Eternal Universe? Do you act in the knowledge that life is a loving experience, where free will is allowed to blossom in order to explore the greatest potentials of the Soul?

Love, as always, is paramount. If it were not that way, there wouldn't be the freedoms that exist. Forgiveness would not be an option; only judgment, with a list of unaccepted prejudices, would prevail. And what good would those prejudices be? You wouldn't be able to enforce rules to punish Souls. That's just nonsense! What are you going to do? Kill the criminals? You can't do that. Lock them up? Send them to Hell? When the scale is based on ignorance and knowledge, sending someone to Hell is not the best way to learn a lesson—especially if one has the ability to affect the reality he experiences. When everything is connected and One, the One cannot separate Itself from Itself, as I mentioned earlier. All we can do is forgive and love. Love is the basis of All. This is what we hear from those who have returned from NDEs, patients who have undergone hypnosis, and spirits who have communicated through mediums or connected to family members through dreams. Love is the sunlight that shines through the entire realm.

The whole dimension of the afterlife does have some similarities to our world—people exist at different levels of the knowledge meter. Emotions are not too terribly different, either. Jealousy, anger, resentment, and other emotions don't disappear, but they do take on a new meaning. Many realize the futility of these emotions when they see how their thoughts create reality. Finally, taking responsibility forces one to think and act in new ways. Once this realization is made, the drive of the future is to learn how to change limiting thoughts and beliefs in order to expand and better express the wonder of the Soul—to love unconditionally all life as a reflection of You, and You of It. This is why education is so supported and talked about by those who speak from the Other Side. It is to help with Soul development, as each person always desires to live a fulfilling life—no matter what dimension they are in.

A special note on suicides. In the decade I have been doing sittings, I have encountered several Souls who have taken their own lives. The prevailing earthly thought about those who commit such an act is that they are sent straight to Hell for punishment, or that they are considered "special cases," requiring a lot of counseling and healing on the Other Side. In about three-quarters of those who I have met, it is the latter that happens.

Once a depressed or fractured person commits suicide, he is immediately put into special counseling and assistance. To kill one's self and then realize that life and mind goes on even after death can add to the already copious amounts of anguish and trauma going on in the individual's life. Once this kind of suicide happens, special teachers and expert counselors are assigned to help the deceased work through his problems and move on to the road of mental (psychic) recovery. It is done in the most loving field of energy, forgiveness, and understanding. It is with the intent that the individual eventually realizes his worth as a Being of all creation and moves forward with cherishing his life and the lives of others. Some of his anguish will psychically be carried over into simultaneous personalities vibrating on a similar psychic wavelength, where they will encounter many of the same problems as the suicide personality and attempt to work them out (or unfortunately repeat the pattern). If these other personalities are successful, this will provide an overall balance to the larger Oversoul, of which all personalities are a part. If not, other simultaneous selves will again address the various challenges. In the field of Time on earth, these personalities may claim to be the reincarnation of a suicide victim.

As I said, this occurs in about three-quarters of the cases I have dealt with. What about the other quarter?

Believe it or not, they are celebrated.

Allow me explain—it was quite a shock the first time I encountered it.

It happened at one of the psychic salons early on in my career. At the time, I had no idea the reading was about a suicide. The woman who had approached me for the sitting remained stone-faced and quiet—she only wanted to see if anybody from the Other Side was willing to talk (at least, that's what she told me). Within a couple of minutes, I had picked up on a brother. His energy was light, not at all heavy or guilty, as suicides typically are. He kept mentioning his throat. I told her he was referring to the loss of air in his lungs; I didn't put it together that he had hanged himself. He started to congratulate his sister for all the wonderful things she had done since his passing—things she wouldn't have done had he not died. Then he acknowledged big changes in the lives of other family members. It was then that my client informed me that her brother had committed suicide. She wanted to know why he did it.

Her brother again praised all the changes and events in people's lives allowed by his passing. They were, as expected, life changing, but also positive. What he said next blew my mind: It was meant to be that way. The drama of his suicide, it appeared, *had been preplanned on some level before everyone was born*. In other words, it was his life's purpose to commit suicide (and yes, I know how fantastic that sounds). His death was needed for the rest of the family to be able to move into areas of development and growth they would have otherwise overlooked or never considered. Again, on the surface, this sounds outlandish, until we realize that some people *do* act as catalysts for enormous change. Prior to being born, everyone already knows he will never really "die," but an act of suicide would create momentum into new areas of experience for each individual left behind. This is the "martyr effect."

For those suicides that have done this, they report that the person who commits suicide in this fashion knows intuitively that he is simply playing a role for the benefit of the others. It will, quite naturally, be as realistic as possible. That is, he may appear to have self-defeating habits or create horrible circumstances to justify the appearance of suicide (in a few instances, this wasn't the case—which made the death even more traumatic, since it was completely without warning).

The playing out of this type of drama requires an entity of advanced knowledge and understanding. The act, underneath, is done out of love to advance and deepen the lives of the others. It is a selfless deed, as opposed to the other kind of suicide, where a person is so wrapped up in himself that he feels he must snuff out his existence to rid the overwhelming sense of inner suffering. Again, consciousness can behave in myriad possibilities and combinations—even with suicide. When it comes to natural death, that, too, in its own way is a form of suicide, for we each choose the time, place, and nature of our passing. Natural death, however, is one where we have all accepted that design and therefore don't condemn the deceased for slipping away.

So where do we go after we have been through the hub? What are the destinations? I can only tell you what I have heard from those who I have communicated with, along with what my guides have told me. In the end, we will find out for ourselves when we arrive. In the meantime, here's the short answer:

Any place you can imagine.

Okay, that might be too short of an explanation.

Most people prefer to inhabit an environment that is very much like earth. Trees, plants, flowers, birds. When my wife's coworker came through, she was ecstatic about studying the flight mechanisms of butterflies. She was a scientist by trade while on earth, and she was overjoyed at being able to study insects and plant life on the Other Side. She said it didn't require microscopes or other equipment—it was a knowledge that would "come through" while studying; that is, it seemed to appear quite naturally, as if she could psychically figure things out without the aid of scientific instruments. She didn't quite understand it, but she was having the "time of her life." She had only been gone a little over a week when I conducted the reading, so she was still in awe at the new surroundings. Part of getting acclimated for her was using her scientific faculties to better understand the environment.

During the discussion, my wife's father, who had died in the 1990s, also appeared. While alive, he was the true outdoorsman. He loved photography and was a part of mountaineering and other nature groups. He let my wife know that he had found a club on the Other Side and was still outside, exploring new and beautiful landscapes with like-minded friends. It appeared that many of the same social groups we love to hang out with on earth also have their counterparts on the Other Side.

Family and friends continue to stay together on the Other Side. Oftentimes, we follow each other around, even as simultaneous personalities incarnated on earth in "past" or "future" lives. Some people refer to these clusters as "soul groups" or "soul families." That phrase "birds of a feather" gives a good impression of this community we share. Many of us are in the process of learning the same or similar lessons of life, so we hang out and share these journeys. It's more fun together than alone!

In various metaphysical circles, I have heard people talk about the Other Side in terms of levels. Some say it is made of seven levels, like the chakras. Others say it's even more. No one really knows. But if everything is frequency based, it stands to reason that multiple realities do exist, and it is not necessarily a status thing or a declaration of stature—it is of a vibrational nature. That is, all frequencies are available—thus, all realities that exist within those frequencies are also available. The question is, what is your vibration? Is your frequency within the range of the frequency-reality you wish to experience? I have heard there are some realities where consciousness doesn't even use a body. That would be an interesting place!

If all advancement is based on a scale of knowledge, then knowledge must create a certain frequency-vibration that determines how high up one could go. This sounds reasonable. When you move out of a state of ignorance into one of knowledge, you certainly feel different about yourself! At one point, you were ignorant on how to drive a car. But now that you've learned, look where you can go. This makes sense when it comes to talking about those entities we perceive as spirit guides and angels.

My guides have told me that some people prefer not to stay in one reality too long—that their greatest joy is exploring different dimensions. This suggests that multiple realities are accessible, depending on your frequency. Each of these realities, I am told, has its own set of "natural laws" for the Soul's experience and expression. Again, it falls to the individual and his invisible psychic network of beliefs, attitudes, and expectations that will grant him where he can and cannot go.

You are immortal!

You are multidimensional!

All in all, everything is possible. As always, what is *probable* depends on You. You may choose to remain in an earthlike setting, or go somewhere completely outside our common notion of reality.

If one is interested in speculation and potential afterlife landscapes, I again highly recommend Michael Newton's *Journey of Souls* and *Destiny of Souls*. The stories related by his clients under hypnosis are indeed tantalizing, as they speak about colossal heavenly buildings and complexes, universities, talking with spiritual masters, and exploring the growth of the Soul.

In addition, if you can find them, I also recommend the three-volume series, *Life in the World Unseen*, by Anthony Borgia. Borgia wrote these books in the mid-1950s, and claimed they were channeled through him by Monsignor Robert Hugh Benson. Benson, son of a former Archbishop of Canterbury, wrote a book titled, *The Necromancers*

(1909), which dealt with spirit-communication and the afterlife in a rather negative fashion, against spiritual mediumship that was popular at the time. According to Borgia, after the Monsignor died, his new knowledge of the afterlife made him wish to correct the errors and inconsistencies of his book, so he went looking for a medium (the only route possible). Borgia, who was gifted with clairaudience—meaning he received psychic information through hearing—acted as the go-between and wrote down everything he heard from the supposed spirit of the dead priest.

Borgia died in 1989, at the age of ninety-three. He truly believed in his work—with such conviction, in fact, that even in his blindness and failing health, he still maintained a sense of humor that stemmed from his beliefs about the afterlife he had transcribed. Whether the books constitute genuinely channeled material or not is always open for debate, but the descriptions of the afterlife and the dying process itself are quite consistent with findings of modern-day research. Much of Borgia's (or rather Benson's) description of life after death makes realistic sense and is in line with other information we have received from psychics, mediums (myself included), and those "regular folk" who have had visitations in dreams from passed relatives. It is quite a comfort to read, as the Monsignor consistently relates the nature of love and acceptance, as well as the growth and expansion of each Soul and the connection between all things. His descriptions of social gatherings, events, and meetings with various departed personalities are both intriguing and captivating. The books are incredibly thorough, and leave one asking: If this is the departed Monsignor, how did Borgia "hear" him?

We'll get to that next.

NOTES

1. From http://www.answers.com/topic/frederic-william-henry-myers.

2. Ibid.

3. From *Closer to the Light* by Melvin Morse, M.D., and Paul Perry, © 1988 by Melvin Morse and Paul Perry. Used by permission of Villiard Books, a divison of Random House, Inc. p. 118-119.

4. Michael Newton, *Journey of Souls: Case Studies of Life Between Lives* (Woodbury, Minnesota: Llewellyn Worldwide, Ltd., 2006), p. 71. Used with permission.

Chapter Fourteen

THE PSYCHIC SIGNAL

Everyone who comes to a reading is always curious about how someone can be psychic. The experience of the reading assures them that such abilities exist, as details about the sitter's past, present, and future come to life, as well as particulars from passed relatives; yet no one quite understands the mechanism behind it. Hal Puthoff and Russell Targ have spent the better part of a lifetime studying it with their ESP experiments and remote viewing. J. B. Rhine of the Rhine Research Institute began his exploration back in the 1930s, starting with forced intention on dice rolls. The foundation is still around today. The Society of Psychical Research (SPR) began during the heyday of spiritual mediums in the late 1800s and is still in the mainstream of paranormal research. These groups have done thousands of tests to validate psychic phenomena, from precognition, to remote viewing, to distant mental influence. Still, all we have are theories.

How does a psychic receive information?

How does telepathy and mental influence work?

Part of my internal struggle in giving psychic readings and mediumistic sittings was a lack of understanding about what was really going on. Being a logical, left-brained, analytical kind of guy, I was always uncomfortable before conducting a sitting because I didn't understand how it worked. Like everyone else, I had read a few books on developing psychic skills and listened to the popular celebrity psychics and mediums. But I never felt the explanations I had heard or read about were speaking to the actual mechanisms of the phenomenon. I wasn't satisfied with the explanation my own guides offered me: "You just know. You are a part of all things, and all things are a part of you. Access is inherent."

This kind of reasoning harkens to the quantum holographic theory, a notion stating that even in the smallest particle exists the information of the larger whole. This theory was first conceived by David Bohm in the early 1970s.

Let me explain through the following example why this may be an appropriate analogy.

The way a typical visual hologram works is that a laser beam is split into two beams. One beam strikes the object to be photographed—say, a rose—while the other beam is ricocheted around by a series of mirrors to collide with the first beam. Together, they blast a piece of film. When the two beams hit the film, an interference pattern is created that looks similar to dropping a series of rocks in a pond, causing a series of concentric circles to form in the waves. Later, when another laser beam shines through the film (or in some instances, a bright light will do), an exact three-dimensional image of the object—our rose—will appear. It is so real, one could walk around the flower and see the thorns winding its stem! Now here's where the really fascinating stuff comes in: If you were to cut the holographic film into tiny pieces and then shine a laser through one of the bits, the same three-dimensional image of the rose would appear! Within each one of the separated bits is an image of the same rose. All one would need to do is shine a light through it to see it.

The more Bohm thought about it, the more he came to believe that the universe was one gigantic, flowing hologram. This led him to write the book, *Wholeness and the Implicate Order*, creating a breathtaking new way of looking at reality.[1] As the interference patterns on a holographic plate appear chaotic and random to the naked eye, so, too, does the universe appear chaotic and random in employing holographic principles. Yet within the illusion of chaos on the holographic plate was revealed the order of our image, the rose.

Bohm believed that since everything in the universe was conceived of energy interference patterns on the quantum level, the same thing must be happening everywhere. He stated that because everything in the cosmos is made out of a seamless holographic fabric, that it was meaningless to view the universe as composed of "parts," as it is meaningless to view the different geysers in a fountain as being separate from the rest of the fountain from which they spout. An electron is not an "elementary particle." It is a name given to a certain aspect of the holographic movement. Dividing up reality into parts is a convention because subatomic particles, and everything else in the universe, are no more separate from one another than different patterns in an ornate carpet. Einstein himself alluded to this when he stated that Time and Space were smoothly linked and part of a much larger whole.[2]

Bohm also stated that just because everything is connected doesn't mean individuality cannot exist. To illustrate this, he pointed to little eddies and whirlpools that often form in rivers. At a glance, such eddies appear to be separate things and possess many individual characteristics, such as size, rate, and direction of rotation. But careful scrutiny reveals that it is impossible to determine where any given whirlpool ends and the river begins.[3]

In terms of receiving psychic information, according to the holographic model, it is accessible from any point at which we might be standing. The "information domain" exists in all places, great or small. All a psychic needs to do is "ask, and it is given."

The Electromagnetic Spectrum
the field of energy in which we reside

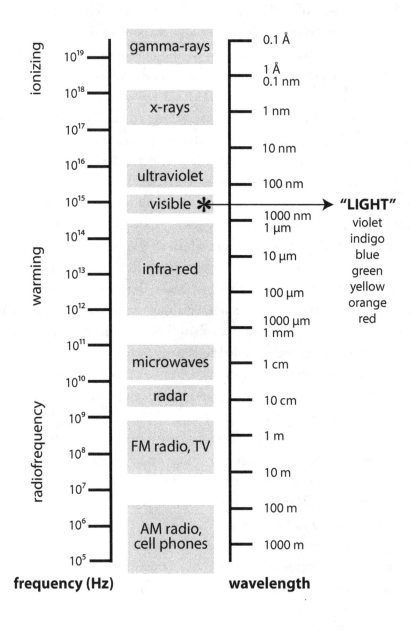

frequency (Hz)

wavelength

Okay. While fascinating, this still seemed too abstract for the left side of my brain when I first began doing readings. The uneasiness persisted for many years. Yes, holography may be a part of the larger picture of psychic functioning, but it still didn't satisfy my desire for understanding the mechanism itself, at least with regard to my own experiences. How was *I* receiving psychic information?

This led me on an interesting search. Since everything is a manifestation or an effect of energy, I went looking in that direction. In particular, I was curious how the human body filtered the energy of reality as a normal process.

I found out that energy exists along the electromagnetic spectrum. Within this scale, between 400 and 790 THz (380 to 750 nm) is the wavelength of light we call visible light, which we are able to see with our eyes.

Between 20 Hz and 20,000 Hz (20 kHz) is the frequency of sound our ears are capable of hearing. All things in the universe fall within energetic frequencies of vibration; however, our bodies aren't necessarily given the gear to incorporate all the information into our brains. Nonetheless, I knew that somewhere along the various frequency spectrums, most likely on the electromagnetic scale, is where psychic information rested. Like everything else, psychic information had to be transmitted via a certain frequency and wavelength.

So how does our body "filter" the information from this spectrum? This was a key to the psychic puzzle.

How do we perceive anything in the world? How do our eyes take a spectrum of light and turn it into pictures that we see *within our minds?* How do our ears take the displacement and vibration of the air and turn it into the sounds we hear *inside our heads?* What about tasting and smelling? In a nutshell, in order to unravel the psychic sense, I needed to understand the standard senses we already use to translate the energy in our environment.

Without getting too technical, here's how sight works:

Wavelengths of light strike our retinas. The retinas, through a process of transduction, convert the patterns of light photons into neuronal (electrical) signals. These signals zoom back into the brain's visual cortex, where they are decoded and created into images that we see "out there."

This is how hearing works: Vibrations enter the ears and are transduced into nerve impulses that are sent back into the brain and decoded into what we hear.

Here's how taste works: A sensory receptor within our taste buds transduces a signal from a vibratory chemical molecule into an impulse that informs the brain how something tastes.

We don't need to get into the other senses, because we can already see what the common denominators are: Turning a certain wavelength and frequency of energy into an electrical impulse that fires neurons in the brain, which allows us to "decode" a signal into a particular sight, smell, sound, or variation of taste or touch. The entrance into our minds is *electrical* and is converted by the body through the process of transduction. It's a miracle going on right under our noses, and we don't even recognize it! How we take our bodies for granted...

Our bodies, it appears, alter an incoming frequency and wavelength into its own brand of electrical impulse that the brain then decodes, much like a computer file. A computer file takes code, strings of 1's and 0's, and connects them into patterns that create programs, sights, and sounds.

It dawned on me: Psychic information would be assimilated through the same mechanical process! How the senses work tells us how the method of "outside" stimuli is filtered and processed inside the brain. Applying it to the reception of psychic information works along the exact same lines.

Say I am communicating with someone's deceased relative. What is the mechanism of that communication, on the basis of what we've learned?

The deceased is transmitting information, whether that be mentally or verbally, at a specific wavelength and frequency. Like light waves or sound waves, a type of energy is brushing up against my body. This energy, like all energy, is vibrating somewhere along the electromagnetic spectrum, but it's very subtle. In some cases, it is *almost* imperceptible. Being sensitive to that energy—sensitive meaning that I am consciously aware that it is striking me—my body takes that subtle vibration—the energy signature—and assimilates it through a similar process to that of other sensory information. It translates the information coded in the vibration through a process of transduction, turning it into an electrical signal that then fires in my brain and decodes itself into the perceived message of the deceased.

Talking with the deceased is not a one-to-one communication, like you and me talking together. No, it requires a unique mode of transmission and reception. Language to us is an adopted use of sounds (words) that we have agreed to have a perceptive meaning (symbols), which we string together to convey an overall message. Without a physical body, the deceased must find other ways of communicating, so the language of the psychic medium is a whole new language—altogether different from what we are used to.

Now, there are some psychics who receive their information audibly—and I am not one of them. Only in small bursts on rare occasions do I actually "hear" anything. Most of what I get is visual snapshots and sensations on my skin, such as tingling, pain, weight, or temperature, along with the emotions of the deceased. Essentially, we as psychics and mediums have to create a *new language*. Our current language is a set of symbols conveyed by words that we can read and decode, or hear and decode. In speaking the psychic language, we still have to create and learn the symbols through a different method of "hearing" and "seeing" than our typical inputs, and this is where the challenge resides. Since everyone creates reality individually within their own minds, it becomes a back-and-forth between the receiver and sender in an effort to understand and decode the symbols being presented.

As to where the psychic signal resides in a frequency domain and at what Hertz, I cannot begin to speculate. One thing that scientists who study telepathy and remote viewing have learned is that there is no degradation in the perceived strength of the signal over vast distances. People have been able to send and receive psychic information from thousands of miles away, on completely different continents, separated by an ocean. The quality of the information appears to be no different than information sent between two people separated by a single wall in an electrically shielded room.

An example of this comes from a famous 1979 study conducted by Marilyn Schlitz and her colleague, Elmar Gruber. At 11:00 AM every day at her home in Detroit, Michigan, Marilyn would attempt to remote-view Gruber wherever he was in Rome, Italy—3,000 miles away. Keep in mind, Marilyn had no idea what his itinerary was or where he might be. Here's an example of one of her transcripts:

> Flight path? Red lights. Strong depth of field. Elmar seems detached, cold...outdoors. See sky dark. Windy and cold. Something shooting upward...Not a private home or anything like that—something—a public facility. He was standing away from the main structure, although he could see it. He might have been in a parking lot or field connected to the structure that identifies the place. I want to say an airport, but that just seems too specific. There was activity and people, but no one real close to Elmar.

Elmar was, in fact, standing on a hill off to the side of a terminal building at Rome International airport.

Marilyn had created ten transcripts for each of Gruber's ten undisclosed sites that he visited. When the experiment was finished, the transcripts were sent to Dr. Hans Bender, a German researcher who arranged the judging by means of using five judges. It turned out that of Marilyn's ten transcripts, six were matched correctly to the target that Elmar was visiting. The likelihood of that happening by chance is less than 6 in 10,000.[4]

What's even more interesting is that somewhere in this psychic signal, information can be embedded about the sender's or the target's emotions (provided the target is a sentient being). When I receive information from deceased relatives, very often I will feel their emotional states. ESP studies also indicate emotions as being a part of the carrier wave information. Galvanic skin response studies have shown receivers picking up emotions of disgust, lust, and feelings of malaise during trials. Since emotions are a by-product of the hypothalamus, somewhere in this psychic signal are instructions to that part of the brain to produce the right chemicals for the receiver to feel.

RECEIVING SYMBOLS

During a particular sitting, a client's deceased father was giving me information about his passing. For some reason, he kept showing me an arm, from the elbow down in a crooked position. It was an enigmatic image, but somehow that arm told me he had been cremated. Ever since, whenever I see that symbol, 95% of the time it means cremation (the other 5% means there was an incident related to an arm). Why this bizarre symbol? I do not know, but somehow it ended up in a library of symbols that I have, and each entity seems to have access to it.

At first this seems quite confusing. It makes you wonder:

1. Where does this library reside? Inside my head?
2. Are there any restrictions on gaining access? Could someone get into my head and find things out about me I wouldn't want known?

Communication, let's face it, is a two-way street. As I said earlier, it is creating a new language. When I do a sitting, I ask the spirit questions, and I have to be "open" to receiving the answers. That openness is an opportunity for an entity to access whatever conscious information is accessible about me. Somewhere, the library of symbols I receive is available, most likely at the subatomic level and not necessarily inside my physical brain. The late Karl Lashley discovered that rats that had 90% of their brains removed were still able to run their mazes as easily as they could when their brains were intact. In humans, memories are divided up between the right and left hemispheres of the brain. Interestingly, tests have shown that stimulation of the same area of the brain twice does not generate the same memories. Additionally, things get really fascinating when you consider that doctors who had started removing parts of people's brains to help cure epileptic seizures found that the surgeries didn't create any loss of memory. It's almost as if memories are processed seemingly at random throughout the mind, or possibly throughout the whole brain in a sort of holographic design, where each part of the "memory hologram" is accessible anywhere throughout the spectrum.[5] However, memories get even more mysterious when we consider the memories retained by individuals who have come back from NDEs. How can these people remember anything if they were declared clinically dead or were in a comatose state?

It is hard to say how memories are stored, but they are kept at some level where the psychic eye can access them. The location may exist nonlocally; that is, it is not confined to any one place or time, but may be accessible anywhere or anytime. The encoding of our memories into this fabric of eternal Space/Time would be at the level of consciousness itself—an area not understood by science. It would not be found on neurons or synapses, or any kind of physical structure, though it may require the possession of a physical brain to unlock the frequency domain of their location to bring it into ego-mind conscious awareness.

The storage medium of this symbolic or memory library would still be some form of energy, possibly interference waves, much like our earlier version of holography, suspended in simultaneous Time and accessible by quantum consciousness. When accessed by consciousness across the domain, the holographic nature of the information is received. As a hologram shows a three-dimensional replica of an object, a universal hologram might also contain a multidimensional component that shares the emotional aspect of the target. This is mere speculation, of course, and there is no scientific method for testing this hypothesis. Nonetheless, some kind of signal is received in the conscious mind that is then decoded to be able to reveal psychic information.

Considering the various kinds of psychic phenomena (such as telepathy and clairvoyance), it raises the question: How is that energy received during remote viewing? Is the receiver actually leaving his or her body and "going" to the location? Many of the descriptions gathered during remote-viewing trials suggest that the receiver is indeed at the location. They describe visuals as "floating above" and "zooming into," as if physically at the location and moving around the environment.

In this case, information isn't being directed at the receiver, as is hypothesized during a mediumship sitting, but rather, the *focus* of consciousness has left the body to dwell in some other location. Remote viewers do not describe leaving their bodies the same way OBEs do, in terms of feeling a shift of energy, tingling, and leaving the body and floating out of the room.

If remote viewers are not traveling astrally, then what are they doing? It is perhaps a different type of consciousness excursion, one that is admittedly hard to pin down. Remote viewers do not claim to be carrying their astral bodies while witnessing a location. But on some subtle level, their consciousness has traversed Time and Space to rest in a different location other than the room they were sitting in. Considering that there isn't any lag time between lying down and mentally arriving at the location, per se, it appears that remote viewers are achieving this sojourn through a nonlocal quantum effect. This is further corroborated by the remote viewing trial mentioned in chapter 3, where Pat Price described the Palo Alto pool, but from the perception of nearly fifty years in the past. Astral travel, to my knowledge, does not include Time travel, but quantum reality does. Though a remote viewer's astral body may not be floating out of the room, through the walls, and then across the ocean, it appears that the mind's eye—which exists independently of an astral body—is.

Since quantum reality states that an observer is needed to collapse waves into particles (or possibilities into actualities), the observer itself is a force of deliberate energy—deliberate in the sense that it can take an otherwise random set of energetic possibilities and turn them into one deliberate reality. It also suggests that this quantum consciousness observer can exist and/or perceive through some kind of nonphysical medium any*where* and any*time*. Therefore, remote viewing takes on a whole new cloud of enigma, tantalizing us with further possibilities and depths inherent within the Soul.

On some level, the mind is able to perceive distant lands, and in some cases different Times. Since the nature of the Soul is Timeless and Formless, eternal and yet physically Nothing but thought, the sojourns and psychic communications become quite natural. As a formless entity shaped only by our thoughts, one could argue that all things and all Time exist as one enormous Mind, expressing itself as many interrelated thoughts. Indeed, many philosophers and scientists believe this to be the case. This, again, demonstrates the unity of all life being One. One thing always has an effect on another. If this were not the case, then the absence of effect would prove the existence of separation and division.

The information obtained by the traveling mind in a remote-viewing situation would be processed by the physical body in much the same way as other sensory data. On a subtle energy level, the consciousness of the observer, through quantum reality, is energetically entangled with the target location. This entanglement of energy is processed by the consciousness to be transduced back into the right temporal lobe of the entangled physical body lying in the viewing room.

This transduction results in a mental (psychic) image of the visitation of the quantum mind's eye at the target. I theorize that this information is transmitted along a similar frequency domain as other psychic phenomena. It is a subtle energy vibration returned to the physical body in order to communicate with a second observer—the listener recording the viewer's findings. In this case, the remote viewer supplies the subtle energy himself, which comes as a result of his quantum entanglement at the location, in conjunction with the entanglement of his own physical body. This is slightly different from spirit communication, in that the spirit provides the energy, in part, for the information he would like the medium to receive.

I refer to this process of psychic energy reception and transduction as SEVC, Subtle Energy Vibration Communication. In a nutshell, it is the reception of psychic energy that strikes the receiver's psychic receptors (most likely the right temporal lobe), and, through the process of transduction, turns the signals into electrical impulses that fire inside the physical brain. This neuronal activity produces images, sounds, feelings, smells, and tastes that otherwise are not being received within the range of the normal senses.

It is a process of communication between the receiver's consciousness and that of a sender. A sender may be someone who is alive—existing in the frequency range of this dimension by using telepathy, for example—or, it may be a deceased person—someone occupying a vibrational frequency range outside the body's normal sensory filters. In some cases, like remote viewing and/or astral travel, the sender and receiver may be the same person, part of whom is focused through nonlocal quantum processes, relaying information back to the physical body, again through subtle energy transduction.

This energy is subtle because it requires focus in order to engage it. It is not typically recognized from a state of normal beta consciousness. The energy exists on a continuum slightly out of the beta brainwave spectrum.

GHOSTS AND SEVC

So, what about earthbound spirits? In some ways, they share the same subtle energy spectrum. Why shouldn't they? Ghosts will speak to me in the same way as a client's deceased grandfather, through telepathic or clairvoyant images and sensations. These same types of communications exist just as same with living people, as we have heard stories of people feeling and knowing what was happening to a distant relative. Since the consciousness of all humanity is, in essence, a gigantic field of undifferentiated energy separated only by our egos and perceptions, beneath all of that, we exist as one Mind. The "I" of me is the same "I" as you, as well as the same "I" of a deceased person. The only separation is the recognition of ego and mental psychic structures rising off that single foundation. Carl Jung discovered this unity when he coined the term, *collective unconscious.*

Now, the human body vibrates within certain frequency ranges. Someone who has died will obviously no longer be vibrating at that rate and speed; the new "spirit-body" will have a vibration all its own. When entering a haunted location, that different energy permeates the atmosphere and can be felt by psychics and other sensitives. For me, the energy affects my legs. If I feel like I am walking through thick mud, there is an earthbound spirit nearby.

Those in the Washington State Ghost Society who consider themselves non-psychics always undermine their abilities. Often, they will walk into a particular bedroom or some other auspicious location, not realizing that they are, on some level, detecting the exact area where an entity is hiding. They could investigate anywhere, yet they are instinctively drawn to where the spirit is located, even before I mention it. This is because all of us are wired to detect these signals to some degree, though some people may not recognize the SEVC signal consciously. Instead, their subconscious picks it up, and they instinctively react to it.

SEVC has its gradations. With anything, it all depends on the mind and on the energy. Some energy is not subtle at all, but still sends a definite psychic message—like when your hair stands on end, telling you to stay out of that dark alley, or the burning in your chest tells you that a deceased person passed from chest-related issues. The more psychics work "in the zone," the less subtle the energy feels. Nonetheless, that is how it begins…the psychic messages don't always enter the consciousness very intensely or "loud" at first—just light and passive. In some cases, it is almost indistinguishable from one's imagination, until you try pushing it aside, and it keeps popping back up like a bad penny (though it usually isn't bad).

TESTING FOR YOUR OWN SENSE OF SEVC

There have been many books written about developing psychic abilities, so I won't spend too much time on this section. However, I do want you to be aware that it is an inherent ability of consciousness and the Soul. If you are interested in exploring psychic abilities further, believe it or not, I found the *Idiots* and *Dummies* versions on this topic to be excellent and would highly recommend them. The ones I have in my library are, *The Complete Idiots Guide to Being Psychic,* and *The Complete Idiots Guide to Spirit Communication.* They are both light-hearted and filled with good, practical information.

The first step in being able to detect an energy that is a little different from your own is to be aware of what your own feels like. You would think walking around with yourself all day would give you an idea. In truth, it's really not something you normally pay attention to. In order to detect a psychic signal, you will need to be able to isolate the sensation of the signal and differentiate it from yourself. You need to be able to feel within yourself that the source of what you are sensing is not of your own mind and energies. You will have to let your own energy recede into the background to "step into" the subtle energy vibration and "turn up the volume" to receive some kind of communication.

The best way to get started is to sit quietly for about five minutes. Make sure there aren't any distractions—you need to be isolated from any potential interference. One of the best places for this...is the bathroom. I'm serious!

Once you have found your ideal place, take a few deep, relaxing breaths. Think about nothing except your breathing. On the inhalation, bring the breath in up to the count of three, hold for two seconds, then exhale to the count of five. By the third time, you should start to feel your body's frequency shift, if only slightly, as the relaxation response kicks in.

Take a few more breaths, only this time, breathe in at more of your usual rate. Don't necessarily make them deep breaths. As your breathing normalizes, start to observe yourself. That is, start looking at what is going on "inside." Ask yourself—"What am I feeling? What do I feel like? What do I—[insert your name here]—feel like energetically?" At first, you may not be able to describe it in words. That's okay, so long as you at least acknowledge your own sense of vibration. Sit with this feeling of yourself for as long as you can. Examine it. Imagine taking a tiny portion of your mind and dropping it into your energy and swimming around like a deep-sea explorer. Discover your energy!

Does your energy inspire a color? Myriad colors? A musical note, perhaps? This is you! This is your vitality—your energy of Being. You may have never noticed it before, but here you are! When you have placed this sense of Self in your memory banks, you are ready for the next step.

PSYCHOMETRY

Psychometry is the act of holding an object and receiving impressions from it. It is the best way to learn and develop your abilities in tuning into the signal. The best items for me are rings and watches, although typically, any kind of jewelry will do. Caution: It should be jewelry worn by one person. If a ring is a hand-me-down, you may end up receiving impressions of a previous owner, which may be difficult to validate. I suggest trying this with a friend and making it a game, if you'd like. You need some way of validating the impressions you receive.

Once you have the object in your hand, take a few deep, relaxing breaths to again find your feeling of Self. Then turn your attention to the object. Don't think about it, just *feel* it. Notice how it has a different energy from you. Ask yourself: Does it feel lighter than your energy, or heavier? Does it elicit a color in your mind? Musical notes? All the same questions you asked of yourself, you can ask of the object in the palm of your hand.

Take it to the next level. Ask, "What does this object have to say about the person it belongs to?" Then, without judging or expecting anything, just observe your body and mind. Notice any thoughts that "pop in" or suddenly fill your mind. Notice, too, if any parts of your body feel different, such as tingling, heaviness, soreness, lightness, or if any colors emerge in your brain across a portion of an imaginary body. Sometimes these things will seem like quick flashes, about the speed of a camera flash in a dark room. Nonetheless, this is reception—you just have to be alert to it. Report your findings to the owner for verification.

Another method of sensing different subtle energies is to go outside and hold the leaf of a plant or touch the bark of a tree—or even a rock. Each one of these will have its own vibration. Though it may seem silly, ask yourself the same questions you did in the previous experiment. Note how the flavor of energy of the object is different from You. Again, it will start out as a subtle energy. But the more your focus on it, the "louder" it will become. It may take a couple of tries before you are successful. If you find you are not sensing the different energies in your hands, try closing your eyes to see if that helps. Occasionally, our eyes might distract our sensing brain with the minutia going on around us.

ARE YOU RIGHT OR WRONG?

It's all a matter of interpretation. Some impressions will be spot-on in telling you exactly what things are. Sometimes they will be odd, disjointed, and perhaps even confusing. There's a reason for this: The information isn't for you—it's for the client.

I carry around a small white board to draw on whenever I give readings. This way, a client can have an idea as to what I am seeing in my mind's eye. In some cases, I don't always know what an image means, but when I draw it on the board, nine times out of ten, the client does. Remember, the information I receive isn't for me, it's for the client—I am just the medium being used to receive it (like a radio tuner). My clients have come to appreciate this method of drawing the images, and I think it adds a greater dimension to the whole experience.

Not every impression you get will mean something or be accurate. You can always be wrong—and there's nothing wrong with that. No psychic is ever 100% accurate; we simply do not know enough about the psychic signal to define it other than that it is some form of subtle energy. When starting out, you may be working to decipher your own thoughts and energies from the psychic signal, and this will no doubt result in a few "misses." It's natural. It's a part of development. Even seasoned psychics will have their "bad" days, where it's hard to get anything, and what does come through gets confused with the psychic's own mental chatter.

After working at psychometry for a while, you will gain wonderful experiential knowledge that the energy of life is eternal; it never dissipates, and—like holography—contains information about a person's larger Self. It opens the door to an understanding of nonlocal phenomena, as might happen if you took hold of a ring only to dis-cover a vacation in the client's upcoming future and that a plane flight will be part of it, to which the client says, "That's absolutely right! How did you get that?" You not only tapped into the information through their energy, but you may also be able to tell them whether or not they will have a good time, or if something stressful will happen. That is first-hand experience of tapping into the ruler of simultaneous Time and witnessing a potential future (it is potential only because after the reading, the client could change her mind and shift her energy com-pletely, thus altering the outcome).

COMMUNICATING WITH "THE DEAD"

First of all, you have to get over the notion that they are dead. They are not. They are simply vibrating at an energy frequency that our bodies have not been equipped to filter in the same way we do in our normal everyday lives. This doesn't mean you can't communicate. I believe that the psychic signal covers many bandwidths, and connect-ing to those on the Other Side occupies one of them. I prefer to think of the deceased as Outside People, meaning that they exist outside the physical body, while my sitter is an Inside Person, still existing inside the body. Both are very much alive and full of energy.

Our discussion of psychometry will have given you the basis for determining whether a separate energy signal has reached you, or if it's just yourself conjuring something up in the corners of your mind. It may not always be clear-cut, but you will have the experience to delve into it with some level of confidence. To connect with the deceased, I would still recommend holding an object that belonged to the person to better connect with the energy. If not, you can use an object from the sitter.

How does this work?

Going through the sitter is another example of quantum

entanglement. The sitter will have had some kind of relationship with the deceased person—therefore, her energy will be the link needed to open the door to the Other Side. Here, you will have double-duty—recognizing the sitter's energy as being separate from yours, then being on the lookout for the energy of the deceased.

The energy field of the deceased is, again, a subtle form of energy. It may be very faint. In many cases it is not, especially if there is a lot to say. At any rate, you will have to be able to distinguish the difference between your energy, the energy of the sitter, and the energy of the deceased.

Once you recognize that other personality in the room, just observe it. Ask it the usual questions. Then, as you have practiced, pay attention to what flashes into your mind and what sensations come across your body. If you are lucky, you might actually hear the deceased speaking words to you—this is called *clairaudience*. I'm not that lucky, although sometimes a spirit will tap my musical memory and use song lyrics to get their message across. This communication with the Other Side may only last a few minutes, or it may last a few hours—it all depends. It takes practice. You may only get one "hit" the first time out. Like anything, the more you do it, the more you learn, the more you recognize, and the more wisdom you gain.

If you do choose to go the route of communicating with the Other Side, understand that it is not something to be taken lightly. You are dealing with real people who do not exist in the same reality you do. They are by no means any "higher" or "lower" than people you already know. They come with their hang-ups, quirks, and personalities, but also with perspectives that are quite different at times than what we are used to. It's a big door to open, and once you do, your life may never be the same again.

Responsibility comes with it.

It's not for people who can be easily swayed by emotions or who like to take on other people's "stuff." It requires grounding, stamina, and a sense of personal space to keep your own identity intact and safe.

And there's risk.

I'm not saying you're going to come across some horrendously evil spirit that will want to posses you, or anything in that kind of dramatic Hollywood sense, but you will have people "knocking on your head" at times when you don't want them to. And yes, you might get some spirits that don't like you or try chewing you out (or are very insistent about butting in and taking up your time). You may even unwittingly attract an earthbound entity, who then creates haunting phenomena in your house. Are you prepared for that? It may frighten you.

If you have trouble identifying with and working with people in the "normal" world, then don't even bother with the spirit world.

The biggest question you need to ask yourself is, why bother going this route in the first place? For me, it was because I wanted to help people, to really make a difference, and to discover for myself what the inner spiritual drive was that continually sabotaged everything I tried to do to be "normal." It is not something you pursue to be "cool" or famous, or rich, or any of that. As soon as your ego comes into the picture during a reading, you will lose your psychic abilities, period. Not because the spirits are punishing you, but because you have to divorce your ego from your mind in order to lock into the psychic signal in the first place. Readings that you give to another person are never about you—it is always about the client.

Now, you will find that there are other psychics out there that do have egos. This is because they are looking to use the psychic tool as a sort of validation for their own sense of worth. It is a ring they wear on their Souls that says, "See, because I can do this, I am special. And because you think you can't—that makes me *really really* special."

No, it doesn't.

It's a gift that everyone has—some people just choose not to believe in it or to cultivate it. That's okay. Everyone—psychic or otherwise—is special. It doesn't matter what one can and cannot do. Egoic psychics, despite what they may preach, use the psychic gift as a tool of division and not unification; it's a "me versus them" mentality, a way for the psychic to feel "extraordinary." Otherwise, she would have to believe herself to be just "ordinary"—and that's boring. "I am different, I am better."

No. We are all One. And each person is worthwhile.

Such us-versus-them mentality has been the downfall of humanity. And as the next chapter demonstrates, this thinking has kept us bound firmly in the shackles of spiritual ignorance, to the point where now, we are in serious woes of division, distrust, and potential nuclear obliteration of millions.

NOTES

1. Michael Talbot, *The Holographic Universe* (New York: HarperCollins Publishers, 1991), p. 46. Used with permission.

2. Ibid., p. 48.

3. Ibid., p. 49.

4. From the book *Miracles of Mind.* Copyright ©1998, 1999 by Russell Targ and Jane Katra, Ph.D. Reprinted with permission of New World Library, Novato, California. www.newworldlibrary.com. See pp. 104-105.

5. Melvin Morse, M.D., with Paul Perry, *Where God Lives: The Science of the Paranormal and How Our Brains are Linked to the Universe* (New York: HarperCollins Publishers, 2000), p. 50. Used with permission.

Chapter Fifteen

A REEVALUATION OF OLD-WORLD RELIGIONS

A book about the Soul wouldn't be complete without touching upon religion. For thousands of years, the Soul has been the province of religion, whether that religion be Judeo-Christian, Hindu, Muslim, Mayan, or any other kind of old-world civilization.

Today, many people hold traditional beliefs about their Souls, as handed down by those old cultures. Still others, though they may not belong officially to any church, search deep into the past for what ancient mystics thought about the nature of man's relationship to the divine. They will quote from sacred Vedic tradition or traditional Native American customs, for instance. They focus the quest for spirituality and the answers to the Soul in the past, as if the past had a wider doorway into discovering the sacred and the divine than the one we have right now. The truth of the matter is, nobody in the past had any more leverage than we have. Not any one of these ancient cultures was any closer to (or further away from) the divine than we are today. The connection to the Age of Miracles, as well as insight to the Soul, is just as available *right now* as it had ever been in the past.

The point of power is always in the present.

Now is always the eternal moment.

This means that the answers to the questions we have about spirituality and the Soul exist *in this very moment*—not in the ancient past. By looking into the ancient past, you confine yourself to limited religious ideologies that resulted from living in an ancient environment and its sociopolitical-economic conditions. Though the ancients may have had some insight, they did not have any greater access to spiritual knowledge than we do today. (Some would argue that the Greek philosophers were extraordinary in terms of deep thinking and spiritual insight. Unfortunately, Greek philosophy was never assimilated into religious constructs.) In fact, when it came to the center of religion and orthodoxy, I would argue that these early believers were far more ignorant of *spiritual* knowledge and enlightenment than we are today. Instead, they created thought-constructs surrounding their environment and traditional customs and claimed that they heralded from sources beyond man's world. Thus, instead of spirituality, we have *religion*. For one, they had no scientific methodology whatsoever to measure the effects of consciousness and define a measurement for life and the nature of the Soul; and second, consciousness as a way to understanding spirituality was completely foreign to them. Possibly, in a very minute way, they may have had a notion of our multidimensional natures, but had a hard time separating it from the other superstitious frameworks running rampant at the time. Many of the ancients did not understand our abilities to traverse time, affect quantum particles, and shape reality. All this was generally attributed to forces *outside* the realm of man, an understandable error when you consider the conditions of the time ancient man was living in.

By accepting the perceived virtues of an old-world religion, one also, by default, must accept its vices. Each era is made up of certain psychological (mental) beliefs, attitudes, and perceptions that inform how doctrine is to be written and addressed to the masses. When I say "to the masses," I mean the masses *as they existed at the time the material was written.* In looking for information about spirituality and the Soul in these past ideologies, you can only see what the ancients *thought* about such things. When we take a look at the other ways they interacted, we must ask ourselves: Should we also believe as they did about the nature of the Soul and spirituality?

The farther back in time we go in the objective search for reason, we can see the ancient world as being completely different from our own. It is safe to say that their thought processes were different, as well. Life back then wasn't just survival of the fittest, it was conquests between kingdoms and empires—a struggle for national identity. Attached to these national identities were perceptions of gods and goddesses, and each group believed theirs was superior to the others. This view was, admittedly, a natural inclination that helped to prop up the tribe—to bring a kind of social encouragement from "on high" and a sense of order out of chaos, a place of being in an otherwise barbaric world. Remember, these people had no knowledge of electricity, magnetism, or even gravity. Nearly 90% or more could neither read nor write, and thus were unable to seek out the knowledge that would have enabled them to effectively form the right questions to help them separate fact from fiction. The world was combative—it was often a struggle to survive amid foreign invaders and, without scientific understanding and modern technologies to enhance the environment, nearly impossible to find the niche for humanity itself within the tapestry of nature. In such an environment, with most of humanity living in ignorance, one could only imagine that God was a being of jealous, hostile, and vengeful temperament and that life was always on the brink of calamity. Yet, this calamity was not God-made—it was man-made.

Since their customs, lifestyle, and way of being are so far removed from our own, it is not only risky business to define modern spirituality according to their texts, but it is, in my opinion, just plain foolish.

As mentioned earlier, they were no closer or further away from the divine than we are today. They approached it in their own manner, on the basis of the civilization at the time. We have evolved thousands of years beyond that *in all other areas,* though so many still cling to a hope of spirituality as they believed it to have been in the past.

This is not to say we should not acknowledge what came before. Absolutely, we should praise and honor any achievements we have made in the past, but we should also not bind ourselves to the shackles of the past when we are meant to be moving forward.

Old-world religions are representative of that old world—its hopes and dreams, its fears and sorrows. It does not and *cannot* represent our world today. The founders of these old religions were completely ignorant about reality and consciousness, in the face of what we know today; they cannot speak to the complexities of our lives and the way we interact with the world and universe—it is simply beyond their comprehension. A "scientist" from the first century would have no concept of the theories of electricity, much less a working computer used on a rocket that could fly to the moon, or a satellite that could photograph what is floating "out in heaven." That he could not think in the *style* we can, on the basis of our evolution of critical thinking, indicates that we must acknowledge that his perceptions of spirituality and the divine are also representative of his time, and are therefore limited to that moment. Likewise, we cannot relate to his style of thinking because we are so far removed from it. However, from where we stand, we can understand his self-imposed limitations, as we would understand the predicament of a child who has yet to learn how to change the television channel or how to tie his own shoes—his mind hasn't developed enough to figure out such things, and until he does, he remains limited in his capabilities. This is not to say that those who came before had less mental capacity than we do today—only that their understanding was limited relative to the circumstances in which they lived.

Too often, we hear people say, "The Bible says..." or "The Koran says..." as if to say the creative life principle that manufactured the entire universe (God) wrote the material. Indeed, there are millions who honestly believe such texts to be a deity's thoughts and even assert that the words arrived by divine inspiration and were offered by supernatural means to the author. (On the basis of its assertion of divine revelation, a great many books beyond the Bible—including this one—could be considered to have been procured via divine inspiration. In truth, with regard to Biblical material, at least, it was a matter of Church elders gathering together at councils and voting about what was to be considered "divine" and "authoritative." And whenever a bunch of men get together to vote—aka exert power—they also come with their own agendas, prejudices, and vices. It's a natural thing.)

Let us remember that men who lived 1500 to 2000 years ago also believed that the earth was flat and that epilepsy was demonic possession. (Contrary to what some people in the modern revisionist schools are postulating, they did *not* believe the earth was spherical, but more like a pie plate, as Biblical passages are reinterpreted). Men mistook the bubonic plague as a manifestation of God's wrath, as opposed to the result of a lack of cleanliness and the pestilence of rats. Man believed in the first century that a woman couldn't be "saved" unless she could transfigure into a man. He also believed the sun rotated around the earth. He believed all of these things and wrote them down, oftentimes believing that God had said them. Knowing this, we must be skeptical when it comes to the notion that any literary passages were divinely inspired by a holy ghost or deity. Indeed, the authors might have felt inspired, but that inspiration would have been couched in the framework of the society *as it existed at that time*. This is the brutal, honest truth, which we in the twenty-first century must come to terms with.

As we look at some of the other customs in those early centuries, it is evident that the religious beliefs become an outgrowth of that civilization and therefore mirror the psychological framework that existed.

Western religion came out of Rome, and the Romans were a highly superstitious people. This bunch read signs and omens from animals' entrails, and believed that trees and rocks could harbor angry or benevolent spirits. Oftentimes, children were told tales of nasty creatures that would eat them if they behaved badly. It was no wonder then that many Romans wore amulets and charms to ward off evil. The Roman Senate, in its infinite wisdom, consulted prophetic books as a way of avoiding a god's wrath during times of crisis, as disasters were perceived by Romans to be manifestations of divine disapproval, and unusual phenomena as portents of catastrophe. No official state business was ever really held without the taking of omens and auspices, based on the movement of birds. The type of bird, how fast it flew, how high, and its direction, could all indicate something about the mind of a god and affect state business. Even the army resorted to consulting auspices, and they carried with them cages of sacred chickens. When cake was crumbled onto the floor before them, if the chickens ate the crumbs it was a good omen. If not, things weren't so cheery.[1] So let us keep in mind that in this context of superstition, the Biblical authors were born, raised, and wrote their material.

Modern humanity has evolved in many areas—technology, science, and psychology—but when it comes to religion and spirituality, we have not evolved much at all. Of course, this has not really happened by choice, as old-world religions have long served as the whipping masters going to work on the backs of our eternal Souls, threatening us with inquisitions and excommunications (aka social suicide). "Turning the other cheek" and "loving thy enemy" held no sway over these ideologies, as they slaughtered millions in conquests for gold and the acquisition of nations. Let us also not forget the thousands of Jews slaughtered in the Holocaust, which the organized religious institutions remained silent about. Today, there are bloody and brutal conflicts going on in the Middle East, costing hundreds of soldiers and innocent civilians their lives every year and warping (emotionally and mentally) the survivors, with fanatics crying "Jihad!" to rally more participants to their cause.

Today we are taught that the writers of these holy books were all pious men that were touched by the Holy Spirit, enabling them to write these treatises. I figured that since my eternal Soul was at stake when I embarked upon my quest for understanding spirituality, I didn't want to take that notion on chance and read up on the subject. I found out that nothing could be further from the truth. Let's take western religion as an example.

What we have today is simply a stack of old-world material that outlived the others through bloody engagements, wars, and attrition. In the case of Christianity, the Bible was not canonized all at once, but rather over the course of 300 years, and even then, some Christian churches refused particular works that were considered by some priests to be inspired, while other works were considered uninspired. These leftover works collectively became known as the Apocrypha.

Most modern churchgoers seem to believe that it was a straight-line process. This, too, is erroneous. Clashes between early Christians lasted for hundreds of years, as sects quibbled over what books were inspired and which ones weren't, and what certain passages *really* meant to say; even the nature of Jesus and the triune godhead were not all fixed theological positions until the fourth century. There was Docetism, which stated that Jesus' body was an illusion, that he was not a man at all, but a pure spirit. Naturally, this was considered heretical. As was Arianism, which stated that Jesus was not the same as God in the Triune godhead, but the highest spiritual being in relation to God. This creed was originally ruled heretical by the first Council of Nicea in 325, then exonerated in 335, then considered heretical again by the Council of Constantinople in 381. Stop and consider that 300 years after the supposed event, they could not say for certain just who or what Jesus was? And we claim to know the answers today, 2,000 years later?

All this raises an important question: Why would anyone base the value of his eternal Soul on any of this old-world thinking? The Bible, like all holy books, is a product of its time—the work of men assembled over a few hundred years, writing text, interpolating passages, and rewriting to present different translations and meanings. In all honesty, this is not God working through men, this is men working to create an institution, one to help create a sense of standards for a community and to help bring order out of chaos in a chaotic world of quarreling nations—noble causes, to be sure. As I have already alluded, most people in these early centuries were illiterate, ignorant, superstitious, and lacked much of the critical thinking skills we have today. This is not meant to degrade them, it is simple fact. And it is from this bunch that the foundation for historical Christian teachings comes, and people 2,000 years later still believe it has a direct effect on their spirituality.

In truth, the only effect this foundation has on one's spirituality is what one *chooses to believe in one's mind.* Even the illustrious figure of Christ himself has no *real* power over anyone's soul (it may sound blasphemous, but there it is). This sort of tale, again, is an outgrowth of limited, first century thinking.

The Jesus of the first century cannot speak to the spirit of twenty-first century man. He does not know his mind, his environment, and his way of life. He could only speak to the people of his time, in the context of his environment and mental processes. Outside of that, confusion abounds and atrocities occur, as time rolls the process of evolution away from the value systems and culture the religion was birthed in. And we have all seen the consequences of that.

Old-world religions stem from old-world thinking. By accepting those ancient beliefs, one also commits to accepting the ancients' vices and limitations, which are totally unnecessary and degrading to the true multidimensional nature of the Soul. It also invites corruption, as doctrine gets twisted away from its roots and becomes "retranslated" to fit newer times. Thus, it's taken out of its historical context and reconstituted to make right any person's view on whatever they wish, with an attempt to say it is "accepted by God" *in the modern world.* Nothing, and I mean nothing, could be further from the truth. Too often, we hear people say, "You are taking the passage out of context." To that, on occasion, they may be right. Unfortunately, today we are taking the whole book and every passage out of the historical and environmental context of its authors, and that is a far more egregious error when it comes to the value of our Souls and its meaning.

THE FLAW OF ANCIENT RELIGIONS

The majority of ancient beliefs share a common denominator that carries the root of their limitations. Spiritually speaking, it isn't right and wrong that matters—only knowledge versus ignorance. Of this, the base, lower-level thinking of old-world illiterate, superstitious, and unevolved psychological man had no idea. Instead, they equated ignorance with sin, and further extended this mistaken view to the greatest error of spiritual ignorance by declaring that humanity was somehow separate or cut off from God. Life in any form is no more cut off from God than your thumb is from your hand. Ancient man, who unfortunately saw with his eyes and not his Soul, allowed the illusion of separation to inform his egoic mind, to which he then superimposed such erroneous vision into his view of God.

The idea of man being separate from God is a very ancient idea indeed. But, as the earth was also believed flat, such an idea is not at all true. If anything, in a holographic universe, God exists in even the smallest particle.

The ancients had the perception of God wrong. To begin with, the force of life and of creation—the Creative Principle—is not a separate deity or entity; it is not an individual form. The perception of "God the Father" is the product of the old-world feudal system, as evidenced by Heaven being referred to as a kingdom and God being the King. Here we have man creating God out of his ancient-world psychological structure and making him male to contrast the pagan, goddess-worshipping centers that were prevalent at the time, and creating for him his own feudal empire, contemporaneous with the times.

The creative principle is seen within all life, therefore God is not an individual being, but rather the summation of all life everywhere. Just as your cells make up your body, we could be likened to the cells of God's body. Our own cells mirror our macroexistence; that is, cells communicate with other cells, give birth to more cells, take in food and excrete waste—they even change and evolve over time. This can also be said of us being cells in the body of God, which means that God, too, is always in a process of evolution—and like us, exists multidimensionally, both inside and outside Space and Time, not separate from us, but part and parcel of us. God is neither male or female, nor wrathful or vengeful—those are human experiences created by human energy interacting with the Zero Point Field to create events and circumstances, on the basis of the thoughts and energies of the observers. Ancient man, who was largely ignorant of his own creative mechanisms and skills, laid the blame on a fictitious source outside his views of understanding—precisely because he didn't understand.

However, as startling as this may sound, an incorrect view of God was not the ancients' greatest flaw in the proselytizing of their ancient religions. The greatest flaw was in the people's view of separation and division through the erroneous concept of "chosen people." In other words—Saint and Sinner, Us and Them.

These old-world religions thrived on the concept of sinners and saints, a division wholly barbaric to the collective reality of consciousness and spirit. For there to be a "chosen people," there must also be a "not-chosen group," which, inevitably, must either accept the religious view of the "saints" or be annihilated as "sinners." This is the grossest and most damning practice of all organized religions. It is also the reason for their failures over the centuries.

It has always been the goal of every religion to convert people to the "one true faith." Unfortunately, the one true faith can never wholly civilize or "save" the world because its doctrine is based on duality and separation, the antithesis of the Soul's nature and existence. In order for there to be saints, these religions also need sinners to contrast themselves against, and it is this flaw that will forever keep organized religion from reaching the true heights of enlightened spirituality.

It may also put the rest of us at risk for the unwarranted massacre of innocent millions.

The more this division is taught and perpetuated, the more polarization will occur between all the major religions—especially those that focus on "sinners" and the need to wipe out "infidels." It is a frightening thing that old-world religions, who are ignorant of the true connection between all life and God, are still in positions of power with the potential to access nuclear weapons. If this doomsday scenario ever comes to pass, the Inquisition of the Dark Ages will be made to look like child's play. It is an ignorance that is barbarously bold, which perpetuates this erroneous belief of separation between life and God. The power of life cannot be divided against Itself—to believe *that* is the great mortal sin. To beat yourself with your own appendage is the domain of a madman, and old-world religions continue to contort modern minds into doing just that.

We must relegate these old-world religions to the past, where they belong. They were never written nor inspired by the Creative Life Principle that fashioned this universe—they were created by men who, with good intention, tried to bring order to their chaotic world by using the only means they had at the time. With their base understanding of the true nature of the divine, which was colored by the circumstances in which they lived, these men fashioned a limited perspective of God and an erroneous view of humanity's relationship not only with God, but also with himself. Ignorant of the power of his own mind, these ancient priests created the most dangerous kind of personal and mass psychology, which was destined to extract from man's consciousness the worst acts and behaviors possible. Let's examine that psychology more closely, shall we?

YOU ARE "BORN A SINNER"

Any psychologist will tell you about the damage caused by repetitive slander. Imagine a small child, as young as two years old, being told that he is a bad boy and that he is a disappointment in his parents' eyes. Imagine the inner damage it would cause, were he to be told that on a weekly basis. How would that repetitious thought inform his consciousness? How would it affect his behavior?

As he grows older, it's pretty obvious that his psychological structure will give way to less than perfect relationships, unsatisfactory physical skills and traits, and negative behaviors. How could it not? He was told from the time of his earliest memories what a disappointment he is! This would also create an enormous amount of internal confusion—second-guessing himself at every turn, oftentimes giving up, because "I can only do wrong." All this leads to depression of his immune system, as he overloads on stress and the conditions of drama playing out around him, which seem to be "happening to him." Soon, he finds himself cut down with disease—cancer, leukemia, what have you.

In today's world, on the basis of our knowledge of how the mind stores memories and acts on repetitive messages, we can see how this youngster's life could unfold. Were he not to unlearn what his parents had guilted him into to believing, he could also become a drug user or alcoholic or engage in any kind of self-abuse—creating additional negative psychological structures capable of blocking him at every turn at he tries to reach for success.

Now, let's take this very real psychological condition and parlay it into the most egregious of the ancient religions' acts of ignorance:

foisting it upon the mass populace.

Let's start with a small group of people. Say this bunch—uneducated, superstitious—believes in their innermost beings that they have fallen short of God's wishes and consider themselves "sinners," requiring some sort of salvation. Imagine that feeling of guilt, sadness, and self-deprecation. Let's say they not only believe it, but they remind themselves of it on a daily or weekly basis for several years. Then they decide to pay a visit to the next village, declaring everyone there to be sinners, as well, and having fallen short of God. Then onto the next town, and the next one. What's worse, they gather followers from each place—and everyone believes they are "less than perfect" and have "fallen short of the mark." Geographically, this belief spreads. Emotionally, it floods the minds and bodies, thoughts, dreams, and limbic and nervous systems of the followers. And, as demonstrated by the Global Consciousness Project, this perceived deficiency is seeded into the atmosphere and is picked up subconsciously by everyone living in the region.

Next, these "hopelessly flawed" individuals tell their children and grandchildren that they, too, have "fallen short in God's eyes." These poor youngsters aren't even given a chance—straight out of the womb, they are branded. And on and on it goes.

Imagine the individual and mass psychology of such a firmly rooted belief system, affecting not only a society over the course of a few hundred years, but *an entire civilization for more than 2,000 years.* If a whole race were to truly believe in their own ineptitude and their inability to rise any higher than a sense of guilt at having been born "bad" in God's eyes, is it any wonder we are living in the current set of circumstances we find ourselves in? The rampant "sinning" committed all over this earth is the sin these ancient religions have seeded inside our mass consciousness. Whatever form of "salvation" these religions offer, whether it be through the Holy Ghost, Christ, or any other entity, does not remove the ultimate sin that constitutes the aim of the doctrine—to shame an individual into the psychological judgment of himself and of every single one of his neighbors.

Again, this is the ultimate example of first century thinking and spiritual ignorance gone awry. I cannot tell you how many ghosts I have encountered that refuse to proceed from the earthly plane to the Other Side, for fear of being judged for their "sins." Further, I have yet to meet anyone from Other Side who claims that their afterlife experience is anything like what has been written in these first century religious texts. They have not been judged by anyone or anything *outside themselves*, nor have they even heard of anyone "being sent to Hell." In fact, departed relatives residing on the Other Side have had *nothing to say about the need for any kind of spiritual salvation to be acceptable to God.* The truth is that we have been fine, all along.

With what we now know about thoughts and energy creating reality, this "being born a sinner" is one of the worst crimes ever perpetrated on the multidimensional Soul and psychological framework of humanity. It is the basis for wars, disease, and unrest (both personal and societal). Within this erroneous declaration, spiritually ignorant men have been allowed to create lethally poisonous doctrines with the intention (whether consciously or not) of separating humanity from God, from nature, and from our True Selves. As soon as one of these "believers" exclaims, "God is Great!" and then opens gunfire on other people, we are unequivocally faced with the insanity that results from accepting ancient, unevolved, old-world thinking.

Of course there will always be those who protest, "Those are extremists! That is not what *we* believe." That may be true—the boundaries of the beliefs may differ—but buried within that centuries-old doctrine, you will find passages that coincide with and exhort the extremists' actions. If it is truly not what the adherents *wish* to believe, then they must abandon their ancient texts and create new ones, based on rational, thought-provoking, evolved thinking and a sense of loving communion, not ancient geopolitical rivalry. Be *inspired* by a *modern* connection to God, not the connection that was perceived to have been during the Bronze Age.

A BOLD NEW WORLD

Come dream with me for a moment. Imagine what this world would be like today, had we not been told for thousands of years that we are born sinners—that we are, in fact, born as a loving reflection of the harmonious Creative Life Principle (God). Imagine if we were taught that when people do bad things, it's because they lacked good judgment and were ignorant—but were free to unlearn such ignorance and become knowledgeable. What if this had been the theme, generation after generation? Imagine hearing and telling your kids that. "You are the loving reflection of the Source Creator." Imagine, too, how the feeling of love would strengthen our connection to our divine source, as opposed to perpetuating the turmoil, guilt, and separation of hearing again and again, "You are a sinner. Repent."

Living life knowing that we are each a loving reflection of Source would make us all more caring people. To see everyone in that light and honor that notion would change all irrevocably. We would be more giving—we would promote more causes of goodwill and charity and experience less fear and suspicion of our neighbors. If everyone believed in the undivided unity created by the fabric of universal love stemming from such a belief, would there have been slavery? Would thousands have been executed in the inquisitions? How about the thousands slaughtered in Holy Wars? Would there ever have been a need for women's suffrage? Would we currently be participating in two simultaneous wars in the Middle East and perpetuating paranoia about the specter of nuclear holocaust always looming on the horizon?

Instead of killing infidels or usurping heathen traditions in an effort to convert a population to an even more disturbing brand of division and bigotry, if we could begin to view ourselves as loving forms of creation, placed on this earth to love and learn from one another, forgiveness would be readily understood and granted when we encountered things that displeased us. As it stands today, forgiveness and acceptance are all too often dangled as some sort of *possibility*—one that can only be officiated by the wrathful, vengeful king who prefers to think of the earth as his footstool (Acts 7:49). This is unacceptable thinking, and it must be stamped out once and for all.

Each of us is born as a loving reflection of the creative Source.

Spiritual ignorance is no laughing matter, and it must be eradicated. Ignorance of the true nature of old-world religions, as well as ignorance of the true nature of our divine union, is no longer acceptable or necessary. It's time to let the possibilities of *learning* come to the forefront of our existence, so that we may *learn* to become the multidimensional beings we are. It is time for us to *learn to become* the loving reflections of God's mind and spirit that we are born to be.

NOTE

1. From http://www.roman-empire.net/religion/superstitions.html.

Chapter Sixteen

A NEW DAWN

Waking up to realize you are the creator of your experience can be both enlightening and terrifying. The power rests firmly in your control, along with the responsibility of how you use it. Do you create a positive and affirming life for yourself and others? Or do you hide away, afraid of your own power and ego? Rest assured, you are not alone—everyone around you is also an individual creator, with the same responsibilities on his or her shoulders. Together, we are all the same in this regard. We now have scientific studies that support this philosophy, as we have read in the previous chapters. Together, we are One magical Being. To recap:

Your Soul moves quantum particles to create reality.

Your Soul traverses Time and Space to create reality.

Your Soul has direct impact on your body and health.

Your Soul contributes to the environment and mass events.

Your Soul is not confined to the physical body.

Your Soul is the harbinger of miracles.

Miracles have happened to people in every time period, from every culture. Ancient Egyptians equated their miracles—sudden cures, wonderful harvests, magical "coincidences"—to any one of their pantheon of gods; the Greeks also. Today, Christians praise Christ for their miracles; Hindus attribute theirs to Krishna or Vishnu (or any other deity in their treasure chest); miracles in the lives of Muslims come from Allah. Miracles happen to everyone, and they are not merely handouts of any of these supernatural deities, for *they* are not the common denominator in these instances. The consciousness of the recipient of these miracles is the tie that binds. Consciousness itself is the glue of the universe—the Soul of the observer that transcends Time and Space. Indeed, the observer might be assisted by deceased relatives or other forces "outside" the realm of his physical body, but it is still the observer himself within the invisible design of his psychic structure, that spiritual architect of existence—the Soul force of life—that initiates the energy for which the miracle occurs. It is the recipient in these other religions that prays for a miracle, not understanding that it is the energy behind the prayer that makes the wish come true, not the cooperation of his perceived deity.

A new day will dawn when all of us can wake up to this realization. Our religious institutions will no longer preach division and sin, dangling the afterlife as a carrot on a stick and abusing the concept of God. Instead, they will teach unity and harmony amongst all life, and they will preach that people on their individual journeys can expect to enjoy unique experiences that will lead them along their path to knowledge. These new churches will preach love for all mankind, not just a chosen few, and in so doing will create an even more prosperous and giving community. Through our sacred Oneness, this planet will heal more rapidly with the cooperation of loving consciousness, instead of competition (leave competition in the realm of economics, where it belongs). When everyone on earth acknowledges each of us to be the wheels of creation in our lives and on this planet, then—and only then—will we be able to broker an eternal peace.

Let us thank the past and acknowledge all that has come before us. Let us be grateful to all the work that has been done. Let us remember the sacrifices humanity has shared along the way. Let us forgive those ignorant actions and beliefs that were inflicted by those who, through no fault of their own, briefly led mankind astray. That is all in the past. And as we learned about the past, it has no effect on the present, save for what our mind wishes to anchor in the Now.

Let us each remember the power of the Eternal and Present Moment—and the unending possibilities of the future. Let us at last greet each other as One entity, enhanced by an invisible network of egos for the sole purpose of all-encompassing eternal expression and experience. Let us hail the Creative Principle—the God incarnate—in each of us.

For thousands of years, we have told ourselves that we were born "less than perfect" or "off the mark." How wrong we were.

Our Souls were created and birthed *perfectly*. We were born perfect, if only for the simple fact that we can change ourselves and our lives within the blink of an eye—simply by altering our thoughts and energy. Perfection isn't a static state, for as soon as you claim something to be "perfect and done," someone else comes along with a slightly different variation that you think is a great enhancement! Perfection is a way of *being—it is your natural way*. It is your unending availability of choices and the ability to experience them that makes you a perfect being. In a single moment, you can choose to become more loving than you were the moment before; you can choose to release anger and fill yourself with happiness; you can choose to see beauty instead of darkness; you can choose to give more charity instead of holding back; you can choose to accept health over illness. That you can do, have, and become all of these (and more) proves that you are a perfect Soul. All possibilities are available to you. If the Creative Principle didn't love you, you wouldn't be able to think your thoughts, feel them, act on them, and become them.

You are a part of God, and God is a part of you. This has always been so, and it always will be.

You are a blessing.

Thank you for being here.

From Jeffrey's Library

BIBLIOGRAPHY

The following is a list of some of the books consulted during Jeffrey's research. Some titles have newer editions available, or the publisher holding the rights may have changed.

Barker, Elsa. *Letters From the Afterlife: A Guide to the Other Side.* Hillsboro, Oregon: Beyond Words Publishing, 2004.

Bentov, Itzhak. *A Brief Tour of Higher Consciousness.* Rochester, Vermont: Destiny Books, 2000.

———. *Stalking the Wild Pendulum.* Rochester, Vermont: Destiny Books, 1988.

Berkowitz, Rita S. & Romaine, Deborah S. *The Complete Idiot's Guide to Communicating with Spirits.* Indianapolis, Indiana: Alpha Books, 2003.

Blum, Deborah. *Ghost Hunters: William James and the Search for Scientific Proof of Life After Death.* New York: Penguin Group, 2006.

Bohm, David. *Wholeness and the Implicate Order.* New York: Routledge, 1980.

Borgia, Anthony. *Life in the World Unseen.* London: Odhams Press Ltd., 1954.

———. *More About Life in the World Unseen.* London: Odhams Press Ltd., 1956.

Braden, Gregg. *The Divine Matrix.* Carlsbad, California: Hay House, 2007.

Braud, William. *Distant Mental Influence.* Charlottesville, Virginia: Hampton Roads, 2003.

Brennan, J.H. *Time Travel.* St. Paul, Minnesota: Llewellyn Worldwide, Ltd., 2003.

Byrne, Rhonda. *The Secret.* New York: Atria Books, 2006.

Campbell, Joseph. *The Power of Myth.* New York: Doubleday, 1988.

Chopra, Deepak. *The Spontaneous Fulfillment of Desire.* New York: Harmony Books, 2003.

———. *The Way of the Wizard.* New York: Harmony Books, 1995.

Cutner, Herbert. *Jesus: God, Man or Myth?* Escondido, California: The Book Tree, 2000.

DeRosa, Peter. *Vicars of Christ: The Dark Side of the Papacy.* New York: Crown Publishers, Inc., 1988.

Dooley, Mike. *Infinite Possibilities: The Art of Living Your Dreams.* New York: Atria Books, 2009.

Dyer, Wayne W. *The Power of Intention.* Carlsbad, California: Hay House, 2004.

———. *Real Magic: Creating Miracles in Everyday Life.* New York: HarperCollins Publishers, 1992.

Edward, John. *Crossing Over: The Stories Behind the Stories.* San Diego, California: Jodere Group, 2001.

Einsten, Albert. *Relativity, the Special and the General Theory.* New York: Crown Publishers, 1966.

Farwell, Larry. *How Consciousness Commands Matter.* Fairfield, Iowa: Sunstar Publishing, 1999.

Gilmore, Robert. *Alice in Quantumland.* New York: Springer-Verlag, 1995.

Goswami, Amit. *Physics of the Soul.* Charlottesville, Virginia: Hampton Roads, 2001.

———. *The Self-Aware Universe.* New York: Tarcher/Putnam, 1993.

Grabhorn, Lynn. *Excuse Me, Your Life is Waiting.* Charlottesville, Virginia: Hampton Roads, 2000.

Graham, Lloyd M. *Deceptions and Myths of the Bible.* New York: Carol Publishing, 1993.

Hay, Louise L. *You Can Heal Your Life.* Carlsbad, California: Hay House, 1984.

Holmes, Ernest. *The Science of Mind.* New York: Tarcher/Putnam, 1966.

Horton, Cody. *Consciously Creating Wealth.* Golden, Colorado: Higher Self Workshops, 2002.

Jung, Carl G. *Man and his Symbols.* New York: Doubleday & Company, Inc., 1983.

Kessler, David. *Visions, Trips, and Crowded Rooms: Who and What You See Before You Die.* Carlsbad, California: Hay House, 2010.

Leedom, Tim C. *The Book Your Church Doesn't Want You to Read.* Dubuque, Iowa: Kendall/Hunt Publishing Company, 1993.

Lipton, Bruce. *The Biology of Belief.* Carlsbad, California: Hay House, 2005.

Losier, Michael J. *Law of Attraction.* New York: Wellness Central, 2006.

Mallet, Ronald, & Henderson, Bruce. *Time Traveler: A Scientist's Personal Mission to Make Time Travel a Reality.* New York: Thunder's Mouth Press, 2006.

Margolis, Char. *Questions from Earth, Answers From Heaven.* New York: St. Martin's Press, 1999.

McEvoy, J.P. & Zarate, Oscar. *Introducing Quantum Theory.* Cambridge: Totem Books, 1996.

McMoneagle, Joseph. *Remote Viewing Secrets.* Charlottesville, Virginia: Hampton Roads, 2000.

McTaggert, Lynne. *The Field.* New York: Quill, 2002.

———. *The Intention Experiment.* New York: Free Press, 2007.

Monroe, Robert A. *Far Journeys.* New York: Doubleday, 1985.

Moody, Raymond A. *Life After Life.* New York: HarperCollins Publishers, 1975.

Morse, Melvin, & Perry, Paul. *Closer to the Light.* New York: Ballantine Books, 1990.

———. *Parting Visions.* New York: HarperCollins Publishers, 1994.

———. *Transformed by the Light.* New York: Ballantine Books, 1992.

———. *Where God Lives.* New York: HarperCollins Publishers, 2000.

Myers, F.W.H. *Human Personality and Its Survival of Bodily Death.* Charlottesville, Virginia: Hampton Roads, 1961, 2001.

Nadeau, Robert, & Kafatos, Menas. *The Non-Local Universe.* New York: Oxford Press, 1999.

Newton, Michael. *Destiny of Souls: New Case Studies of Life Between Lives.* St. Paul, Minnesota: Llewellyn Worldwide, Ltd., 2002.

———. *Journey of Souls: Case Studies of Life Between Lives.* St. Paul, Minnesota: Llewellyn Worldwide, Ltd., 2004.

Ostrander, Sheila, & Schroder, Lynn. *Psychic Discoveries.* New York: Marlowe & Company, 1997.

Pert, Candace. *Everything You Need to Know to Feel Go(o)d.* Carlsbad, California: Hay House, 2006.

Pierce, Penney. *The Intuitive Way*. New York: Atria Books, 2009.

Radin, Dean. *The Conscious Universe*. New York: Harper Collins, 1997.

————. *Entangled Minds*. New York: PocketBooks, a division of Simon & Schuster, 2006.

Roberts, Jane. *The Nature of Personal Reality: A Seth Book*. San Rafael, California: Amber-Allen Publishing, 1974.

————. *Seth Speaks, the Eternal Validity of the Soul: A Seth Book*. San Rafael, California: Amber-Allen Publishing, 1972.

Robinson, Lynn A., & Carlson-Finnerty, LaVonne. *The Complete Idiot's Guide to Being Psychic*. Indianapolis, Indiana: Alpha Books, 1999.

Rogo, Scott D. *Leaving the Body: A Complete Guide to Astral Projection*. New York: Fireside Publishing, 1983.

Ronson, Jon. *The Men Who Stare at Goats*. New York: Simon & Schuster, 2004.

Russell, Peter. *Waking Up in Time*. Novato, California: Origin Press, 1992.

S., Acharya. *The Christ Conspiracy: The Greatest Story Ever Sold*. Kempton, Illinois: Adventures Unlimited Press, 1999.

Sage, Michael. *Mrs. Piper & The Society for Psychical Research*. New York: BiblioBazaar, 1904, 2007.

Saltmarsh, H.F. *The Future and Beyond: Evidence for Precognition and the Survival of Death*. Charlottesville, Virginia: Hampton Roads, 1938, 2002.

Schwartz, Gary E., & Simon, William L. *The Afterlife Experiments*. New York: Atria Books, 2002.

————. *The Truth About Medium*. Charlottesville, Virginia: Hampton Roads, 2005.

Sheldrake, Rupert. *The Presence of the Past*. Rochester, Vermont: Park Street Press, 1988.

Talbot, Michael. *Beyond the Quantum*. New York: Macmillan Publishing Company, 1986.

————. *The Holographic Universe*. New York: HarperCollins Publishers, 1991.

Targ, Russell. *Limitless Mind*. Novato, California: New World Library, 2004.

Targ, Russell, & Katra, Jane. *Miracles of Mind*. Novato, California: New World Library, 1998.

Targ, Russell, & Puthoff, Hal. *Mind-Reach: Scientists Look at Psychic Abilities*. Charlottesville, Virginia: Hampton Roads, 1977, 2005.

Tart, Charles, T. *Body, Mind, Spirit*. Charlottesville, Virginia: Hampton Roads, 1997.

Tiller, W., Dibble, W., & Kohane, M. *Conscious Acts of Creation.* Walnut Creek, California: Pavior Publishing, 2001.

Tucker, Jim B. *Life Before Life.* New York: St. Martin's Press, 2005.

Van Praagh, James. *Heaven and Earth: Making the Psychic Connection.* New York: Simon & Schuster, 2001.

Vasiliev, L.L. *Experiments in Mental Suggestion.* Charlottesville, Virginia: Hampton Roads, 1963, 2002.

Wattles, Wallace D. *Financial Success: Harnessing the Power of Creative Thought.* Rochester, Vermont: Inner Traditions International, 1990.

Weiss, Brian L. *Many Lives, Many Masters.* New York: Simon & Schuster, 1988.

————. *Mirrors of Time: Using Regression for Physical, Emotional, and Spiritual Healing.* Carlsbad, California: Hay House, 2002.

Wolf, Fred Alan. *Mind Into Matter.* Portsmouth, New Hampshire: Moment Point Press, 2001.

————. *The Spiritual Universe.* Portsmouth, New Hampshire: Moment Point Press, 1999.

————. *Taking the Quantum Leap.* San Francisco: Harper & Row, 1981.

————. *The Yoga of Time Travel.* Wheaton, Illinois: Quest Books, 2004.

Learn more about books by Jeffrey Marks at

www.aragopress.com

CPSIA information can be obtained
at www.ICGtesting.com
Printed in the USA
BVHW031349201221
624338BV00012B/317